6·99

WHITE LIGHTNING
ALLAN DONALD
THE AUTOBIOGRAPHY

Patrick Murphy is BBC Radio's Sports Correspondent in the Midlands, specialising in cricket and soccer. He has covered England cricket tours for the BBC and is a prolific author in his own right, having written in tandem with cricketers such as Alec Stewart, Jack Russell, Dermot Reeve and David Gower.

First published in hardback in 1999
by CollinsWillow
an imprint of HarperCollins*Publishers*
London

First published in paperback in 2000

1 3 5 7 9 8 6 4 2

A CIP catalogue record for this book is
available from the British Library

ISBN 0 00 218899 6

Set in Linotype Sabon by
Rowland Phototypesetting Ltd, Bury St Edmunds, Suffolk
Printed and bound in Great Britain by
Clays Ltd, St Ives plc

Photographic Acknowledgements
All photographs supplied by Allan Donald with the exception of the
following: **Allsport** pp 9 and 10 (all), 11 (top, centre) 12 (top right,
centre), 13 (bottom left), 15 (bottom left and right), 16 (top, centre);
Patrick Eagar pp 11 (bottom), 12 (top left), 13 (all except bottom
left), 15 (centre right); 16 (bottom); **Mark Leech** p 5; **Roger Wootton**
pp 1 (top), 3 (centre, bottom), 4, 6, 7 and 8 (all), 15 (top).

Contents

	Acknowledgements	v
	Foreword by Nelson Mandela	vii
1	Thank you, Mr President	1
2	A Life in 'Bloem'	7
3	From School Blazer to Springbok Cap	21
4	The Bloemfontein Brummie	40
5	Breakthrough to the Big Time	57
6	A Wake-up Call	67
7	A Momentous Year	80
8	Back in the Fold	89
9	Learning to Win at Warwickshire	113
10	Climbing onto the Treadmill	123
11	To England – At Last!	147
12	In Lara's Shadow	165
13	Falling at the Crucial Hurdle	185
14	Time Out	197
15	A Hard Slog	204
16	Failure Against England	226

17   Who'd be an Umpire?   261
18   What Makes a Fast Bowler?   271
19   A Dramatic Series   280
20   Just One Run!   297
21   Looking Down the Barrel   316
     Career Statistics   337
     Index   365

ACKNOWLEDGEMENTS

There are so many people I wish to thank for helping me to have a career that qualifies for an autobiography. There are my team-mates from the three sides I have played for in professional cricket – Free State, Warwickshire and South Africa. My family, of course. My wife, Tina, my parents and my uncle Des, who fostered my love of cricket. Dr Ali Bacher has been tremendously supportive of me down the years, while Alan Jones has been a great psychological help since we first met in 1993. Early on, Johann Voldstedt was very important as coach and mentor in Bloemfontein while Bob Woolmer's imaginative coaching methods and hard work have helped me enormously with both Warwickshire and South Africa.

I'd also like to thank Marc Archer and John Bredenkamp of Masters International for their career guidance in recent years, helping to make my life much easier since we linked up. Finally, to the BBC's Pat Murphy, who has been part of Edgbaston since I've been at the club, and who helped compile this book with me.

Allan Donald

To Tina and all my family

FOREWORD

by *President Nelson Mandela*

Sport played an immensely important role in uniting the people of South Africa as our country emerged from decades and centuries of racial division. Some of the most joyous and spectacular celebrations of our new found unity and common patriotism were connected with the achievements of our sporting teams, whether it was the Rugby Springboks winning the World Cup, our national soccer team Bafana Bafana triumphing in the African Nations Cup or the gallant performances of our Protea cricket team around the world.

Sport often produces individuals who serve as role-models and sources of inspiration to millions of followers, aspirant sportspersons and to the general public. Allan Donald is one such South African sportsman. He is universally acknowledged as a superb athlete and one of the all time great practitioners of fast bowling. Even in a sports mad country like South Africa he stands out as a national hero and idol.

His autobiography is more than merely the story of sporting achievement. It is a very human tale of an Afrikaans-speaking young man from one of our rural provinces battling against odds to reach the highest pinnacle.

It tells of dedication, hard work, lessons learnt about the importance of humility, the importance of self-belief, the disappointment of setbacks and the ability to rise from adversity.

It is also courageously honest in portraying how a young South African who, because of his background, grew up with a very restricted view of the politics of his country, was prepared to listen and to learn of the other side when it became possible. He is generous in his recognition of the role played by the libertarian movement and the new democratic government of his country in making his international achievements possible. His book is therefore as much the narrative of our new South African-hood.

We are confident that Allan Donald will continue to impart of his experience and knowledge to the new generation of fast bowlers that are emerging in our country. The relationship between sports and politics, and between the identification of merit and the need for development is often complex. The balanced wisdom of persons like Allan Donald, who had the privilege of observing conventions and customs in many parts of the world, will be invaluable as we progress towards being both representative and competitively successful with our national sporting teams.

We are proud to know that this great athlete and fast bowler is a son of South Africa.

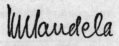

CHAPTER ONE

Thank you,
Mr President

As usual the handshake was firm, the smile warm and the gratitude sincere. Again it struck me how bizarre that the man thanking me for being a decent cricketer was the most admired statesman in the world, that it should be me expressing appreciation to him for what he had done for South Africa. President Nelson Mandela prefers to encourage South Africans to be leaders in their own personal fields, rather than have the spotlight turned on him and that's why he was so gracious to me on the night of 15 August 1997. I had flown back to South Africa for a special moment in my career and my life. A great honour had come my way – I was to be presented with a special lifetime achievement award in South African sport, one of only six recipients in history. At the age of 30, I was the youngest and not even a NatWest trophy semi-final was going to stop me getting there for the ceremony. Just a few hours earlier, in Birmingham, I had polished off the Sussex batsmen, taking five for 43 to help book Warwickshire a place in the NatWest Final at Lord's. It had been touch-and-go whether I would catch the plane to Johannesburg, because rain had caused a spillover day in the match at Edgbaston, and I had been anxiously scanning the local weather forecasts. So there was an extra incentive as I tore into the Sussex batsmen on that second morning. I caught the plane, just in time, delighted that my county was again booked for a Lord's final, but thrilled that I would keep my appointment with President Mandela, a man who had done so much for my country's reputation. The fact that he was honouring me was particularly memorable.

My wife, Tina, accompanied me to/the ceremony and we were both moved by the gracious words of the President. Steve Tshwete, our Sports Minister was there, and he was as kind and supportive as usual. Mr Tshwete had played a notable part in persuading South Africa's black community to get behind cricketers of all colours and since the start of the decade, the change in attitude towards cricket in my country had been remarkable. The African National Congress, at the instigation of President Mandela and Steve Tshwete, had been fully behind our reinstatement to international cricket in 1991 and had done everything since to try to heal the divisions in our society, by using sport to unite all South Africans in the common cause. It had been a very successful campaign. I had noticed the change in support over the years. Before, when South Africa was still in isolation, there was no black support for us when we played against 'rebel' sides who came to our country. Not that we deserved to be supported by the black community – we were hardly playing these sides to improve their lives, we were doing it because we were mad about sport and would take on anybody who would give us a game. We were thankful in the 1980s for any sort of competitive action. Yet since we came back into the fold, all sections of South African society seem to be behind us. Whenever I go into a shop, walk down the road or put petrol in my car, I get black people shouting across to me, 'Well bowled, Allan!', and they come and shake my hand. At last they are supporting us because we are South Africans, and our colour is irrelevant. Without the inspirational leadership of Nelson Mandela and the support of the ANC, that wouldn't be the case. I'm prouder now of representing South Africa than a decade ago. I now realise we deserved to be boycotted economically and in sport, and have enormous respect for the statesmanship of President Mandela and F. W. de Klerk, a white man brave enough to stand up to the extreme elements in his country and hammer out a deal with a black man still in custody, on Robben Island. Mr de Klerk showed the vision and guts necessary to lead South Africa out of the wilderness years, and even though it made him unpopular with some sections of the white community, his leadership was instrumental in the remarkable changes of the past few years.

Yet President Mandela has been the inspiration and it was a humbling experience to receive that sporting award and to be told by him that South Africa was very proud of me. Nowhere near as proud as I was that my country was led by the most respected and popular leader in the world. Growing up in Bloemfontein, the heartland of the Afrikaaner, I had been led to believe that Nelson Mandela was a bad man, that he had blown up factories and railways, caused a lot of deaths and represented a serious threat to law and order. He was, basically, a terrorist and deserved to rot in jail. I believed what I was told by the whites in Bloemfontein, without realising that many Afrikaaners wouldn't be exactly in favour of black people seeking racial equality. Mine was an insular world in those days, with the television news giving the National

Government slant and just mentioning more disturbances in the black townships, without bothering to examine why they were rioting. As a sports-mad youngster, growing up in a secure, loving family, I had no interest in looking beyond the boundaries of my happy existence. I realise now I was too laid-back, in common with many others of my background. It was to be years later, when I read Nelson Mandela's autobiography, that I realised why he was such a hero to so many others in different parts of the world. I was amazed at the depth of his moral bravery; he was like Martin Luther King in the way he stood up for black people's rights. When you read about the Sharpeville Massacre, thirty years later, and take in Nelson Mandela's words from the dock in the Rivonia Trial, you soon understand why South Africa was isolated for so long. And justifiably so. Who would want to invest in our country after all those atrocities? Now I understood why it was wrong to fly the old South Africa flag once we were readmitted to international sport. There had to be healing, the whites had to accept the need for conciliatory gestures, with a new national flag and national anthem. And a new leader who saw himself as a South African, not as a black man.

I first met the President in November 1992, when he came to the Wanderers Ground in Johannesburg to meet the South African and Indian sides during a Test match. I was struck by his physical stature. Although in his mid-seventies, he was a tall man, physically strong, with massive hands. When he shook hands, I could tell he used to be a boxer, he had a vice-like grip! The man had huge charisma, a natural smile and a calm dignity. He treated everyone with charm and respect. Our players were simply bowled over by him. He had a personal word for each of us. When he came to me, he said, 'How's Bloemfontein? I can't remember the last time I was in the Free State', and I felt like telling him to pop in for a barbecue (or a 'braai', as the South Africans call it) at my place when he was next in town! To every South African player, he said, 'Thanks for what you're doing for us', and you felt like telling him the gratitude should be all ours. His dignity and personal example had been instrumental in helping us to play international cricket for the first time since 1970. I think we owed him, rather than the other way round.

The President really wants us to win in all sports. A real South African! He makes it clear to us how important sport is to our country and that winning is always preferable to taking part, something we can all relate to. So he's a regular visitor to major sporting events, and his presence is definitely a plus. I'm convinced his support at the Rugby World Cup Final in 1995 helped us beat the All Blacks and lift the trophy. The All Blacks, Jonah Lomu and the rest, were favourites that day at Ellis Park, yet President Mandela lifted us before the start with an amazing gesture. Among politicians, only he could have got away with walking onto the pitch, wearing the South African jersey, with the number six on the back – the number of the captain, François Pienaar. The home crowd went absolutely wild, they were initially stunned but then roared the roof off. I'm sure that gesture was worth a few points that day. It was the action of a genuine sports lover and proud South African. It would have looked like a cheap gimmick if anyone else in politics had tried it. Yet just five years before, he was still on Robben Island. He is equally inspirational whenever he pops in to see us playing cricket. You always know it's on the cards because the helicopters are hovering, you see scores of security guards using their walkie-talkies and you suddenly see him there, in the stand. During the one-day international against England at Port Elizabeth in 1996, I was fielding close to the boundary, noticed a bit of a commotion, looked up and there he was – in South African cap, blazer and white flannels. I thought that was a brilliant statement and when I told him later that he looked smart, he gave that famous chuckle. And we proceeded to hammer England once the President had arrived! That certainly pleased him.

So you can see that a two-day trip to South Africa and the inevitable jet lag was a small price to pay for being honoured by a man who is South Africa's finest export. Wherever I go round the world, I am asked about Nelson Mandela. I say that it has been fantastic to be a South African under his leadership, seeing him try so hard to move us forward, to heal deep divisions. As an international sportsman, you obviously want to win for yourself, your team-mates and your country – but we have also wanted to do it for this man. President Mandela has made me even prouder to wear the South African blazer. That's something I never thought I'd be saying all those years ago, when growing up in Bloemfontein.

CHAPTER TWO

A Life in 'Bloem'

The city of Bloemfontein doesn't have the brightest image among South Africans. Many say it's best to bypass it in a plane or by car, and don't bother to stop. Bloemfontein's detractors say there's nothing to do there, everybody speaks Afrikaans and the locals are unfriendly to outsiders. It's an area dominated by farmers, rugged characters of few words and devout religious tendencies. Even though other South African cities are now more progressive, Bloemfontein is still proudly, even aggressively traditionalist and many from other parts of the country like to poke fun at it. I suppose it's the same as Yorkshire if you're a Brit. The locals take pride in their toughness, self-discipline and just being different from the rest. Growing up in Bloemfontein certainly did me no harm in my chosen career, and I won't hear a word said against the place. Even my English wife, Tina, has become a convert. When we first married, she wanted to move from 'Bloem', because she found it hard to adapt to its particular lifestyle and people, but now she loves it. She's made many friends there and thinks it's an ideal, safe place to bring up our kids. Bloem is known as 'the City of Roses' and the parks and rose gardens are beautiful, but to those who prefer the sophistication of Cape Town or Johannesburg there is no contest. That doesn't bother me. I'm very happy to come from Bloemfontein. I like the values instilled in an area where you're not allowed to get carried away with your own importance or success.

My parents were very strict with their three children and I'm glad of it. That upbringing has certainly helped make me a better cricketer. They told us to stay level-headed if we'd done well at sport or in school. I can hear them saying, 'That's very good, but don't go on about it – you'll get a big head'. I'd race back from the playing fields, full of myself, only to be told not to boast. I haven't forgotten that message, even though at times I admit that I've slipped my standards. Now, when I've done very well and been inwardly pleased, I'll keep that satisfaction to myself. I'll go home, tell Tina how I've done and after she's said 'well done', we'll talk about other things. I can hear at the back of my head the words of my mother, telling me to take things in my stride and not be boastful. If you can't be level-headed as a sportsman, with all the hype that flies around, then you won't do yourself justice.

My mother, Francina was the driving force in our family. I was the eldest of three – two boys and a girl – separated by three-and-a-half years, and we all knew what our responsibilities were at home. My father, Stuart, worked incredibly hard as a senior TV and licence inspector at the Post Office, leaving home at five in the morning and not getting back till twelve hours later. Mother didn't exactly sit around either, working as a nursery school teacher at the local hospital, starting at six in the morning till four in the afternoon. My brother, Andrew and I would get up at five, go to the hospital with my mother, sleep in the

8

creche for another hour, then walk to school. So hard work was something we all knew about very early in life. There were no servants in our house – unlike many white South African families – and we three kids knew what chores were down to us. We'd organise the dinner before Mum came home to cook it, and if anyone came to visit, it was our responsibility to make them tea or coffee while our parents made them comfortable. If anyone came inside, we'd have to stand up immediately, shake hands and ask them what they'd like to drink. No alcohol – Mum was very strict about that. Her family background was even stricter than Dad's, so she'd tell us 'bars are where bad things happen, you get influenced'. Now, when she comes to my home and sees me enjoying a beer or glass of wine, she keeps quiet. I think she puts it down to the English influence – I'm much more outgoing socially since playing in England – but I hope she says nothing because she realises I'm happy with my family and different way of life.

My parents weren't dull and mindless when it comes to discipline. We were happy children, we knew we were cared for and accepted that our elders knew better than us. That might sound very old-fashioned and passive to kids who are used to getting their own way, sitting in front of the television, waiting for their Mum to make them something to eat. I'm glad that our way was different. Kids need clear guidelines of what they can't get away with and when I see some of the sloppiness of certain young guys in the South African side, I'm grateful for my upbringing. Shaun Pollock can be very sloppy and untidy in the dressing-room, dropping coffee cups or apple cores, assuming others will pick them up for him. Others like Mark Boucher and Paul Adams need constant reminders as well. During the 1998 tour to England, I was pleased to see that at last Shaun had started to say 'please' and 'thank you'. Jonty Rhodes and I had been on at him for some time about showing more respect and we seemed to be getting through to him finally. All that might seem as if I'm an old fuddy-duddy, but I really believe that attention to detail and personal cleanliness helps make you a better cricketer. Years ago, my mother made sure that we tidied away our school gear as soon as we came home, did our homework conscientiously and kept our bedrooms immaculate. Now I get annoyed at the lack of discipline from a player in the dressing-room environment, when he just dumps his equipment down, sprays it around and expects someone to clean it all up for him over the next few days. I believe that discipline is the key to success in any profession, it shows a clear mind. I always clean my boots before I go out to bowl, and I must have clean flannels when I take the field. My South African team-mate Daryll Cullinan is the same. He cleans his bat minutely, taking great care over it. He often says 'I like a man whose house is in order' when he sees me cleaning my boots, and to me it's just a case of taking pride in your profession. I don't see the advantage in not being able to put your hand on a piece of your cricket gear straight away, rather than rummage around in a panic.

I think my strict upbringing helped me overcome the inevitable knockbacks every youngster experiences. You weren't encouraged to mope around, expecting sympathy. It was a case of getting on with it: hard work was expected to solve any problems. My first major disappointment came when I was around twelve, when I was told I wasn't academically bright enough for the school I'd set my heart on. The school was Grey College, Bloemfontein's pride and joy, one of the most prestigious schools in South Africa. The sports facilities there were fantastic, and a host of South African Test rugby players had come from Grey's. Cricket didn't quite have the same prestige, although the facilities were wonderful and in years to come, two former pupils captained South Africa in succession – Kepler Wessels and Hansie Cronje. Many reference books have added my name to the illustrious roll-call of Grey's, but that would be distorting the true picture. I only lasted two years there, before the headmaster wrote to my parents to say that I just wasn't up to the required academic standard. My English was particularly weak. We spoke nothing but Afrikaans at home and I didn't utter a word of English until I was fourteen. Some might say I'm still not that fluent at it even now! I was devastated to leave Grey's. The sports master, Mr Johann Voldstedt had spotted I was good at sport and had encouraged me with just the right amount of sympathy and discipline. One day, he sent me off the field because I wasn't batting well. He was umpiring and wasn't impressed when I missed three balls in a row. I was warned, 'Don't waste my time – miss another and you're off' and he chased me away when I did just that. I felt inadequate and burst into tears when walking off the field. To make it even worse, I caught sight of my father, who had got off work early to see me play. I can't blame Mr Voldstedt, though – he was very good to talk to, even though he pushed me hard. He would inspire the young boys with details of marvellous performances on the rugby field by former pupils and he was full of praise for Kepler Wessels. By then, young Kepler was making his way in county cricket with Sussex and he was offered up as the role model for all aspiring cricketers at the school. 'He'll be the best player you've ever seen' we were told, and we were shown details of his scoring prowess in the cricket magazines and the old scorebooks at Grey's. It was drummed into us that to succeed in sport, you had to be as mentally and physically strong as Kepler Wessels. Years later, Kepler captained me for South Africa and Mr Voldstedt's words would ring true. He remains the toughest cricketer I've ever played with, the benchmark for any aspiring cricketer. The Afrikaaner upbringing in Bloemfontein made Kepler Wessels.

Rejection by Grey College wasn't the only setback for me. My next choice of school, Brebner Primary School tested me and also ruled me out because of my poor standard of English. I cried when I was turned down, but my father made sure I didn't feel sorry for myself for too long. The local Technical High School agreed to take me on, and Dad told me I should learn to become a mechanic or carpenter or electrician, because I obviously wasn't going to win many academic prizes. He wasn't being hard on me, he was right to spell it out honestly, there was no point in deluding myself. At least they played good-quality rugby at the High School. In those days, I was fanatical about rugby, along with almost everyone in Bloemfontein. It was the most popular sport in the area, and if you had won your school colours, you were someone to be respected. Cricket didn't compare in appeal or status. Every Saturday in winter, rugby matches would be played at the schools from ten in the morning till three in the afternoon – and the whole school would turn out in support, plus the parents. I've seen crowds of ten thousand watching schools rugby games in Bloemfontein and the local rivalry was huge. In cricket, for similar games, you'd be lucky to get a thousand spectators.

The fanaticism for rugby in Bloemfontein made my next failure even harder to bear. I was mad on rugby, and my ambition was to play fly-half for South Africa. My hero was Naas Botha, another Afrikaaner, who had made his name as a brilliant tactical kicker for the national side. His critics said he overdid the kicking, but he could do no wrong for me, and of course, I copied his style of kicking for distance, rather than running with the ball, creating openings for the backs. Unfortunately, I was dumb tactically, kicking at the wrong time and sometimes straight to the opposition. I managed to get into the first XV at Technical High School, but only for two matches. I was a mobile, wiry fly-half, but kept choosing the wrong options when we had possession. I'd hear the groans from the crowd, and my team-mates would give it to me, straight in the face. On Mondays, I'd hear them saying openly, 'Donald's useless, he should be dropped'. I was and I deserved it. That didn't make it any easier to swallow, though, nor the words of my father – 'This game doesn't suit you, you'd be better off at cricket'. That was no consolation, because I'd set my heart on being a top rugby player. I never played again after the age of nineteen, when I was in the Army, yet I still have a great passion for the game.

Those early setbacks helped me, although I didn't think so at the time. You need to show character to succeed in top-class sport, to bounce back from adversity and you realise eventually that getting kicked in the teeth hardens you up. So, after trying most sports, I eventually specialised in cricket. I was good at athletics at school – throwing the javelin, the high jump and long jump – but after straining my side in a javelin event, that was the end of my athletics career. There was no cricket coaching at the Technical High

School, so I relied on my father to foster my interest at his local club, Old Andreians. My grandfather kept wicket, and he used to talk to me for hours about the game. Dad had a really nice bowling action, modelled on the great English fast bowler, Frank Tyson. He had a great outswinger, delivered at pace, but he just gave it up one day. I never knew why. But he took me to the nets and we took it from there. I'd started off bowling leg-spin when I was eight or nine at primary school, but one day I was told by my teacher that I had to bowl fast because our regular opening bowler was sick. I took seven for 9, and that was the end of my spinners! Somehow, I bowled big inswingers and at Grey College, I had an action similar to Mike Procter, bowling slightly off the wrong foot. I must have decided to copy Procter, after watching him on television, but Mr Voldstedt was sufficiently impressed to ask me to practise with the Under-15s at Grey's, when I was just twelve. But soon I was out on my ear at Grey's, looking for my Dad to help me at his club.

My uncle Des was also influential. He'd coach me at my grandparents' house after cutting a strip with a lawnmower. We'd use a hard cricket ball and Des would show me no mercy, telling me I had a bat in my hand, and couldn't complain if I missed the ball. He really made me understand what was needed to stand up to the big boys. One day in the nets at Old Andreians, a quick bowler called Arthur Baker knocked out my stumps five balls in a row and I burst into tears through sheer embarrassment. Uncle Des said, 'Get out of the nets if you can't stand up to him', while Dad just said, 'Come on, stick at it'. Just a few years ago, I played against Arthur Baker for the first time since we were at school. It was a club game in Bloemfontein and when he came into bat, I reminded him of those days when he was quicker than me. It took only a few balls to get my revenge!

When I was about thirteen, I started knocking around with Hansie Cronje, who was later to be my captain at both Free State and South Africa. Hansie and his brother Frans were still at Grey College while I had gone to the High School, but we hit it off together and I used to go to their house to play cricket and rugby. Their father, Ewie, had played for Free State, becoming an important administrator, and he became a great advisor to me in later years. But his main role at this stage was to act as umpire in fierce contests between his sons and myself. We played many games of imaginary Test cricket on the Cronje turf, and it's amazing to realise that Hansie and I have travelled all over the world together since as Test cricketers, while Frans and I eventually opened the bowling for South African Schools. They were both hugely talented sportsmen – Frans played rugby for South African Schools, Hansie for Free State Schools, as well as playing tennis to a high standard. It used to annoy me so much that Hansie could bat too easily against me, as I tore in off my long run – and yet he was three years younger than me. We'd try our damndest against each other in that back garden, and I'd look enviously at the Cronje brothers, thinking 'I've got to go some to be anywhere near their standard'. But right from the earliest days, I've always been a great trier and I hated losing at any time, even if the Cronje boys were obviously more talented than me. It's in the South African genes, I suppose. When you start playing sport in my country, you soon realise that there's no such thing as a social game, that winning is everything and coming second doesn't interest anyone at all. Even in the winters, we'd go full on at each other with a rugby ball, with Hansie getting a few of the first XV over to his back garden. I'd take out my frustrations on them, because I hadn't really made the grade, and we never pulled out of any tackles. I suppose we South Africans know no other way.

Obviously, I didn't realise it at the time, but the ability to bowl fast was just a natural thing for me. Throwing the javelin seemed easy to me, and the fast bowler's action has something of the same about it. Perhaps I inherited my father's smooth bowling action, because the rough edges were soon smoothed out in the club nets. I remained wild and erratic in direction, but my basic action hasn't altered a great deal over the years – I've just managed to get it in the right area a little more consistently! I was lucky to have inherited my mother's suppleness, something that's been an important part of my bowling. I bowl well when my rhythm is good, and that stems from being supple and coordinated. When it's all in place, I glide to the crease. Mum was a very good netball player and gymnast at school, and even now, after two hip operations, she can touch the ground flat with her palms while standing up straight. That's also one of my party pieces, although I'm glad to say my hips are in better shape than Mum's! When I was still at school, I'd go and watch how the senior Free State cricket side prepared before taking the field. They did a lot of stretching, and I'd go back to school, and amaze the boys with my suppleness. I suppose I was showing off a bit, but there's no doubt that helped me bowl fast. The long cycle rides to get to school also gave me strong legs, which fast bowlers need. We'd moved further away from school, so I'd cycle sixteen kilometres a day. I shall never forget some of those bitter winter mornings, when the balaclava over my head and the gloves proved very useful against the freezing temperatures – yes, it does get cold in South Africa!

So I suppose that God-given ability to bowl fast was in me, it was just a case of having the desire to capitalise on it. After getting over my disappointment about rugby, I was certainly enthusiastic about playing cricket. My grandfather did a lot to fire my imagination by telling me all about the great names of world cricket. He bought every cricket magazine that came out and I read particularly the English ones – the *Cricketer* and *Wisden Cricket Monthly* – from cover to cover. He'd point to pictures of the great players and tell me all about them. I remember he was especially keen on Australia's Allan Border, he admired his guts. The cricket grounds in England looked particularly interesting, especially the beautiful ones in the country, with all those trees around the boundary edge. I thought how lucky were Mike Procter, Clive Rice and all the other South Africans to be playing in English county cricket and secretly I told myself that I'd try everything I could to play over there one day. I read all about the great South African side of 1970 that had been barred from Test cricket because of apartheid, just when it was set to be the best in the world. Granddad told me the rest of the world wanted us to get our act together over apartheid before we could return to international cricket. 'When will that be?' I asked him. 'About ten years'. He reassured me it would happen one day, but for now, the only way for the South Africans to prove themselves internationally was to play World Series Cricket for Kerry Packer. I was hooked – somehow I had to play in England, prove myself over there, and then play for my country. That's if Granddad's forecast about the timescale was to be right. It was, give or take a couple of years.

Apartheid had only entered my thoughts for the first time during those cricket discussions. Occasionally, we would see examples of unrest in the townships on television, but they were just snippets, and I was a typical Bloemfontein teenager – mad on sport, living in an insular world, knowing no black people educated enough to make me appreciate the evils of apartheid. Not until I played cricket in England did I start to understand the realities of apartheid. I remember watching a BBC documentary about the struggles in my own country, and being appalled at the way black people had been treated for decades. I was ashamed. I'd been brought up to believe that the blacks were always fighting each other, burning down their own schools, that the whites were just trying to keep the peace. Now I could see why the black people wanted equality and why Nelson Mandela was such a hero to them. I was a typical product of my particular society, in Bloemfontein. The Nationalist party had been formed in the city in 1914, and it was the Nats who administered the doctrine of apartheid with great severity. The Dutch Reformed Church is also very strong in Bloemfontein and many used their religious beliefs to justify apartheid. It is a region that is proudly and distinctly separate from most other parts of South Africa. It isn't an area known for radical changes. Many of the bloodiest battles of the Boer War were staged around Bloemfontein and there are many battlegrounds and monuments still there. As a result, the British aren't very popular with the older generations and it's no surprise to me that English is rarely spoken in Bloemfontein shops. There are a lot of people there with social and political views that could be described as 'Far-Right', and so the support for apartheid would linger longer in Bloemfontein district than a more progressive area like Cape Town. I would say that there is a sizeable amount in my home city who aren't too happy with the way things have changed so dramatically in South Africa in recent years. I mention that opinion not as a criticism, but as an explanation of the environment in which I grew up, and my unquestioning acceptance of the way things were.

By the time I was nineteen, I was getting practical experience of apartheid's bloody legacy. I was conscripted into the Army. That was a harsh introduction into reality. It was in the mid-eighties, during the State of Emergency, when so many parts of South Africa were vulnerable to civil war. The black community seemed close to revolt after so many years of repression, and within a few months I had gone from being told by Mum not to watch blacks killing themselves on TV to walking into townships with a rifle in my hand, wondering if I was going to stop a bullet. I remember one particularly scary day, when we had to patrol one of the townships, just outside Bloemfontein. We were told to carry live ammunition but not to return fire unless absolutely necessary. That didn't seem a particularly good deal to me, and I was genuinely frightened. We were a troop of fourteen, on a four-hour beat, there to impose order after a flare-up. I'll never forget that dry feeling in the mouth, as I saw kids darting across the road out of the corner of my eye, wondering if they were setting us up for an ambush. Behind me, my corporal was on the walkie-talkie, and you just knew that if one of our guys panicked and fired off a round, that would be curtains for all of us. I saw death that evening – the remains of a guy who had been 'necklaced', burnt alive with a tyre around his neck. He was still quite warm, burnt to a cinder.

Now I could see the point of all the harshness associated with basic training in the Army. You needed discipline to get through days like that awful one in the township. The first three months were incredibly hard. They tried to break your resistance, making you do so many mindless things, with just a few hours sleep, just to see if you could stand it. One day the fire alarm went off and a few of us were a bit sluggish at turning out. As punishment, we had to go under the shower, wearing all our gear, and then every piece of clothing had to be dried, washed and pressed by five o'clock next morning. And that was only after we had been marched over every bed in our quarters. There were so many drills, and they were just waiting for you to answer back. I never saw that happen, though. It wasn't a period I look back on with any fondness, but at least it taught me how to look after myself if I was totally isolated, relying on myself to get out of danger. Out in the bush, with the freezing mist hanging around you, as you dig your foxhole to get some shelter – it's a glamorous life! Compared to all that, bowling at Brian Lara on a flat wicket in exhausting heat is a doddle. The discipline involved in just surviving the Army training did help me as a cricketer later on. To succeed you just have to bite the bullet, get on with it, don't look for short-cuts or excuses. Oh, and a bit of ability helps as well.

My Army stint lasted two years, but after the first year, I got lucky. I had suddenly become one of Free State's brightest prospects as a cricketer, and training with my team-mates seemed to take up an enjoyable amount of time. Cricket has been kind to me in many ways!

CHAPTER THREE

From School Blazer to Springbok Cap

Once I had decided to dedicate myself to cricket, things moved forward at a bewildering pace. I had no idea if I had the ability to be a fast bowler at the highest level, but I wouldn't miss out through a lack of commitment. Yet within the space of fifteen months I went from schoolboy to national player. In South Africa, they do like to 'fast-track' youngsters, but even this rate of progress was exceptional. To me, it was mind-boggling. When I was given my Springbok colours for the unofficial 'Test' at Port Elizabeth against the Australian 'rebel' side, I looked around my new team-mates, pinching myself that I was in the same team as legends like Graeme Pollock and Clive Rice. Just over a year earlier, I was sitting in the classroom at the Technical High School, wondering what sort of career lay ahead of me. Then I just got carried along on a rapid tide of events that ended up with me playing English county cricket at the age of twenty. It's been one long rollercoaster ride since.

Those Australian 'rebels' were a godsend to cricket in South Africa. We knew that Kim Hughes, their captain had sparked off a storm of protests back home, by agreeing to lead a tour party to South Africa for two successive seasons, but we were only bothered at the time about playing against as many top-class players as possible. We were, of course, aware that apartheid had led to our ban from established, official international cricket but our top administrators felt that they owed it to our game to attract big-name opposition, to keep interest going in our country. To a naive kid like me, who just wanted to bowl as fast as possible, political considerations were irrelevant. Statisticians and world cricket's rulers would say the matches against these Aussies would not count as official Tests, but South Africans were happy to describe them that way. Certainly the way both sets of players approached the contests didn't indicate any reduction in commitment. For my part, those two Australian tours came at exactly the right time for me. They gave me the opportunity to shine against glamorous opposition, rather than just working away with Free State, relying on the odd first-class game to gain practical experience. Kim Hughes' side gave me the best possible platform when I was hungry for exposure and desperate to succeed, despite all those rough edges.

In fact, my promotion to first-class cricket was so rapid that I didn't represent South African Schools until after I'd played two games against the Australians and had a couple of Currie Cup matches for Free State. The previous season, at the age of eighteen, I'd opened the bowling for Free State Schools with Frans Cronje and then had to settle for being twelfth man for the national Schools team. I was happy enough, though, and treasured my South African cap, even if I hadn't made the final eleven. Soon I was scrapping away against hard-nosed Australians, and one of them lost no time in telling me I should be back at school, rather than trying to match up with the big guys.

My last day at school coincided with my Free State debut,

and the Aussies were the opposition. I was given special dispensation to take a science exam at seven in the morning, so that I could be free to play. I was so excited that I'd finished my efforts with more than an hour to spare and I vividly recall ripping off my school tie for the last time when I was picked up by Corrie van Zyl, who was to open the bowling with me that day. Corrie was a very fine fast bowler at the time, an automatic choice for South Africa and an inspiration to Free State cricket as its players had to come to terms with the increased pressure from being promoted to the premier section of the Currie Cup. Although injury cut short his fine career, he later became a fitness specialist and assistant coach to the South African national side, so he has been a great help to me over the years. That particular morning, in November 1985, he tried hard to calm me down as he drove me to the Ramblers ground for the biggest day so far in my life. When we got to the ground I was presented with my Free State gear and I just couldn't wait to put it all on. I shudder now whenever I see the team photo taken that day – I looked so skinny, with white, straight, short hair! It was the classic Army haircut, hardly surprising because I was due to report for my national service in a few weeks.

The match itself was uneventful and drawn. I bowled reasonably enough, taking the wickets of Steve Smith and Trevor Hohns, but I don't have special memories of my part in the game. I was too shy and unsure of myself to do anything other than speak when a team-mate talked to me, and kept quiet the rest of the time. I was thrilled to be playing, though, and it was great that many of my friends were there for the big day. Hansie Cronje, who was sixteen at the time, operated the scoreboard for the sum of five rands a day and he and his family were very pleased for me. It wouldn't be long before this hugely talented cricketer would be making more important contributions on a cricket ground.

I can't have done all that badly on my debut, because a few days later, I played in Pretoria for the President's X1 against the Aussies. Corrie van Zyl was also picked, so it was good to have his company and experience. But no amount of words of wisdom from Corrie could prepare me for the verbal onslaught I copped from Rodney Hogg. A fast bowler good enough to take more than a hundred Test wickets, and a fierce competitor, Hogg was known for his fondness for 'sledging' – giving out the verbals to the opposition, with plenty of expletives thrown in. He lined me up in the second innings when I came out to bat. I was last man and the Aussies were looking for an early finish, as I joined Hugh Page, a fine all-rounder from Transvaal. Hugh was a very good batsman, who tried his best to protect me, but eventually I was exposed to Hogg, who was unimpressed when I kept playing and missing, then fluked a legside three. Hogg started to bowl bouncers at me and when another whizzed past my nose, he followed through to me and shouted in my face 'Listen, you little . . . , I'll bounce you back to f****** school!' I was shocked, I'd never been sledged before, and I was so upset I thought I was going to burst into tears. I had no idea how to handle it, and Hogg kept bouncing and cursing me. That made me angry and I steeled myself not to get out to this rude guy. Hugh Page helped farm the bowling, keeping me away from Hogg, and I was eventually run out for twelve. But at least Hogg hadn't got my wicket, so there was a certain satisfaction in that. Afterwards, Hugh Page told me 'This is what you'll get if you play for your country, they do it all the time'. I would have to toughen up – and quickly. Somehow I'd get even with Mr Hogg. I had to wait a year for the chance.

In a hectic summer, I then played at last for South African Schools at East London against Border – possibly a little lucky, because I had actually left school, but when the season had started, I was still a schoolboy. Then it was time for Army service. In between the harsh early training, I managed to play cricket as well for Free State. Luckily, I was based at an Army camp near Bloemfontein and I'd manage to catch a couple of hours' sleep at Hansie Cronje's home, which was nearer to the camp than my parents'. I'd suffer the training, crash out at the Cronje home, go to nets, then return to the camp for guard duty. It was very, very hard work, but I got through it and I'm glad I passed the tests of character. It certainly toughened me up mentally, as well as physically, and I lost some of my painful shyness. Hugh Page's wise advice stayed in my mind: I would have to be strong in self-belief if I was to have any chance of making it as a cricketer.

I was very lucky to be surrounded at Free State by supportive, experienced team-mates who clearly wanted me to improve. And two Test players from other countries were very influential at that time. Vanburn Holder, the West Indian fast bowler, was coming to the end of his long career, but gave valuable service to Free State during that time. Vanny was tremendously helpful to me, passing on so many fast-bowling tips. A cheery guy, he's now a relaxing umpire in county cricket who never fusses, but lets the players enjoy the game, without taking any liberties. He talked to me about how to handle tight situations, how to spot a batsman's weakness and just how I should toughen up my whole approach. Chris Broad was Free State's captain that season and he gave me a lot of sound advice. Having batted so well for England the previous year against the likes of Malcolm Marshall, Michael Holding and Joel Garner, he knew a fair amount of what a fast bowler can do to trouble batsmen and it was very interesting to hear his perspective. He understood the mentality of the fast bowler, and he kept on at me about the need to exert pressure, that you can get wickets by frustrating the batsmen, giving them few scoring opportunities. He pointed out how little the West Indies quicks give the batters, and although I was still very erratic at the stage, I could see the sense of it all.

It was Chris Broad who broke the news to me that I was going to make my first-class debut. I'd travelled to Johannesburg with the Free State squad, expecting to be there just for the experience, to soak up the atmosphere and watch at close quarters the powerful Transvaal side, the best team in the country, known as 'the Mean Machine'. The night before, Chris came to me and said I was playing. It had been fantastic to play against the Aussies, even though the games weren't designated first-class, but now I would forever be known as someone who had played first-class cricket. Even if I never played another game, I would have achieved something. And just a few weeks before, I'd still been a schoolboy!

I was incredibly nervous the following morning, and it was a blessing in disguise that we had to bowl first on a good Wanderers pitch, because it meant I was right in at the deep end. I opened with Corrie van Zyl, and my first delivery was wide down the legside. Our wicket-keeper,

Robbie East just got a glove to it, saving byes and he shot me a dirty look. Next over, I was more successful. My first victim in first-class cricket was an illustrious one: Jimmy Cook, one of the best batsmen in the country. I managed to clip the outside edge and the faint nick was taken by Robbie behind the stumps. That was to be my only success that day, and in the match. Henry Fotheringham got after me, smacking me for sixteen in one over and I started to feel sorry for myself. That night, Chris Broad reassured me. 'I'm really proud of you', he said, 'you kept going. Don't worry about that one bad over, these things will always happen'. I didn't believe him – what young bowler would? – but it was good of my captain to think about my morale. We didn't get another bowl at Transvaal, because they steamrollered us to an innings defeat, but after the game Jimmy Cook said some kind things about me to the press. He said that I was wild and woolly, and sprayed it around, but I was definitely quick. He forecast that I'd be a fine prospect once I got the ball in the right area more consistently. That was great to hear from such a fine player, and now all I wanted was another chance with the first team, as quickly as possible.

It came a week later, when I played in Durban against Natal. I was still so naive and inexperienced in the ways of the world. It was only the second time I'd been in a plane and when we got to the hotel, I showed how little I knew about life's practicalities. We were told to get an early lunch, then be ready for nets at four in the afternoon. So I walked into the dining room, and marvelled at the fantastic buffet laid out. Joubert Strydom, one of my team-mates, told me 'Help yourself, and put it on your room bill'. I thought 'This is nice', and climbed in. I did the same for the next four days, under the impression that it was all paid for by Free State and it came as a shock when I was presented with my bill. My daily allowance of fifteen rands didn't quite stretch that far! Robbie East had to bail me out with a loan. I wasn't exactly sophisticated!

My cricketing naivete was also shown up again in this match, when the West Indian batsman Collis King took me apart. King had been part of the West Indies 'rebel' tours and it had made financial sense for him to build a new career in South Africa. Batting without a helmet, he treated me with complete contempt, scoring 154 and toying with me. I felt intimidated by the way he'd pull a good-length delivery over midwicket, just swatting me away. I had no idea of how to bowl at him, and although I got him out cheaply in the second innings, that was due to a magnificent catch by our wicket-keeper, rather than any skill on my part. It was a bitter experience for me. I knew that King had been a fine batsman – he'd destroyed England in the 1979 World Cup Final – but he had the reputation of being erratic. He was not in the class of a Viv Richards, an Allan Border or a Gordon Greenidge, yet he had made me look an amateur. If I was to get anywhere near to achieving my ambition of playing for my country, I had to toughen up and become more consistent.

I improved in the next Currie Cup match, against Eastern Province on my home ground. I took five for 46 and bowled well. My rhythm was good, I generated good pace and I even managed to move the ball away from the bat at times. At that stage, I was more of an inswing bowler, or moving it around off the seam – subtleties like the outswinger were beyond me then! The idea was just to get the ball down the other end as fast as possible. When their final wicket fell on the stroke of lunch, the South African team for the next 'Test' against the Aussies was read out over the tannoy. We were all delighted to hear that Corrie van Zyl was in it, and I was stunned when Robbie East turned to me and said, 'It's a shame you didn't take those wickets earlier, because you'd have had a chance the way you bowled today'. I was amazed that anybody would think of me as an international prospect, let alone my wicket-keeper. Later that day, I had my first newspaper interview. Ray Williams, who was working for the South African equivalent of the Press Association, and had been around the cricket scene a long time, told me that I should have been in the squad, and coming from such an experienced reporter, I took notice. Perhaps people were starting to become aware of me after all.

Robbie East was responsible for something even more significant in that match than just telling me I was getting better as a bowler. He told me, 'Allan, you learn about this game in the opposition dressing-room' and he marched me in and sat me down alongside the great Graeme Pollock. I had already delighted myself in the game by bowling at Pollock, and not being smacked around the park by him. Mind you, it was only one ball and he pushed it defensively to mid-off! As I ran in, I thought 'I'm bowling at Graeme Pollock!' and was mightily relieved when he played defensively. He was out next over, so I only ever bowled one delivery at one of the greatest players of all time. When I sat alongside him in the dressing-room, I realised that everyone else there was also in awe of him. He was quiet, modest and very impressive. He eventually turned to me and said 'Now, what do you want to do with yourself?' and I blurted out 'Play for South Africa'. He smiled and said 'I like that attitude – do you think we'll get back in again?' I hadn't a clue, but we all agreed that we hoped it would happen one day, the sooner the better. It would come too late for Graeme Pollock, but I'll never forget the day a legend took time out to talk to someone like me. His good manners and interest were an object lesson in how great players can inspire youngsters. I wish all top cricketers were as helpful as that guy was to me.

My first Currie Cup season ended with two more games, a rain-ruined match against Border in East London and a significant one at home against Northern Transvaal. What made it memorable for me was the bitter lesson I learned about handling pressure. Quite simply, I bottled it, letting the pressure get to me and I let the side down. My bowling was satisfactory enough, with figures of five for 43, but I failed badly with the bat when the heat was on. When I walked out to bat, we needed just six to win, and I was the last man. Brad Player, a great friend of mine, was at the other end and he told me not to worry about the spinner, Willie Morris. 'Look, it's not turning, don't worry about it' he told me, and yet the first delivery turned square. I played a poor defensive shot and nicked it to Anton Ferreira at slip. As I walked off in despair, I burst into tears. Anton, one of the nicest of guys, had his arm around me, trying to console me, saying, 'This'll happen to you again, son , you've got to get used to this. It's not your job to score six runs at number eleven, those guys sat up on that balcony should have got them for you'. It was nice of him to say that, but I couldn't be consoled. I was crying my eyes out, because I had turned to jelly. When I got back to the dressing-room, I could see in the eyes of some of my team-mates that they believed I had bottled it. I had to go onto the outfield to compose myself, rather than face them. I felt so small, so inadequate. Cricket at this level seemed so harsh. It felt that I had buckled at the first hint of pressure. I just had to work out how to handle it, otherwise I'd never make the grade.

Despite those misgivings, my first-class bowling figures in my debut season were good. In seven Currie Cup games, I had taken 17 wickets at an average of 21.50, and the *South African Cricket Annual* selected me as one of the five most Promising Young Players of the Year. All very gratifying, but I saw no reason to brag about my first season. I had the raw material – pace – but there had been enough sticky moments against good batsmen for me to understand I had so much still to learn about fast bowling. And as for coping with the mental demands of first-class cricket, I was a world away. Being shy and tongue-tied didn't help, and I knew that somehow I had to be more aggressive on the field and to stand up to fiery characters like Rodney Hogg.

So it was back to the Army after those few cricketing interludes and over the next six months, I certainly did toughen up my approach to life and cricket. At the start of the 1986/87 season, I took seven for 63 and eleven wickets in the match for the South African Defence X1 against Griqualand West in Kimberley. It was such a treat not to have to make our own beds for those four days in Kimberley – when you're on national service, you appreciate little things like that. Our captain, Roy Pienaar gave me a good report for my efforts in that match, and it clearly did me some good in the eyes of the selectors. I was quicker than in my first season, after a year of hard physical work in the Army and one batsman on the Griquas side was made painfully aware of that. Andy Moles, the Warwick-shire opener was out in South Africa that year and I wasn't impressed to see him walk out to face me, without a helmet. Roy Pienaar said to him, 'This bloke's got a bit of pace, you know – be careful'. Andy said, 'We'll see' – and we did. The first bouncer I bowled at him saw him fractionally late on the hook shot and he top-edged it straight over the wicket-keeper's head to the boundary. Andy then called for his helmet. We've often joked about that down the years after becoming great friends and Warwickshire team-mates, but for me it was important that I got riled at the batsmen. He thought I wasn't that quick? We'll see about that! It had dawned on me that you need a bit of the bully in you to dominate as a fast bowler. A touch of the Rodney Hoggs, in fact.

A month after that Kimberley game, I got my revenge against Hogg. Kim Hughes' squad were back for another tour and we squared up to them on a dead pitch at Bloem-fontein, which led to a dull draw, followed by a President's XI game in the gold mining town of Virginia, a short drive out from 'Bloem'. The match was played at the Harmony Oval, but there wasn't much harmony out in the middle. I decided to impose myself on the Aussies, rather than be the quiet guy who just wanted to concentrate on his bowl-ing. In my second spell, I worked up a fair old pace and I was angry when Roy Pienaar dropped Carl Rackemann at slip off my bowling. We felt we had a real chance of victory and I was frustrated when that chance went down. Yet two balls later, I squeezed a yorker through him and when the stumps went down, I did something I'd never tried before. I gave the batsman the 'send off', pointing him in the direction of the pavilion. By then, I was really pumped up and Rackemann was the recipient of something that happened purely on the spur of the moment. I've done it many times since, in common with every fast bowler, but it was new territory that day for the quiet guy from Bloemfontein. I was getting harder in my attitude on the field and there was some satisfaction knowing that the Aussies would expect exactly that sort of behaviour. After all, they were the past masters at it.

So, with Rackemann out of the way, Rodney Hogg walked in. He didn't seem all that bothered about the possibility of defeat, and he chatted away to the close fielders as if it was a friendly. Now there is no such thing when South Africans are involved in a cricket match, never mind the Australians, and I was determined to give him a wake-up call. I hadn't forgotten how he talked down to me a year earlier in Pretoria, telling me to go back to school. Since then the shy Afrikaaner had become more committed to his career, more determined not to back down against verbal intimidation. Those back-breaking months of Army training had given me a backbone and Hogg was about to get what he deserved. As he walked to the crease, some of the guys said to me, 'Come on, Allan – it's time to get even with this bloke. Be hard-arsed, give it to him'. I knew exactly what they meant. My first ball hit him straight on the helmet. He swore as the ball bounced just over the stumps and I followed through, all the way for a close-up chat. He had a massive smile on his face and I said 'What the f*** are you grinning at?' He then told me to f*** off, that I'd only been in the game five minutes, and that my time would come. That didn't stop me, and I proceeded to give him the full treatment – stares, short-pitched deliveries whizzing just past his nose and a few verbals thrown in.

He didn't like it, and when he was reminded about Pretoria from a year ago, he was even less impressed. To be fair to him, he didn't give it away and hung around long enough to win the game for the Aussies. Afterwards, he came up to me, shook my hand, asked how old I was and said, 'That was good to see, mate. Let's hope you play in the next Test, and we'll see how you go'.

That's the way it should be in cricket. I see no problem in giving out the verbals as long as racial or physical abuse aren't drawn in. It's often just banter, but it's a hard game out there. The crucial thing is not to get distracted, as Glenn McGrath was against Alan Mullally during the Melbourne Test in 1998 when he gave away vital runs. McGrath was too good a bowler to be put off by a 'bunny' like Mullally. Those extra runs proved decisive in England's narrow win and McGrath did his team no favours by getting carried away.

Rodney Hogg's sudden respect for me meant a lot. I was coming more and more out of my shell every time I played a big game, and I couldn't wait to get the ball in my hand and impose myself on the batsmen. Now I could understand the surge of adrenalin and power that fast bowlers like Dennis Lillee, Jeff Thomson and Michael Holding experienced, that feeling that no one could withstand them for very long if it was all working for them. I wouldn't have put myself in their class for a moment, but in terms of raw power, I could relate to the feeling that the fast bowler could turn a game if he was powerful enough psychologically. That was an area I had to work on, quite apart from all the other technical skills needed. I felt I was getting there, especially after taking eight for 37 against Transvaal at the Wanderers. It all slipped into place that day, against some fine batsmen. I had pace, bounce, control and rhythm and there was the perfect finale to the match for me when Clive Rice, the Transvaal captain came into our dressing-room. He was also the South African captain and he was there to tell me I'd been picked for the next 'Test', at Port Elizabeth. Clive also said that I wouldn't be twelfth man, that I was going to play. I clutched my face in pleasure and excitement and for hours afterwards, just floated away. Already, my mind was racing ahead to St George's Park, wondering about the atmosphere and what it would be like to walk onto the field as an international cricketer. Was it really only a few months ago that I had been a schoolboy?

All I wanted was to try on that blazer with the Springbok cap. I then thought about the great South African players of the past, including that marvellous 1970 side – Barry Richards, Graeme and Peter Pollock, Eddie Barlow, Dennis Lindsay and so on. What a thrill to be following on from those guys. I thought of one of our opponents, Kepler Wessels, the idol of Grey College. After playing in World Series Cricket, he had married an Australian girl and qualified for Australia. He was back playing for Eastern Province, and yet he would be lining up against us. That wasn't a very popular move in our country, and it gave us an extra incentive to blow him away. It made no difference – Kepler scored a hundred in each innings, showing all the discipline and stroke selection that Mr Voldstedt had raved about to me when I was at Grey College ten years earlier.

I didn't lack support on that great day of my career. Dad got to Port Elizabeth to see me take the field, after a terrible journey that involved flights from Bloemfontein to Johannesburg, then to East London and finally to Port

Elizabeth. The Cronje family was also there to support me, just a few years after all those hugely committed games on the back lawn of their house. Hansie's father, Ewie was particularly delighted I'd been picked, because at the end of the previous season, he'd said, 'We've got to look after this boy, he's going to be big one day'. He'd also been instrumental in getting me some time off from Army duties to train with the Free State boys, so I owed Mr Cronje a great deal. When his son was first picked for South Africa, then became captain, I was thrilled for Ewie Cronje. There can't have been a prouder father.

I got three wickets in the match and of course the first one sticks in my mind. Greg Shipperd tried to pull a short one and ballooned it up to Brian Whitfield at midwicket. A lot of the guys said afterwards that I didn't look too happy at getting the wicket, but that was because I was frustrated after bowling a lot of overs and getting nothing back on a flat wicket. Later, I got Kim Hughes twice – bowled through the gate in the first innings, then he dragged one on, a widish delivery that didn't deserve a wicket. In the second innings, I went for around four an over, with Wessels feasting on too many legstump half-volleys. So I wasn't all that pleased with my debut, although Clive Rice was very positive. He told me, 'Well done, I hope that's been a fantastic experience for you, I'm sure there are many more to come'. That was very reassuring to a young man out of his depth and I appreciated his support.

Another great player was equally supportive of me in that game: Graeme Pollock. He stood there at mid-off, saying, 'Just enjoy it' to me, and it was a special thrill to be on the same side as him. One of my genuine claims to fame is that I played in the same team as Graeme Pollock, in his last game for South Africa. Within a month of his 43rd birthday, he was still good enough to score 144, looking a great player after his usual shaky start. He was nearly out first ball to a brilliant delivery from Rodney Hogg that clipped the edge of his bat and dropped just short of the wicket-keeper. Hogg bowled very fast at him, giving absolutely nothing away, and it was a fantastic contest. After a time, Pollock just pinged the bowling to the boundary. I was amazed at his unbelievable timing, the way he just leaned into the shot. There was a huge gap between his feet at the crease and he did that because if the ball was full, he didn't have to move that far and could just then lean into the shot. If the ball was short, he'd lean back and probably not offer a stroke. His balance was perfect, his bat was heavy, he had great physical strength and a very fast bat swing. He made it look so easy. Hogg got him out eventually in his farewell innings, but not before he had shown his genius. I count it a great privilege to have started my international career in the same game that Graeme Pollock brought down the curtain on his. He must have been a fantastic player in his prime, judging from what I saw when he was in his forties.

After my debut in Port Elizabeth, I was delighted that Clive Rice was as good as his word and picked me for some of the one-day internationals. Corrie van Zyl was injured, which obviously helped me, and although he replaced me at Johannesburg, I was happy enough with my efforts and both Rice and the chairman of selectors, Peter van der Merwe said they were very pleased with my introduction to the big time. My first experience of one-day internationals at Port Elizabeth is still the best game of its type I have ever played in. We scored 316 for six, and after I'd been carted for 32 off just four overs, the Aussies needed just eighteen to win off eighteen balls with nine wickets in hand. Hughes and Wessels had both scored hundreds and they were coasting to victory. Yet Rice somehow kept his cool and bowled some brilliant yorkers. The Aussies threw it away, couldn't take the pressure and we bowled them out for 310, to win by six runs. An amazing performance, and when the last wicket fell, the noise at St George's Park almost blew off the roof.

When all the international games were over, and I could reflect on a fantastic season for me, I couldn't have been happier. I'd taken 47 first-class wickets at 23.74, and only Garth le Roux, with 49, had taken more. Many good judges were talking about me and Corrie van Zyl being South Africa's opening pair for some time, and I was very excited about the prospect. Sadly for Corrie, it wasn't to be as the injuries mounted up. He lost his competitive edge when various stress fractures to his back meant he could only bowl off ten yards in the nets. He had been a great help to me in those early years at Free State, and I'm glad he hasn't been lost to South African cricket, doing a fine job as a fitness specialist.

Just to finish off an amazing few months for me, I was then offered a contract to play county cricket in England. I couldn't believe my luck when the Warwickshire manager, David Brown approached me during the 'Test' in Port Elizabeth. David was a very good friend of Dr Ali Bacher, Managing Director of the South African Cricket Union who was becoming very influential in South African cricket at that time. Dr Bacher approached me on Warwickshire's behalf; did I fancy a season's trial at Edgbaston? I didn't ask for any details at all, I just said 'yes' over and over again. David told me I'd get £6,000 for the summer contract, but I wasn't bothered at all about the money. The challenge was the thing. Many of the world's best players were still involved in county cricket in 1987 and I wanted to match myself up against them, to stretch myself. My imagination had been fired years earlier, listening to my grandfather telling me all about county cricket, showing me those magazines. I was like a ten-year-old kid at the prospect.

There was one thing I needed to keep in mind, though, and Hansie Cronje's Dad spelled it out to me when I called in to say goodbye. 'Remember to work on your English, boy', he said. He was right – there was work to be done in that area, as well as my bowling. I was about to start learning in all sorts of areas.

CHAPTER FOUR

The Bloemfontein Brummie

I couldn't wait to get to Birmingham and start learning about county cricket and its various disciplines. I imagined what it was like bowling at great players, and told myself that this is what I really wanted to do. Before leaving Bloemfontein, I'd told my good friend, Hansie Cronje, that I'd give everything at Edgbaston, that no one would ever accuse me of not trying my best. I wanted to make a career out of professional cricket. At the age of 20, I had many rough edges – including a very strong Afrikaaner accent that tended to distort my faltering efforts at speaking English fluently. It would be some time before I could honestly say that I'd made myself understood in English! In fact, in that first season, I kept misunderstanding the difference between 'optional' and 'compulsory' nets. Whenever the coach or captain said the nets were 'optional', I'd make sure I got there early, ready to bowl for ages, desperate to get stuck in. I had no idea what 'optional' meant. I soon learned!

From day one, it's been a fantastic experience to play for Warwickshire. I've learned such a lot at Edgbaston, not just about cricket but also life. I was picked up at Heathrow Airport by Andy Moles, and on the way up to Birmingham,

he marked my card about the various possible social pit-
falls. He told me it was a great life on the county circuit,
but to avoid too much alcohol – no problem there, I'd
never touched a drop in my life – to stay away from drugs
(which just made me laugh), and to give the newspapers
no reason to write about me unless it was about my cricket.
He was being very protective even though I wouldn't have
stepped on an ant in those days, never mind cause a fuss
in a bar or club. I hadn't a clue about drugs or alcohol,
but I was impressed at Andy's concern for me. He couldn't
believe that I'd brought three suitcases over from South
Africa, and we spent ages trying to cram them into his car.
One of my suitcases was full of shoes, which I admit is my
one major weakness. I collect shoes like others accumulate
beer mats, although my hobby is rather more expensive!
Don't ask me why, but I've always loved having lots of
shoes – one of my Warwickshire captains, Andy Lloyd
used to call me 'Imelda', after Imelda Marcos, who had
cupboards full of them when she was the big name in the
Philippines a few years back.

The chaos at Heathrow Airport absolutely amazed me
and yet Andy Moles assured me it was always like that.
Coming from Bloemfontein, it was certainly a contrast in
airports. It seemed to take ages to get away, and yet the
journey up to Birmingham was fascinating. I loved all the
greenness of the countryside, and I just sat there, wide-eyed,
not saying anything until Andy spoke to me. Near to Birmingham, I saw some gasometers, and asked Andy if that
was where they played cricket, at the Oval. I'd seen the
Oval gasometers in one of my grandfather's cricket magazines, and I was disappointed when Andy told me that
particular ground was behind us, in South London, as we

drove north to Birmingham. I had absolutely no idea of the geography of England. I was so naive, so short of knowledge.

My digs were to be a flat above the pavilion in the Edgbaston ground, and Andy, at the time a single guy, was also living in the ground area. So the most natural thing was to go out together on my first night in England. He took me to a pub – the Old Varsity Tavern, in Selly Oak, five minutes' drive away from the cricket ground. That's when I had my first alcoholic drink: a lager shandy. In my 21st year. What a sheltered life I'd led! Something more significant happened that night in the Varsity Tavern. I met Tina, the girl who was eventually to become my wife four years later. She was studying at Birmingham's College of Tourism at the time and we chatted about South Africa the first time we met. I was painfully shy, short of many social graces, with a thick Afrikaans accent and a military haircut that certainly wasn't all that stylish for the English way of life. But Tina and I hit it off. We didn't really get together until the following year, but settling down was the best thing I've ever done. I've always been a big family man, and Tina was one of eight children, so she shared the same attitude to kids and looking after your parents. We have two lovely children and a stable and secure family life that is absolutely essential to my happiness. There's no doubt at all that I've become a better cricketer through the peace of mind you get from being very happy at home. The travelling and the hotel life on tour are definitely a hassle, but the knowledge that you are coming home to loved ones who are special is so reassuring.

I enjoyed everything about England that first summer. The social life was fun, the younger guys in the Warwickshire squad were always very kind with me – and the learning curve in my cricket was massive. There was so much to pick up from talking to team-mates with such deep experience of the game. I met Gladstone Small on one of my first days at Edgbaston and he was so friendly and cheerful. He'd just come back from a very successful tour to Australia with England, and of course I knew how well he had performed. But he went out of his way to make me welcome. It was another totally new experience for an Afrikaaner from Bloemfontein to change in the same dressing-room as a black guy like Gladstone, but there was never a problem for an instant. I may have been naive but I wasn't that daft and I knew that with my background, there might have been potential problems. But I was never embarrassed. I knew that people would talk to me about apartheid, with Nelson Mandela still on Robben Island, and a hero to so many others throughout the world. I was determined not to get drawn into long discussions about the situation, not least because my command of English wasn't all that great, and I could easily let myself down. Would people call me a racist? Would a guy, aged twenty, with little experience of the outside world, get all the flak about South Africa's policies? It's not as if I knew all that much about my own country. Growing up in a sheltered part of South Africa, with no great knowledge of what was going on outside the Afrikaaner community in Bloemfontein didn't exactly equip me for great debates over a pint in a language that wasn't all that natural to me. I got to know more about South Africa from watching television programmes in Birmingham, once I'd turned up there at the age of 20 – so what could I contribute to serious discussions, other than the obvious remark that people should go over there, experience various things, then make up their own minds? Geoff Humpage, the Warwickshire wicket-keeper, was a great help to me in those early days at Edgbaston. Geoff had been a policeman, so was used to difficult social situations. He had also toured in South Africa, as one of the Graham Gooch 'rebel' team in 1982, and knew about some of the complexities involved in making blanket condemnations. So Geoff protected me, making sure things didn't get too heavy. There was never a dull moment with Geoff Humpage, he had such a ready, quick wit that he kept me laughing all the way on our many car journeys to away fixtures. While Geoff drove, I'd bombard him with questions about professional cricket and life in England. His ears must still be burning, all those years down the line. I'd ask him about the wickets in England, the line I should bowl, the quality of the balls, where to place the field. I'd keep it up in the bar after a game, or in the dressing-room, and Geoff would sometimes say 'Al, do you always talk this much?' The very idea; I've always been a quiet guy, but not when it comes to learning about cricket. I hadn't forgotten that important lesson from Free State, that you learn quickest of all about the game by sitting in the dressing-room and asking questions. Basically, I was a student cricketer and the senior Warwickshire guys were willing to share their knowledge.

When I arrived at Edgbaston, I knew I was on trial. Tony Merrick, the West Indian fast bowler, was in contention with me for the overseas place, and we obviously eyed each other up over those early weeks. Tony was a different sort of bowler to me – he liked to bang it in, short of a length, in true Caribbean style, whereas I was very wild and didn't really know where I was pitching the ball. Tony and I never had a particularly close relationship, which was hardly surprising, because we were professional rivals. We got on well enough, but I could sense he was determined to see me off, and we never really shared much in tactical terms. Tony was quicker than me in those days. I remember one spell against Essex that was seriously fast. He hit Allan Border over the ear, which prompted a volley of foul language from Border in the physio's room as he was being treated. But he recovered to make a hundred in the second innings, which showed how much guts that little guy had. Border was such a hard character; I'd look at someone like him and appreciate how vital courage and mental strength were to succeed in top-class cricket.

So Tony Merrick and I alternated in the first team over the first two seasons I was on the staff at Edgbaston. But I put down an early marker in the indoor nets before I played for the first eleven. Dennis Amiss was having a net, preparing himself for what turned out to be his last season for Warwickshire. I knew all about his prestige and was determined to impress, by a hostile attack on the fast, bouncy indoor wicket. His rib cage was tickled up a few times by some deliveries I managed to get in the right area and it was reassuring to see a batsman of his class hop around. Just because he was 43 didn't mean I should go easy on him, I wanted that first team place ahead of Tony Merrick. So I put Dennis through the mixer and I noticed that he kept turning round to talk to another first-team batsman, Andy Lloyd, who was standing outside the net. Dennis wasn't wearing a helmet and yet I kept on peppering him. I bowled him a short one, he ducked out of the way just in time, then threw the ball back at me angrily. He shouted 'F*** off, youngster.' He was clearly ruffled and

I wondered what I'd done. I apologised afterwards and Dennis said 'It's very quick in these nets, we don't try to kill each other, and the bowlers go for line and length. Show us your frustrations when you play county cricket, then you can bounce the opposition as much as you like'. Andy Lloyd enjoyed it, though. I could tell he was impressed, even though I sprayed it around a lot. Over the next few years, Andy was to prove very helpful to me. He'd coached me for a couple of days in Bloemfontein a few years earlier and when he finally became my captain at Warwickshire, he handled me very well, using me in short spells, encouraging me to blast out batsmen with sheer speed, rather than just settle for line and length. In those early days at Edgbaston, I was very wild in my direction, and it was sensible just to encourage me to bowl fast, and worry about accuracy at a later stage.

There were so many positive guys in that Edgbaston dressing-room that I couldn't fail to learn quickly. I'd just sit in the corner drinking it all in, listening to bubbly characters like Andy Lloyd, Geoff Humpage, Gordon Parsons and Andy Moles, while the wiser, older heads like Dennis Amiss and Norman Gifford would offer sensible words of advice. Norman was my first captain at Warwickshire, and he was excellent with me. He was still playing county cricket at the age of 47, which amazed me, and he had so much knowledge stored away. He was also willing to share it generously, which I respected greatly. He told me early on that he thought I was a great prospect, but quickly added 'But that's between you and me'. Norman didn't believe in a youngster getting big ideas. He'd puff on his pipe, offer a quiet word and usually, you'd be amazed that he'd spotted something that was useful for you. He'd be hard on younger players who didn't match up to his high standards, and there's nothing wrong with that. I was so fortunate with the wealth of experience available to me. Our cricket manager, David Brown was a top guy. He'd been a fine fast bowler with Warwickshire and England a few years earlier, but never dwelt on the past, you'd never hear him talking about his experiences. He was the nicest bloke you could ever wish to work with – he'd see the funny side of things, but always had the consoling word when he sensed you were down. When I was vulnerable, he was there, with an arm around my shoulder, always encouraging me if I felt that I should be playing in the first eleven, rather than Tony Merrick. He talked a lot to me about attitude, that he knew all about the South African philosophy of aggression, and that he wanted me to show that hostility to batsmen. He said that I should never feel overawed at bowling at great players, that I must always have a positive attitude. Brownie was so calm about set-backs. He'd have a quiet chat after a bad day and just say 'Have you thought about bowling this way at that bloke?' Then he'd talk me through it all with so much authority and clear language that I couldn't wait to get out there and put it into practice. He also knew so much about English conditions that his advice was always valuable. David Brown only worked with me for one season – but he made a great impression on me. You wanted to do well for him, as well as for your own sake.

In fact, Brownie was delighted by my bowling in my early county games, even though I put an opposition batsman in hospital when we played Essex at Chelmsford. I broke Paul Prichard's finger with an accidental beamer, as umpire Dickie Bird hopped around, fussing about the fading light.

I just got on with it, tried the yorker and got it totally wrong. I was very sorry about the injury and apologised profusely to the Essex captain, Graham Gooch, but he wasn't too pleased with me. I found out years later that Dickie Bird had been impressed by my pace and hostility and told our manager, 'You've got a good 'un there, Brownie'. I wish Dickie had given me a few more lbws down the years, so that recommendation from him might have been more appreciated!

That particular delivery which injured Paul Prichard actually put me out of the first team for a while, because I ricked my back, striving for the extra pace. Tony Merrick got in while I recuperated, but he played more championship matches than me for the first two seasons – 30 compared to my 18. Of course, I was frustrated and as I kicked my heels in the second eleven, I kept an eye on his progress in the first team. It was nothing personal, just professional rivalry. When I did get back in the first team, my performances were mixed. I cleaned up the Leicestershire tail to take five for 42, then got taken apart by Derek Randall when we played Nottinghamshire. Richard Hadlee also bowled me twice with unplayable deliveries. In the next game, I watched Malcolm Marshall closely, to see just how he managed to swing the ball so late, the way he used the crease to vary the angle slightly, his mastery of the slower ball. It was a tremendous bonus for me to watch the likes of Hadlee and Marshall in successive matches – you just had to be able to pick something up from world-class performers like them. In those days, county cricket was full of terrific overseas players. Martin Crowe took me to the cleaners, scoring an unbeaten double-hundred for Somerset on a green seamer. He played so straight, and he left the ball so late; the best batsmen have always been superb at judging instantly when to leave the ball, just when you believe you've got them playing away from the body. Crowe gave you nothing at all, he was the supreme technician. Watching at close quarters top players like Crowe and Border made me realise the importance of patience when batting. The best batsmen are like hunters, knowing when to go for the kill. They never get too eager, they don't press too soon, they just bide their time and pick you off when the loose ball comes around.

At the end of that first season with Warwickshire, I feared the worst. I'd taken 37 wickets in ten championship matches, while Tony Merrick had 57 from fourteen, and I wondered who they really preferred. I wondered if they were shielding me from too many matches with an eye on the future, making sure I wasn't overbowled. Yet that didn't apply when I had to bowl 37 overs in one innings on the flattest deck of all time against Sussex at Nuneaton! But the hard work didn't frighten me at all, and even though I did get a little fed up of second-team cricket, after bowling at guys like Crowe in the first team, I was fairly happy with that first season. Yet Merrick and I couldn't play in the same first team, due to restrictions on overseas players – so what would Warwickshire do about us? Before the season ended, I got the good news. A two-year contract, with my wage leaping up from £6,000 a year to £15,000. Very nice indeed, but it was the professional challenge that appealed the most.

I returned to South Africa for the 1987/88 domestic season, feeling happy about gaining vital experience in England and a more confident person socially. My friends in Bloemfontein were amazed at how outgoing I now was, compared to just a few months earlier. They told me I had a Birmingham accent, but I wasn't so sure of that! One thing had to go when I came back – my long hair. I'd made sure my severe Army haircut had been replaced by something more fashionable during the English summer, but it was back to square one in Bloemfontein, because I still had some months to serve in the Army. This time, the last few months were easier; I'd been transferred to the sports office just outside base, after Ewie Cronje had pulled a few strings, so that I could train and play for Free State.

That season was a rude awakening for me. I took just 25 wickets at 30 apiece for Free State and didn't bowl well at all. I was so disappointed, because I thought that I'd come back from England a better bowler. I didn't deceive myself, I knew I was still erratic, but I was building up to a consistent pace and felt I ought to have done better. My basic problem was that I tried too hard, my rhythm suffered, and I sprayed the ball around all over the place. My line was never right that season, I couldn't stop myself bowling the English length – fuller, to make the ball swing, as if the pitch was slow – whereas I needed to come back a yard and bang it in shorter on the faster South African decks. I had a nightmare in one particular match, when Kepler Wessels smashed me all over the place in a Nissan Shield game. I was moping in the dressing-room at tea-time, feeling sorry for myself when our coach told me, 'You're bowling the biggest load of crap I've ever seen'. He was right, but it was painful for me to hear those words from Johann Voldstedt, my old sports master at Grey College, who was now helping out Free State. I had great respect for Mr Voldstedt and his words cut home to me. I had to walk out of the dressing-room in frustration and anger.

There was no one to turn to – the harder I tried, the worse I bowled. It wasn't a very pleasant experience. At that stage in my career, I just didn't have enough inner calm, to tell myself I just had to slow things down and think it all out. I was just rushing at my bowling, thinking that guts and all-out effort would be enough. There was also some criticism flying around in the press to the effect that I was coasting for Free State, that I thought I'd cracked it now that I had a county contract. That was so unfair, because I certainly didn't believe I was anywhere near as good as the favourable press cuttings had suggested the season before. I never believed all that hype, I was a fairly humble guy who didn't believe in shouting my mouth off. At no stage had I ever talked myself up in the press, but others had clearly done it for me, so that when I failed to deliver, I copped the flak. I simply had to get used to the criticism in South Africa, because for the next few years, I was to read that I was delivering for Warwickshire, but not Free State. That really upset me, because I have always tried my hardest for my side. I didn't know how to cope with that unfair criticism, except try to ignore but I was disappointed how anybody could think I would ever coast when playing for Free State. It simply isn't in my nature or in the way I'd been brought up by my family.

At least Free State was starting to gel as a unit after getting promoted to the senior division of the Currie Cup. We had some good young players coming through, as well as top performers like my Warwickshire team-mate, Alvin Kallicharran, Corrie van Zyl, the West Indian fast bowler Sylvester Clarke and the England batsman, Allan Lamb. I thought Lamby was a brilliant player against fast bowling and he scored an astonishing 294 that season against

Eastern Province, when he was almost bowled first ball, and then proceeded to smash everything out of sight. Unfortunately, that was the best we saw of Lamby, because he then went home to England for most of our domestic season, and only returned when Free State got into the Currie Cup Final for the first time. In my opinion he wasn't a good communicator and had a rather hard attitude to his team-mates. Sylvester Clarke was different. A great guy, who bowled in pain for long periods but never complained. His right knee was blown away with all the wear and tear of fast bowling, but Sylvers carried a syringe around with him to inject cortisone into the knee, and he always got on the park for us. Sylvester Clarke was the most frightening fast bowler I've seen and I thank God he was on our side, not the opposition's. He'd bowl big in-duckers at you, then line you up for the short delivery. He seemed to love hitting batsmen and he did that for a pastime. His control was immaculate, and whenever he went round the wicket to the batsman, you knew he'd be looking to ping him. His pace was serious – a consistent 90 miles per hour – and even in a one-day game, he'd have three slips, gully, short leg and a silly point. In that Final against Transvaal – which we lost inside three days on a green wicket – Sylvers almost ended the career of Louis Vorster. Bowling from round the wicket, he hit him on the head two deliveries in a row, and after the second, Louis fell onto his stumps. He hadn't been wearing a visor, just a helmet, and didn't have a clue where he was when he got up. He had to be escorted to the pavilion, after starting to go the wrong way. I'm sure it was unintentional on Sylvers' part, but it was scary. I'm convinced that Sylvers bowled just within the laws of the game, although it was wide of the crease and usually aimed at the neck of the batter. It was his control that made him so fearsome. Once he'd got his range, you were in trouble.

So, after a season of frustration in South Africa, I pitched up at Edgbaston for the 1988 summer, determined to smooth out a few rough edges. Warwickshire could only play one of their two registered overseas players because regulations were being tightened up to give England qualified players more of an opportunity in county cricket. Therefore I knew it was either me or Tony Merrick who would be in the first eleven. It proved to be another tough time for me. I just didn't bowl consistently enough, and with my overseas rival Tony Merrick starting the season well, I had to be content with filling in for him. He played in fifteen championship matches, I only got six, taking 26 wickets. I spent a lot of time in the second eleven, still trying my hardest, but I did get discouraged at times, especially towards the end of the season, when I realised I hadn't learned all that much in the summer. We had a new cricket manager, Bob Cottam, who came with a high reputation as a bowling coach. Certainly Bob was very good. He spoke clearly and openly, was honest with the players and didn't shirk from telling us how it is. He was an 'In Your Face' sort of coach, unlike David Brown's more subtle approach. At the stage of my career, not yet 22, I probably needed the arm around my shoulder, rather than Cottam's straight talking, but I'm not saying Bob was wrong to deal with us his way. He's one of the best technicians I've worked with, who understood the mechanics of fast bowling, how a bowling action can go wrong and what then to do about it. He didn't blind you with science and he could explain things concisely. But Bob liked to test you out, to see just how mentally tough you were. In that 1988 season, I bowled very well for the first team at Leeds, when I took nine wickets in the match. Everything felt right, and I couldn't wait for the match against Kent at Edgbaston straight afterwards. Before we played Kent, Cottam said to me 'That was great, that's how I want you to bowl all the time. Now you've got to go out and do it against Kent – then again in the next game. Can you do it? Are you up to it?' I thought that a little hard. He was clearly testing me out, seeing how far he could push me. I was a quiet lad, who needed more sympathetic handling at that stage, even though I could see what he was trying to do with me. I did need to get harder, to develop consistency – it's just that there are different ways to get there when the bowler's just a shy kid who desperately wants to learn.

There were two other significant developments for Warwickshire in that 1988 season, that helped mould us into the hugely successful outfit of subsequent seasons. First, Andy Lloyd became our captain, and his positive approach started to rub off on all of us. Andy liked a gamble on the horses, and his captaincy was like that. He'd back a hunch and go for it. He didn't like draws or attritional games and he encouraged us to play aggressively and take chances. Andy was great for me, he really looked after me, coaxing me towards the idea of short spells, rather than all-out assaults that took too much out of me. Andy and I had many chats in the Extra Cover Bar at Edgbaston during that 1988 season, and he made it clear to me that I was his man for the future, the fast bowler he wanted to rely on. I wouldn't ask him about Tony Merrick's prospects, because that was basically between club and player, but Andy was always very good at encouraging me, boosting my confidence that was at times very low during that period when I was learning my trade. Andy said I had a long-term future at the club, telling me 'Just hang on in there, Al', and I liked the feeling of confidence shown in me by my new captain. He told me that he saw me as the spearhead, the guy who gives it everything for around five overs, and then comes back for regular assaults on the batsmen, rather than bowling me into the ground. There was no point in pushing my body beyond the point where I might be effective, so it was better for all concerned that I wasn't stretched too far physically, too soon in my career. That decision by Andy Lloyd proved to be spot on – in later years I'd be able to sustain long spells, but not at the age of 21, when I just wasn't sure where the ball was going and how much I should be putting into each spell.

Warwickshire was on the move under our new captain, and the signing of Dermot Reeve that same season was to prove even more influential. Andy Lloyd rated the competitive instincts and all-round abilities of Dermot when he played for Sussex and he was keen to get him signed up for us, once Dermot had decided to move on. It was a crucial signing. I'd played against him in second eleven cricket and I recall how unpopular he was with his own team-mates. He was a niggler on the field, and convinced he was a better player than he appeared. Yet there was something about Dermot Reeve, even in those early days at Edgbaston. He had an inner confidence that I wish I'd been able to call on, and a competitive edge that he'd learned by growing up in Hong Kong and playing grade cricket in Perth, Western Australia. So Dermot was never lacking in confidence or guts. No one ever forced Dermot Reeve to back down. Years later, I offered my own tribute to Dermot when I said 'I'd rather he was on my side, than against me', and that was because he never gave you much peace on the field. Even when he was trying to outwit you tactically, he was telling you that you weren't all that special as a cricketer. That's why Dermot was never fondly regarded, because he just got on your nerves. But you'd want him in your corner; he was physically brave, imaginative as a tactician, and bright enough to create a winning environment. That was all in the future, though. In 1988, when he joined us from Sussex, he was okay as a player, but nothing out of the ordinary. If someone had told me at the start of that season that Dermot Reeve would make such an outstanding contribution to our later success, I wouldn't have believed it.

After two seasons with Warwickshire, I knew that the club was on the move, and I wanted to be part of its future. The problem was that Tony Merrick probably felt the same way. He was there before me, and would surely expect to get preference ahead of me. I had just one year left on my contract, after an unsatisfactory second season at Edgbaston. The 1989 season with Warwickshire was going to be a crucial one for me. I was impatient, running out of time in my own eyes. There was another level of performance that I needed to get to. The quicker the better.

CHAPTER FIVE

Breakthrough to the Big Time

I'll never forget the day I realised I might just be on the way to being a proper fast bowler, rather than a wild operator, capable of occasional fast spells or the odd rapid delivery. It came towards the end of May 1989, during a county match at Edgbaston against Middlesex. I ripped out the first four batsmen, hit John Carr on the arm, forcing him to retire hurt, and ended up with seven for 66. Everything felt right that day, and one of my team-mates spotted that. As we gathered round, waiting for the next Middlesex batsman to walk out to the middle, Paul Smith came up to me and said, 'It's just a matter of you pitching it up these days, Al. You seem to have it all worked out now'. I must admit it felt that way, but it was hard work that was the basis. That and inspiration from some fine fast bowlers.

The first to influence me during that formative period was Clive Rice, who had forgotten more about the art of fast bowling than I knew at the time. He taught me how to bowl the outswinger, which greatly increased my chances of getting out the best batsmen. Before, I'd been predominately an inswing bowler, and I knew I needed something extra. Clive worked with me in the nets during the 1988/89 season in South Africa, getting my wrist cocked high, and getting the seam to move towards the offside. He filmed me on video and I saw that I was still opening up my action too early, so that my left side was dropping, with the ball automatically spraying down legside. Clive told me to remember two things: 'You must get off the ground higher and earlier, and your left arm should be aimed at the keeper. He's your target. Pull that left arm through and across your left leg, to give you zip'. We tried all that off a short run and it clicked straight away. Clive explained that the left arm acts as a lever on the body, and it's vital to stay balanced at the height of the leap, to take aim without any loss of control. Rhythm is crucial – as I've discovered painfully many times when I've lost it!

I was full of confidence when I came back to Edgbaston, determined to bowl the outswinger consistently. There were some early teething problems, though. Bob Cottam confused me a little by demonstrating correct grips and wrong grips, and after a couple of net sessions, I was not sure in my mind. So I bought a Richard Hadlee video in the club shop at Edgbaston, and it was a fascinating master class from this great bowler. He talked about how to bowl the appropriate deliveries, and made it all seem clear and concise. Yet it was the mental aspects that fascinated me. The video went through all eleven wickets he picked up in the Wellington Test, when New Zealand surprised everyone with such a great victory over England. To me, the guy had a microchip in his brain. He knew just how to outfox the batsman. He showed how to get David Gower out, because of his habit of playing from the crease, with little foot movement. Allan Lamb was vulnerable to one that left him late, because he was predominately a backfoot player, and couldn't get out of the initial movement across his stumps, when the ball was moving off the seam. Sure enough, Lamb was caught behind. So it went on. His homework on each player was detailed and he had the ability to tailor his bowling line for each player's weaknesses. It gave me a frightening insight into just what's needed mentally to succeed at the highest level. Hadlee talked about the mechanics of fast bowling – the need for balance at the crease, good rhythm and an action that won't let you down, that is grooved and reliable. Before all this, I knew I had the raw ability to bowl quickly at times, but now I could see how I could reach consistency, if I worked hard enough and remembered the basic simple messages Hadlee hammered out.

I knew I had to sort out my run-up. There was no point in getting the mechanics right once I'd got to the crease if I'd arrived there too early, and wasn't in control of myself. So I looked for inspiration to another fast bowler and his name will surprise many. Devon Malcolm. Now I know that Devon has been criticised by many purists throughout his career for technical defects, for an action that falls away at the wrong time and because he's just not reliable enough – but to me, he has always been a magnificent athlete with a marvellous approach to the crease. I'd watched Devon closely during the 1988 season in England, and was intrigued by his rhythm as he ran in. He wasn't just a muscular fast bowler, he'd glide into the crease on his toes, with lovely rhythm. In comparison, I was very flat-footed and didn't seem to be able to generate a balanced run-up consistently. So I copied him. For the next two seasons, I tried to run in exactly like Devon Malcolm. It worked; I was getting to the crease with greater rhythm. For the rest of my career, if ever I have trouble with my rhythm, I think of Devon, and if it's a fault in my wrist action, I visualise that Richard Hadlee video. For me, Devon Malcolm has been the most impressive fast bowler England have had in my career, and I'm not just basing that on his fantastic bowling against us at the Oval in '94. Most of his rivals have been hard-working, bustling bowlers, but Devon glided in and was consistently quick. His example spurred me on and helped me make that transition from being right-arm fast medium with the odd speedy delivery to right arm fast.

So it was starting to fall nicely in to place in the first month of the 1989 season with Warwickshire, and things bucked up even more for me when Tony Merrick came back late from Antigua – and overweight. Andy Lloyd and Bob Cottam weren't too pleased, especially as Andy had made several calls to the Caribbean, trying to track Tony down. Out of the blue, he then pitched up, not in the best condition. He was given a severe rollicking, and although he took out his frustration on the batters in the indoor nets, I felt I'd moved ahead of him in the overseas pecking order. Andy encouraged me, I started to feel really confident, and after getting into the county side early on, never looked back. My captain used to say to me, 'Ease and grace, Al – ease and grace' and Gladstone Small was always at mid-off, giving me sound advice if ever I got carried away on the adrenalin of bowling fast. Glad would just say, 'Don't go overboard, mate – ease and grace, calm down'. As a current England fast bowler, he knew what he was talking about, and he was full of compliments. 'You've got a big future here, Al – you're on the way, just keep working hard'. Andy Lloyd's policy of using me in short, five-over spells was ideal for me. He told me that the very first ball of my new spell had to be hostile, that I was expected to be at the batsman straight away, with no coasting up to high speed. So I'd do a lot of stretching to get loose, and often bowl a bouncer first ball, catching the batter by surprise. In the morning, when I knew I'd be bowling first, I'd get the blood rushing by running on the spot in the dressing-room, then throw a few balls into the wicket-keeper's gloves to be sure my wrist was flexible enough. Andy used to say in that season, 'Get me a couple out early, come back for the middle order, then you're back for the rabbits. Another six wickets, Al!' and yet there were times when he'd deliberately save me for the second innings, when I was looking to knock over the tail. He'd say that he was saving me, that I'd be no use to him later if I'd been overbowled. He was right, although you don't expect a raw 22-year-old who just wanted to bowl to see the point!

I played in 19 of the 22 championship matches in 1989, taking 86 wickets, at a strike rate of one every 39 balls. I was delighted with those figures, because as a strike bowler I was doing my job. That season was the start of Warwickshire's rise to becoming the outstanding side in the country for a couple of seasons. Between 1993 and 1995, we won six trophies, including two championships, and the confidence we developed in ourselves as a unit stemmed from the hard work put in a few years earlier. We became a very aggressive side in the field from 1989 onwards. Dermot Reeve loved to mix it vocally. He was like an Australian out there, saying things like 'He doesn't fancy it, Al' or 'Look at his grip, Al – he's going to be shovelling it to leg every ball'. Dermot simply loved getting up people's noses and Andy Lloyd wasn't far behind, either. He'd prey on the nerves of the batsmen in silly ways – for example if I told the umpire I was going to bowl around the wicket, Andy would shout, 'Oh no, Al! don't do it!', as if my new line would mean physical danger for the batters. At short leg, Andy Moles would be shouting 'Don't worry, Al – I'll push him back, he's all over me at the moment!' a subtle hint from Moler that the batsman was backing away! All designed to disconcert the opposition and I loved it. Behind the stumps, we had a chirpy little character called Keith Piper, who made his first-team debut that year, and contributed to the general air of vocal aggression. Keith has been great for my career at Edgbaston, because he has snaffled the half-chances that wins matches. He's always been a noisy lad because he's basically insecure, but I've enjoyed hearing him shout 'Come on Al!' as I paused at the top of my run. He is so athletic, so spring-heeled. I can bounce it high and Keith still gets up and claws it in, without conceding byes. Both Bob Taylor and Alan Knott have told me he's the most naturally talented English keeper, and I haven't seen one better. I've broken his finger four times, but he still keeps taking unbelievable catches off me. One of the most amazing claws was the catch to dismiss Steve Marsh at Canterbury, the game that clinched us the '95 championship. It was an inside edge, going at speed, and he flung himself to his left. Those catches have the mark of genius, and when they come on flat pitches and you're looking for inspiration, that can be a matchwinner. People go on about Keith's batting defects, but he's okay if he can manage to concentrate. That's a red herring anyway, because England should pick the best man for the specialist job – and that's been Keith Piper for years now.

Keith Piper's amazing work behind the stumps was equalled in the field over the next few years at Edgbaston by another man who made his debut in 1989 – Trevor Penney. He grew up in Zimbabawe, played all sports to a high standard and quickly became the best fielder in county cricket at cover point or deep backward point. He's been so quick to the ball, with such swift footwork. I've been spoiled by the presence in the field of Trevor Penney for Warwickshire and Jonty Rhodes with South Africa. I'm often asked to compare the two. They're both brilliant and inspirational. Rhodes is lower to the ground, keener to dive around, while Trevor hangs back a little, preferring to advance on the ball, stay on his feet and cock the trigger. With their hockey player's wrists, both are very good at getting the ball in without too much backlift, although Trevor seems more accurate, I think he hits the stumps more. What's going to happen to me when either of these aren't around in my side? Time and again, they cut off a high percentage of shots hit at pace through the point area. That lifts your morale, because the bad ball hasn't been punished and the batsman is fretting. These fielders get you wickets by exerting pressure, and they also save you a fielder, because they cover such a vast area.

So with Piper and Penney coming through, our work in the field was improving greatly. I also found an excellent bowling ally to supplement Gladstone Small. Tim Munton established himself in 1989, bowling himself into the ground every day, never giving the batsmen a moment's peace. Bob Cottam had spent a winter with him in the indoor nets, teaching him how to swing the ball and he emerged a very fine bowler. It was great bowling in harness with Tim. He'd block up an end for you, and on flat wickets his level of performance never dropped, because he had the ability to adapt so quickly. The pressure Tim exerted by nagging away has given me so many wickets at the other end, with the batsmen trying to get after me, because he's given them no peace. Tim Munton was to prove a hugely influential figure in Warwickshire's rise to the top.

With these younger players coming through, we had an excellent blend in '89 between potential and guys nearing the end of their careers like Geoff Humpage and Alvin Kallicharran, who were hungry for one last trophy. It came at Lord's in September, when we won the NatWest Trophy, beating Middlesex in the last over. Before then we won what was almost as big a game, beating Worcestershire in the semi-final, in front of a packed, noisy crowd at Edgbaston. In 1989, Worcestershire weren't just our local rivals, they were one of the best teams in the country, having won a lot of trophies in recent years. We were the underdogs, but that's how we liked it. We managed to scramble 225 on a dry pitch and needed to bowl very well to win. In the dressing-room, we kept telling each other, 'Come on, just sixty overs and we're at Lord's'. We needed to get Tim Curtis out early, he was their lynchpin and I nailed him lbw second ball. When umpire Barrie Leadbeater's finger went up, I saw Gladstone leaping up at mid-on in delight. We were on our way.

Graeme Hick came in, the key wicket. All week the papers had been full of the duel between Donald and Hick, but after he smacked me for two boundaries, I was taken off. Dermot Reeve came on, and the Golden Arm did it again, getting a faint nick. With their best two batsmen out, we were hyped up and just steamrollered them to win by a hundred runs. We could barely get into our victorious dressing-room, for all the friends and well-wishers, but the excitement was understandable. Warwickshire hadn't won a trophy since the Sunday League nine years earlier, so it was about time we changed all that.

My duels with Mike Gatting and Desmond Haynes were heavily featured in the press build-up to the Final, but I just knew it was to be a massive day for me, no matter what happened. Andy Lloyd told me, 'This is what it's like if you play for your country, only it's even more pressurised. Just go out and enjoy the day'. When I stood on the players' balcony, watching all the supporters pour into Lord's early to get the best seats, I felt inspired – but very nervous. I had never played before at Lord's, and knew it was unique to all professionals. As I walked through the Long Room, then onto the field for our warm-ups, I felt a fantastic buzz about the place, but also I was apprehensive. Maybe all this was too much for me, at the age of 22? Gladstone must have spotted something, because he came over, put his arm round me and said 'How you feeling, old chum? Nervous? You will be, but just get through the first over, and you'll be fine'.

We lost the toss and fielded first, which suited me. It meant I just had to get on with my bowling. I started from the Nursery End, and initially bowled too full a length. Desmond Haynes drove me down the ground for a couple of boundaries, but I felt better after switching ends. I bowled Mark Ramprakash, and although they recovered towards the end of their innings, a target of 211 was definitely on for us. Between innings, Andy Lloyd said, 'Look, lads, this wicket is very slow, so we can't just go in and smack it around. We've got to look for quick singles, dab and run, mess up their line'. Yet our batters kept getting out at the wrong time, trying to break the stranglehold and it was building up to one of those tense Lord's finishes in the gloom. Dermot Reeve, though, was ideally suited to this sort of situation. He seemed to be the master of the calculated gamble, and he got out the slog/sweep to get some precious runs in partnership with Asif Din. When Dermot was run out, Neil Smith came in. Fresh from his 161 not out the day before in a championship match against Yorkshire, Neil was clearly in decent nick, but he has always been a poor starter. He struggles to see it early on, and I was dreading having to go into bat if he got out. I had the pads on, willing Neil to do it for us. We needed ten off the final over, and Neil just lined up the bowler, Simon Hughes. After Asif Din lost the strike early in that final over, we were worried that Neil wouldn't see the ball, because it was so dark. He managed to spot Simon Hughes's slower ball and hit him straight for six. I was standing on the balcony, straining to see where the ball was going, but gave up looking for it when I saw our two batters hugging each other out in the middle! After that crucial six, Neil saw us home, to total pandemonium in the dressing-room. My nerves were completely shredded. I honestly don't know if my legs would have carried me down those steps out to the middle if I'd had to bat. Instead, I could join in some serious celebrations.

It had been the perfect end to a golden summer for me. I felt I was advancing as a proper fast bowler, rather than someone who can turn it on now and then. Warwickshire had at last ended a long run without a trophy and I was sure that the young players coming through and this boost to our confidence at Lord's would set us up for some great seasons, and some trophies. Yet just a year later, I was preparing to leave Edgbaston, disillusioned that the club didn't seem to want me around.

CHAPTER SIX

A Wake-up Call

When I returned to South Africa after the 1989 English season, I thought I had it made. I'd won a medal with Warwickshire, seen off the challenge of Tony Merrick and bowled well all season. My career seemed to be on the move and life was good. The next year was to be a rude awakening for me as I showed there was a lot of growing up to do. Putting it bluntly, I needed a kick up the backside, and that's exactly what I got.

My uncle Des spotted straight away that I'd developed an attitude problem as soon as I got back to Bloemfontein in September '89. I was brash, not interested in other people's opinions and he soon pulled me up short. 'Have you ever heard of the word humble?' he asked me, and I said, 'No, what does that mean?', which wasn't very clever. Uncle Des told me I hadn't yet done all that much in my career, and that the game could easily kick me in the teeth, but I wouldn't listen. My parents were concerned about my attitude, with my mother saying she didn't know me anymore, that I was acting way over-the-top. My relationship with my Free State colleagues and our coach, Johann Voldstedt wasn't very happy either. I was even speaking like an Englishman to them, which didn't go down very well. I reckoned I was a bit suave, having played in England and done well for one season. It all got out of proportion for a time, and it definitely affected my form that season in South Africa.

After a long chat with Uncle Des, I did start to see sense and toned down my brashness. Things got better with my team-mates, but my form suffered all season. I finished with 37 first-class wickets at 21 each, but that flattered me. Perhaps I just didn't respect the game enough at that stage. I certainly tried very hard, after getting through that unfortunate early period. I think I tried too hard, actually – I was bothered by some of the newspaper stories asking why Allan Donald appeared to be able to succeed with Warwickshire, but looked jaded when he came back to Free State. That has been something I've had to live with over the years, but I've never felt that bowling a lot of overs in England has affected my bowling for Free State. The criticism has made me even more determined to give of my best when I got back to Bloemfontein, and that extra keenness has probably affected my bowling at times, unbalanced me. Perhaps I should have reined in some of my desire always to bowl, something I've learned about in recent years. Not enough 'ease and grace', as Andy Lloyd used to say.

I look back on my brash period in 1989/90 and use it positively when I deal with some of the young pups in the South African side a decade later. On the '98 tour to England, we were very down after failing to go 2–0 up at Old Trafford. I heard one of the young players say, 'We should beat them three nil in the series' and I cut him off straight away. With some force, I said, 'We've won f*** all yet, so keep your mouth shut until we do'. I was annoyed at such complacency. It was typically South African. We didn't think England was in the same league as us, and I know our supporters shared the same view. That was madness. South Africans don't expect failure in any sport, and we really go overboard when we win, even more than the Australians. There was a lot of frustration about being out of international sport because of apartheid, and now we're back in the mainstream, we feel we should be winning all the time. That's wrong and unbalanced, but I'm lucky that living in another country helps me not to tempt fate. I can see banana skins along the way and respect the English attitude, which is not to make disparaging comments about the opposition and just look at your own game. Yet I can now see that, at the age of 23, with just a little success behind me, I was behaving like a typical brash South African sportsman. I needed that knocked out of me and I'm glad the events of the next year did just that.

As I struggled with my form in the 1989/90 season, momentous things were happening in my country. Nelson Mandela was finally released after prolonged negotiations with President F. W. de Klerk, and we entered into an exciting, historic period that eventually saw Mr Mandela elected our President four years later. At the same time as Mr Mandela's release, Mike Gatting had brought over a team of 'rebel' English cricketers, and their presence just complicated matters. Gatting and his players thought they were doing something to help dismantle apartheid, but they were irrelevant – that was going on already in much more meaningful areas, with Mr Mandela dealing directly with our President. Those English players did well out of a tour that was called off early. They not only got their full amount of money for that and subsequent years, but some of them were back playing Test cricket within three years. So they got the best of both worlds. Meanwhile, financial resources that could have benefitted South African cricket at all levels went out of our country into the pockets of rebel tourists who were only in South Africa for a few weeks.

I admit that when the Gatting tour was announced in the summer of '89, I was all for it, believing that rebel tours benefited us, because it gave South Africans a chance to test themselves against international opposition. But the intervening six months gave opponents of the tour more time to mobilise resistance and the atmosphere was very unpleasant when Gatting and his team flew in. We all underestimated the passion of the black people and the understandable actions they took to disrupt the tour. There was a massive demonstration at the airport, no black people would serve us in the hotels, and a turnstile at the Newlands ground in Cape Town was blown up. It was getting nasty and I wasn't sure that our safety could be guaranteed in the scheduled games. Some pitches were damaged, many demonstrations took place and opinion hardened against the tour daily.

During one game against the English in Bloemfontein, I saw the tension among the Afrikaaner farmers as they watched Mike Gatting take a leaflet from one of the protesters inside the ground, while a demonstration went on outside. Thousands of people were walking up and down, waving placards and chanting slogans, and I wondered what the Afrikaaners were thinking after turning up, wanting only to watch the cricket. It was a recipe for chaos and violence, and Gatting's team had become the focal point for the anti-apartheid philosophy that had built such momentum over the years. It was too risky to carry on with the tour, so it was aborted after just five weeks.

Dr Ali Bacher was the organiser of the tour and I think he was very brave to call it off and big enough to admit he'd made a mistake. Dr Bacher's dream – his Development Programme – was in grave danger of collapsing, especially in the townships, where coaches were being physically assaulted and cricket was suddenly insignificant amid all the rising tension. He had made a huge commitment a few years earlier to bringing cricket to the poorer people of South Africa, and it became his life's work. He has faced death threats over the years for sticking with his Development Programme, and his bravery and commitment have been remarkable. Gatting's tour wasn't worth persevering with if Dr Bacher's lifetime ideal was going to be destroyed and he took the only sensible course of action. We didn't know it at the time, but happily this was to prove the last 'rebel' tour we would host.

A few weeks after Mike Gatting and his team flew back to England, I was heading in the same direction, eager to get stuck into a new season. I told the press that my aim was to take a hundred wickets for Warwickshire in the championship, and even though I'd heard that the seams on the balls were to be smaller in the coming season, I wasn't bothered about that. There'd been a lot of talk in England about the wickets being too seamer-friendly, and that the balls needed to have a less pronounced seam, but I didn't think that this would affect me all that much. What difference would a reduced seam make to a genuine fast bowler like me? I soon found out. Within a few months I was facing the sack because my club felt an overseas batsman was a better, long-term bet.

The Australian Tom Moody had been signed to alternate with me, depending on the pitch, and pretty soon it was clear to me that Tom had jumped ahead in the pecking order. Only one overseas player could be selected for each game, but every time Tom went to the middle, he reeled off a hundred. The balls were no use to the seamers that season, the pitches were usually flat and the hot weather also favoured the batsmen. The bowlers were slaughtered all over the country and I barely got a look-in. I picked up a side-strain injury, which bothered me for a long time that year, and Tom lashed the bowlers everywhere, ending up with an average of 86 for the season. I couldn't believe how big he was, how quick he looked between the wickets and how far he could hit the ball. Bob Cottam, our coach, was clearly impressed and I started to feel vulnerable. I looked up to big Tom in more ways than one – he'd played Test cricket, he had this effortless air of superiority that the Aussies always seem to possess and he made me feel insecure. I was jealous of him. He seemed to be in total charge of his game. Tom scored a thousand championship runs in just twelve games, including seven centuries in eight innings, plus the fastest hundred of the season, in just 36 balls. I was twelfth man in a lot of those games and every hundred seemed to be another nail in my coffin. It was so strange not being part of the action after seeing off Tony Merrick's challenge the year before and playing in almost every match. I just wanted to get on the field eventually, as Tom continued to outplay me. One game, against Lancashire, I found myself substitute fielder in the unaccustomed position of short leg. Graeme Fowler nearly killed me, flicking one off his legs just past my head, and he turned to me and said 'What the f*** are you doing here?' I didn't know, either – I was just happy to get out of the dressing-room.

Tom got into all the one-day matches ahead of me, bar one, because his handy medium-pace and good catching were extra strings to his bow. He was also one of the most destructive batsmen around at the time, so I could understand why he was preferred to me, but that didn't make me feel any better. By the start of August, I had prepared myself for the sack. I'd had no contact from the club officials, and had no faith in their loyalty to me. I was an overseas professional coming to the end of his contract, and realised that if they had someone better to replace me, that would be goodbye. My captain, Andy Lloyd said little to me that was reassuring, other than 'I'll vote for you when the committee meets, but it's not up to me'. That didn't exactly inspire me with optimism. I didn't feel Bob Cottam was on my side. I got the feeling he believed I was still a little soft. At times, when I got into the first team and did well, he'd challenge me to deliver the goods again next day, and the vibes he gave off were that I wasn't tough enough, compared to the big Aussie. Perhaps Bob was just trying to motivate me in his own brusque way, but I wasn't comfortable with him during that 1990 season. I was still a young lad, not mentally strong enough, with little practical experience of dealing with knockbacks in life. I couldn't stop those pangs of jealousy when I saw Tom getting ready to play in every game, as I just sat in the dressing-room, aware that days of twelfth-man duties or second-eleven cricket stretched ahead. Tom was also very popular with our team-mates and with the members – something he had over Tony Merrick – and to me he was the obvious man to get the nod. I started to lose a lot of self-motivation as that season wore on. I kept wondering why Warwickshire had wanted to sign Tom Moody when they already had me on the books as a successful overseas player. It seemed a denial of the investment they'd put in since I'd joined them in 1987. Hadn't I done well in one-day cricket the year before? Why did they need Tom? I was conveniently ignoring what Tom could offer in a summer where the bat dominated the ball, and feeling sorry for myself. Every night, I'd be out having a few beers, trying to blot out the reality of getting the sack. It was my way of preparing myself for the inevitable, and I convinced myself I wasn't good enough, that I hadn't produced the goods. Tom was the better option, and I had to go.

Early in August, Bob Cottam put me out of my misery. I was doing the inevitable twelfth-man duties at Edgbaston, when Bob called me up to the committee room and said they were going to go with Tom. If the wickets and the reduced seam on the balls were going to remain the same, season after season, they needed Tom's batting rather than my bowling. I wasn't surprised at the decision and as I stood up to leave, Bob asked me if I needed any help in finding another county. I said I'd sort that out myself and I went straight downstairs to phone Duncan Fearnley, the chairman of Worcestershire. Duncan had been keeping tabs on the situation at Edgbaston and made it clear that he would like me at New Road if Tom was preferred. Duncan was delighted to hear from me, called me back that night and offered me a three-year contract, with more money than I was getting at Edgbaston. It all seemed perfect. I looked forward to playing with guys like Ian Botham, Neal Radford and Graeme Hick, they were a side used to winning trophies and I wouldn't have to leave home. I really didn't want to leave Warwickshire because I'd grown up with the boys there, I loved the place, and there was always the worry that a new county might not have that special chemistry for me in the dressing-room, but this move to Worcester seemed the best solution after a sad few months for me.

But then it all changed round again. It seemed that Bob Cottam jumped the gun a little. A few days later, I was playing in a second-eleven match against – coincidentally – Worcestershire when M. J. K. Smith, the cricket committee chairman walked up to me when I was fielding at fine leg. 'What's all this about you leaving Warwickshire, Allan?' he asked, and when I told him what Bob Cottam had told me, he said, 'That's a load of rubbish, you just leave this to me'. So now, I was really in limbo, and it dragged on for another six weeks. Tom Moody and I had become great friends during the summer, drinking in the pub at night, laughing about the dilemma we found ourselves in. Although our team-mates were at times embarrassed at the situation, not knowing who to side with, we didn't let it affect our relationship. The press had sniffed out the story, building it up as a head-to-head, but there was never any grudges between us. We'd often joke over a beer, 'So which one of us is going to Worcester, then?' and that relaxed attitude helped us both get through the difficult weeks ahead. Duncan Fearnley had made it clear he wanted whichever one was rejected by Warwickshire, but I was still convinced I would be the one to go.

In the end, and to my great surprise, I was offered a new contract and Tom was let go. He told me there were no hard feelings, that it made sense for the club to stay with a fast bowler, that overseas batsmen like him were, in his own words 'a dime a dozen', but it seemed a remarkable turnaround by the club. Andy Lloyd said, 'There you are, Al, I told you I'd get you back', which was a bit of a contrast to what he'd told me earlier about it not being up to him! Tom Moody went to Worcestershire, where he had a great career, and it's worked out fine for both of us. I think the New Road wickets might not have helped a bowler like me who likes to hit the deck and get bounce. The wickets there are low and skiddy, and a seamer like Stuart Lampitt and Neal Radford, who kiss the deck rather than hit it hard, have been better bowlers for those surfaces than me. And the extra bounce at Edgbaston has certainly favoured me through the nineties. So it all panned out satisfactorily enough, but it was a tough time for me, a period when I had to dig deep, to stop feeling sorry for myself and get on with the job. That 1990 season was by and large a bit of a party for me, with just 28 championship wickets at 35, and too many evenings spent looking at a glass, looking for comfort. My team-mates kept saying 'You'll be alright, Al', but they had no better idea than me about the outcome. I played ahead of Tom in the last two championship matches of the season and bowled well, managing to snap out of my lethargy. At least I'd ended what was a difficult season on a positive note. A month later, Bob Cottam resigned as Warwickshire coach, and 'policy differences' was the official reason. To this day, I don't know if the Donald/Moody dilemma contributed to his departure. Certainly it seemed odd that his information to me about Tom staying was rescinded by the cricket committee six weeks later. There didn't appear to be much communication during that painful period and the two players involved were the most affected by it all. Luckily, we could stay friends and laugh at the absurdity of it all.

After a disappointing season then with Warwickshire, I needed to kick-start my career with some consistent bowling performances when I got back to South Africa. I just couldn't manage it, though. It was the old story – I was pressing too hard, trying to bowl too fast. I was still experimenting with my run-up, trying to glide in like Devon Malcolm, rather than roar in, and that change of style obviously didn't impress some of my critics. *Wisden* reported that 'Donald bowled in cruise mode for much of the season' and referred to 'much bitterness' at Free State because of that. I certainly wasn't aware of any bitterness, but we did finish bottom of the Currie Cup table, and I took just 29 wickets at nearly 26 apiece, so nobody was particularly happy. I don't think my team-mates had any lingering bitterness against me for my immature behaviour the year before. I had certainly become more humble after my experiences at Edgbaston in 1990, and there was never any danger that I wouldn't be giving everything to Free State cricket. I've never been the type of cricketer to do things half-heartedly and those who referred to my bowling being 'in cruise mode' ought to have taken the trouble to ask me why I had altered my run-up. I just wanted to get better, and all of us at Free State were disappointed we'd had such a bad season. Our squad lacked depth and talent, we were still waiting for young players like Hansie Cronje to come through, while older guys like Corrie van Zyl weren't being adequately replaced. Meanwhile, I continued to worry why I couldn't bowl as consistently well as I'd like for Free State, convinced it was a red herring for people to claim that it was my periods in England which affected my performances. I simply didn't believe that. The English experience definitely made me a better bowler and eventually I won over most of my detractors in South Africa.

Allan Donald's faltering form in the 1990/91 season was nowhere near as significant as the changes to our domestic structure that summer. Steps were taken to integrate black people further into the mainstream of cricket, rather than continue with a structure that seemed to alienate them in the past, leading to them playing in their own leagues. More and more white players were going to play at non-white clubs, including the Western Province captain, Adrian Kuiper who joined Primrose, a mixed club in Cape Town. The United Cricket Board of South Africa was set up, co-ordinating all the other hierarchies that had never managed to be assimilated. The new Board's managing director was the dynamic Dr Ali Bacher, and ideas and initiatives just poured out of his office. While Dr Bacher pressed ahead with his Development Programme, bringing the game of cricket into the most hostile of areas, he also set to work on creating the framework for South Africa to return to official international cricket. Dr Bacher had worked tirelessly to persuade the International Cricket Conference that we had put our cricketing house in order and deserved reinstatement, but as long as Nelson Mandela wasn't free and apartheid remained on the statute book, our return was unlikely. But Mr Mandela's release opened the floodgates and the pace of reform quickened over the next few months. Dr Bacher was instrumental in getting rid of the Springbok symbol under the new colours of the United Cricket Board. He felt that the symbol was too representative of the old South Africa and he wanted everyone associated with our cricket to know that we were now on the move, building towards a more equal structure, where players are encouraged, irrespective of their colour. There were, of course, a few grumbles when the Springbok had to go – and don't forget, Ali Bacher had been proud to wear it as both player and captain – but we had to move forward. So the Protea – a South African flower – became the new symbol. Soon we would be wearing our new national colours with pride. The momentum wasn't slackening. We were on our way back.

CHAPTER SEVEN

A Momentous Year

I heard the news that South Africa was back in international cricket from the man who had done so much to get us there. Ali Bacher rang me one day in July 1991 and I'll never forget his words: 'Allan, we are going to the World Cup next year – we've just been voted back'. He was calling me from Lord's, at the end of the historic ICC meeting which had voted for our readmission. I was in tears as we spoke, and so were my parents when I rang them in Bloemfontein. I felt so happy for my country, because I knew we deserved it, as we'd done so much work to make our sport multi-racial at all levels. Also, we were on the way to democracy with Nelson Mandela now out of jail, heading the African National Congress, and things being set in motion for a general election, when non-whites would have a say in shaping South Africa. It was a great day. Ali Bacher reminded me of a conversation we'd had in 1988, when I had wondered whether I'd ever get to play official representative cricket for South Africa. At that time, I could understand why the likes of Robin Smith and Allan Lamb had decided to play instead for England, because there seemed no prospect for us getting back into the fold. I didn't blame those guys at all, but I hoped that it would never have to come to such a choice for me. It would be wrong to say I was tempted to qualify for England, but it was important to be reassured by Dr Bacher in 1988.

'Don't worry, Allan', he said, 'We'll be back in within the next two years, just be patient'. He was one year out, but he obviously knew a lot more about the political niceties than me.

In the back of my mind, I know I'd have been saying 'What if?' during my qualification period for England. I'd never have had real peace of mind if I'd thrown in my lot with England, rather than wait for Ali Bacher's forecast to come right. Now I could wear my South African colours with extra pride, because this time we were kosher. No more 'rebel' tours, every wicket I would take from now on would be official, it would be in the record books forever. To be involved in the 1992 World Cup in Australia and New Zealand was a fantastic way to return to the big time. I couldn't wait.

Before all that, I completed a memorable 1991 season with Warwickshire. We really fired as a unit that year, finishing second behind a strong Essex side in the championship and I was very pleased with my 83 wickets at 19, a strike rate of one every 47 balls. I later learned that seventy per cent of my wickets that year were either bowled, lbw or caught behind the wicket or at slip. That's the area where a fast bowler should be claiming the scalps – you don't get many caught at cover or long-off! – and that statistic suggested I was on my way towards consistency. For that, I had to thank our new coach at Edgbaston, Bob Woolmer, who was a revelation to me in 1991. Although Bob lived in Cape Town, I knew very little about him, because he had been out of the game in recent years.

I knew he was big mates with Dennis Amiss, from their England days together, but it was Andy Lloyd who marked my card about him. The captain was very excited that we'd got Woolmer. He said I'd find him very enthusiastic, with the ability to motivate players in different ways, rather than Bob Cottam's clenched-fist style, and that he had great imagination. He was spot on. Woolmer quickly showed an ability to get the best out of players by getting on their wavelength. He would sympathise, offer a constructive suggestion and get to the point quickly. He had this ability to look ahead, to stretch you. Bob liked to hear us talk cricket, and he'd initiate discussions in the dressing-room about the game. He was very good with players on their own, saying things like, 'What's your game plan for bowling in one-day cricket – and if you haven't got one, then why not?'

Bob was so meticulous. A great planner, he liked to play every likely scenario out. He'd come into the nets and say, 'Right, we're playing Essex in a one-day game today. How are you going to bat against their spinner, John Childs?' and then he'd have us batting specifically against a slow left-armer, practising the appropriate shots. In 1991, you'd see a lot of flowing drives being played in one-day cricket that went straight to the fielder for no run. Bob didn't like that, he wanted the ball to be put into open spaces because that meant runs. He got us involved with the slog/sweep – a distinctive shot against the spinner that has been the hallmark of almost every Warwickshire batsman since 1991. When played properly – and Bob insisted it was practised on before being brought out in a match – it is a destructive shot against a tight spinner, with Dermot Reeve and Nick Knight particularly adept at it.

But it was Woolmer who drew our attention to it. Bob looked at all angles and methods to change the game, and challenge conventions. He nagged everyone to back up the right way out in the middle, to avoid just turning blind, looking for another run. He advised us which hand to hold the bat with when running between wickets, so that there was more chance of squeezing out an extra run. We had to pressurise fielders every time, use soft hands just to drop the ball down defensively, and steal a single. His attitude was that there was a run available every ball, it was just a case of working out the methods of accumulation. Bob found kindred spirits in Andy Lloyd and Dermot Reeve, and they all helped spark us off, making us think hard about our individual responsibilities within a team game. We talked and talked about cricket, and it never felt as if we were going to work. This is where we started to move ahead of other counties, who had a more stereotyped approach. The results would come later that proved to the outside world that we were the best around, but the groundwork was done in earlier seasons under Woolmer, Lloyd and Reeve.

Bob was great for me as a bowling coach. That's not something you can often say about someone who was primarily a batsman himself, but he seemed to understand the frustrations of being out of form with the ball, as well as the bat. One day he said to me in the nets, 'You're bowling very well. Never come to the nets and abuse good form. Don't pick up the ball and just bowl for the sake of it. Feel how it's coming out of your hand. Practise hard for half an hour of good quality, then leave it. So when it goes badly for you – and it will – think back to when it was good, and piece together what's missing'. That's the biggest lesson I've learned in practice: don't just do it for the sake of it, think hard about it. I watch Steve Waugh in the nets and he has the same attitude. He hardly plays a shot in anger, he just defends. He likes to get in the focus area, knowing that you don't get many loose balls in Test cricket, so there's no point in blazing away in the nets. You need a good defence, then you build from there. Bob Woolmer taught me in '91 that I have to know just why I'm bowling so well in the nets. He felt that you must feel as good as you did the day before when it went so well in the nets, that you have to take the responsibility for finding that magic formula yourself. Get the rhythm right, the hand action, the run-up, the precise moment to release the ball – it must all gel. Under Bob Woolmer's guidance, I started to ease into my bowling in the nets. For my first twelve or so balls, I just want to get the batsman leaving my deliveries, so that I can line them up and groove my accuracy. Then I'll bowl straighter, aiming to attack the batter and dismiss him. You just go through the gears until the engine is fully warmed up. Then you must know when to stop, in case you lose that fluency.

With our batsmen, Bob used to look for specifics. He didn't believe it was enough to have someone throwing a ball down at you, as you stroked the ball back against the boundary boards. He wanted to know where you thought the ball should be going, how well your feet were moving, and why did that shot go in the air? The bowlers should be warming up on the square on the morning of a match, with a proper run-up in simulated match conditions. He liked us to bowl no more than twelve deliveries out in the middle, after a good net. I haven't prepared any differently since, because it's important to feel good after practice.

Bob was great at spotting things I'd got wrong in the previous session. It could be that I was striving too hard, that my rhythm was out or that I wasn't shaping the ball in the right channel – invariably he had it sorted out in his own mind before I asked him in the interval what was wrong. His advice was responsible for me nailing so many batsmen in the slip/wicket-keeper area in that 1991 season. Bob suggested I should bowl a fuller length than in previous seasons, because I was beating the bat too often and getting nothing for it. He said that batsmen on English wickets tend not to get a full stride on when going forward, they play a little half-cock and were therefore vulnerable to the surprise element of a fast, fuller length. Once I got used to the risk of being driven off the front foot, I was happy to keep the ball up, with the short one there as the surprise factor. My outswing worked well throughout that season, my rhythm was good and Bob's practical experience of being a batsman himself was ideal in helping me try to understand what the batter was thinking.

I was also much stronger than at any stage in my career up till then. We'd trained in April at Birmingham University, and I'd taken advice on what fitness regime was best for a fast bowler. I was told that repetition with light weights was better than bulk work. This certainly improved my muscle flexibility, and the work on shoulders, back and legs gave me increased confidence for long spells.

Andy Lloyd warned me midway through the season that I had to prepare myself for a heavier workload in August and September if we were continuing to challenge for the championship, and I was glad I'd done the hard gym work earlier on to build up my stamina. There were times when I was desperate to bowl and Andy would insist on keeping me in reserve. He used to say, 'Games are won in the second innings, so we'll keep you fresh. Hadlee used to win matches in the second innings' and so mention of the great man was enough to keep me quiet. If it was good enough for Hadlee, who was I to complain? Andy used to tell me that Gladstone Small or Tim Munton would look after the tail, that I was more vital to him later on in the game. He captained the side so well that year, setting a positive example when he batted, firing off shots at number three, and handling me exactly right. When he really needed me bowling for a long time towards the end of the season, I was able to answer the call, and I was proud of that. It was the home game against Northants that we had to win to stay in contention for the final round of matches the following week. I took nine wickets in the game, bowling twenty overs unchanged in the second innings, to get them out cheaply. We sneaked home by three wickets, and it gave me great satisfaction that I could bowl a long spell when it was really needed. So it was off to Taunton, where we won another close game by five runs, but Essex had wrapped up the title on the first day, by bowling out Middlesex for just 51. Essex were a stronger unit than us, with class players like Graham Gooch, Salim Malik and Neil Foster, but we had led the table for three months, and the fact that we were winning close contests like the Northants and Somerset games showed our self-belief. We won five games away from Edgbaston, so our home pitches weren't that much of an advantage to us, and every one of our victories was a genuine one, with none of them a run chase after a declaration. Our seam bowling quartet of myself, Gladstone, Tim and Dermot Reeve was the strongest in the country and Dermot was full of ideas as vice-captain. His bubbly enthusiasm and competitiveness was rubbing off on everyone. Dermot used to say in those days, 'Let's get used to the feeling of winning. Don't wait till it really matters, let's get into the winning habit straight away'. I enjoyed that positive approach, and from then on we usually managed to win matches that came down to the wire. That was to be a feature of the outstanding couple of seasons we enjoyed a few years later.

I really enjoyed the surges of adrenalin and sustained confidence I had all that summer. I'd go to the ground, fully expecting to take nine wickets because I'd done the hard training. I was thinking analytically about my bowling and there was Bob Woolmer as my back-up, another pair of eyes to tweak the engine if it spluttered. I felt I couldn't go wrong. My pace was seriously fast at times that summer. There was a Sunday League game at Worcester, when I had just two fielders in front of the square, against Tom Moody and Graeme Hick. Off just fifteen paces, the ball was going through very rapidly. I had a fly-slip, a third man, slips and a gully – all this in a one-day game, when you're normally looking to contain the batsmen. Against two superb front-foot drivers, I had the confidence to dispense with a mid-off, and my pace managed to keep Hick and Moody quiet. I ended up with nought for 25 in my eight overs, and I was very happy that I hadn't forced my run-up, that I just glided in and felt everything flow from that relaxed rhythm. Doing this off a short run-up was even more satisfying.

My morale in September '91 was unrecognisable from the year before, when I was sure I was going to have to leave Edgbaston. Now I felt so much stronger as a fast bowler, and, thanks to Bob Woolmer's coaching skills, I had a lot more in my armoury. Life was marvellous. I married Tina that month, and it's been the best decision of my life. I loved being part of a new, large family, with all the appropriate responsibilities of being an uncle. Later, I'd be a father and that's been an unbelievable thrill. A settled, happy home life has definitely helped me as a cricketer, even though the times away are hard. On top of my marriage, the good news kept coming. I was nominated one of *Wisden's* five Cricketers of the Year, alongside Phillip DeFreitas, Richie Richardson and two handy fast bowlers in Waqar Younis and Curtly Ambrose. Distinguished company for a 25-year-old who had been unsure about his prospects just one year earlier. And I was about to start my international career with South Africa taking a short trip to India. All this and the World Cup just around the corner. It was an exciting, memorable time for me.

CHAPTER EIGHT

Back in the Fold

I f you wanted to know just how much it meant to us to be back playing international cricket, you should have been on our flight from Johannesburg to Bombay in November 1991. Talk about adults behaving like kids! We were chattering away excitedly like children on Christmas morning ripping open their presents, or as if we were going away on holiday for the first time. The build-up to this historic tour had been hectic and frenetic, with the television bulletins full of the countdown information, profiles of both our squad and our Indian opponents. We were seen off by thousands of well-wishers at Johannesburg Airport, and on our chartered flight there were a lot of supporters and friends who stayed with us on that short tour. It was great to feel such warmth of support, and we were very proud to be making history. That aircraft from Johannesburg was the first from South Africa that ever touched down on Indian soil, so we were making history in more ways than one. We knew how much we owed India for casting the decisive vote in our favour at the ICC meeting at Lord's in July. That tipped the balance in our favour, and it was therefore only right that India should be the first country we played. It had also been confirmed that India would be the first side we played at home in a Test series a year later. We South African cricketers were now on a fast learning curve about the racial policies of the past, and we read about the Indian influence on the ANC, of the passive resistance policies of Mahatma Ghandi, popularised by him when he lived in South Africa more than seventy years ago. Nelson Mandela had paid tribute many times to the Mahatma, and so it seemed absolutely right that we should share such historic sporting times with India.

The welcome we received in Bombay exceeded everything we'd imagined. It was overwhelming. Excited, passionate, in danger at times of spilling over into unruliness, it all stemmed from a desire to make us welcome. From the airport to our hotel is normally a 20-minute journey. This day it took two hours. The whole of Bombay Airport was shut down to accommodate our flight and the massive welcoming committee – heaven knows what other passengers on other flights from around the world must have made of that! The scene from airport to hotel was mind-boggling; every piece of earth seemed to be occupied by humanity, all of them screeching best wishes. That was so reassuring. We genuinely didn't know how we'd be welcomed in India. How could we? We had never played them at cricket, there had been little trade or diplomatic relations at all between the two countries because of apartheid, and although things were moving along rapidly at last in our country, we players on that trip were taking nothing for granted. We were swiftly made aware that we were in the vast company of cricket fanatics who were delighted to see us there. I was absolutely stunned by the force and warmth of that welcome in Bombay. Our captain, Clive Rice made a brilliant public relations gesture halfway through our tortuous journey to the hotel, when he asked our coach driver to stop and he stepped outside. Clive thanked the people for their support and enthusiasm, bowed with his palms together in traditional Indian style, then waved to the crowd. They loved it and we were genuinely moved by that moment. When we got to the hotel, we were bowled over by the generous hospitality, but one of our party was keeping his eyes open. One banner said 'Welcome to the Springboks' but Dr Ali Bacher made sure it was taken down and kept away from the TV cameras. Ali had worked so hard trying to modernise our cricket structure – even down to replacing the Springbok symbol with the Protea – that he wasn't going to have the traditional image represented, even on a well-meaning banner. This was a team representing the NEW South Africa in Ali Bacher's eyes, and he was very sharp indeed about possible public relations blunders. He hasn't changed a bit since then!

We were treated like gods during that fortnight in India. We played only three games, all of them one-dayers in the space of five days, but the experience of being in India was marvellous. Thousands would come to our hotel every day, just to stare at us as we walked through the foyer or got onto the team coach. At practise, the crowds were enormous, and their astonishing passion for the game of cricket amazed us. We were used to full commitment back home, but these fans were stunning. Our captain, Clive Rice was faultless in his public relations, proving a great ambassador for our country.

He made it clear that we were there to play entertaining cricket, that winning wasn't the most important part of the tour (and that was very un-South African!), but the experience of just being there was the most meaningful part. He told the press, 'I know now how Neil Armstrong felt when he stood on the moon', and the locals loved that. Clive was a terrific, diplomatic captain on that tour, with the intelligence and approachability to win everyone over. He had waited a long time to get back into the official international fold, and although his playing career was coming to a close, he was the best man for the job on that unique tour.

That first game, in Calcutta was a mind-blowing experience. The biggest crowd I'd played in front of had been around 20,000 in the NatWest Final at Lord's, but this one was officially logged at 90,800, with the general feeling that there was more than that squeezed into the ground, and several thousand outside, unable to get in. Before the start, the whole South African squad walked out to greet the fans, and to release some doves to symbolise peace, and the reception we were given was overwhelming. The noise during the match was deafening, with firecrackers being let off all the time and any success for the Indians greeted with astonishing fervour. Yet whenever we got a wicket, the silence was eerie. I took three wickets in my first four overs and all you could hear in front of 90,000 people was my squeals of delight. Yet if their batsmen pierced our field, bedlam reigned as the ball sped to the boundary.

We batted first, even though the ball was looping around in the nets before. In the early morning smog, with a nine o'clock start, it was an ideal time for swing bowling, but the wicket looked good and we decided to have first go on it. We lost Andrew Hudson to the first ball of the game, which increased the volume a little, and the ball swung all over the place. We only managed 175, and although we defended hard, we still lost by three wickets. I took five for 29 and felt inspired by the occasion, pumped up with adrenalin. If this was a foretaste of international cricket, I couldn't wait to play it all the year round, throughout the world. I got the ball to swing, but nowhere near as much as the Indian bowlers. This caused the first diplomatic incident of our international return, and it was set in motion by Dr Ali Bacher, who had been so keen to avoid any public relations blunders. Adrian Kuiper came into our dressing-room after getting out and swore blind that he had seen the ball being gouged. That's why it was swinging so much, in the eyes of many of our guys. Dr Bacher told us to say nothing, that he'd deal with it. He made an informal protest afterwards about the state of the ball, the Indian Cricket Board weren't too impressed and our Board president, Geoff Dakin was left to tidy things up, and issue a hasty apology. Just as well the allegation didn't come from a player, because I'm sure Ali would have been down on him very hard. I can understand that someone probably leaked the story, because Ali would have wanted the matter dealt with secretly, but it didn't exactly help relations with the Indians for the rest of that short tour. Not that the vast crowds were bothered – they kept on throwing firecrackers at any time during the game. One exploded between the legs of Jimmy Cook as he was fielding on the boundary and he was deaf for a few days after that. It was hazardous fielding at fine leg or third man, because stones were thrown regularly from the crowd. That gave the police an excuse to wade into the crowd and the punishment they dealt out was pretty strong! India was proving a volatile place to make our international comeback.

The Indian fans even singled out their own players with

a few rocks in the next match, at Gwalior, when Sidhu and Raju were hit. We never understood the reasons for these sudden attacks, but it made all of us even keener to field in the ring! That Gwalior game was lost by us by 36 runs, with Sidhu and Srikkanth smashing us all over the place, but we got some revenge in the final one-dayer, winning by eight wickets on a very good pitch in New Delhi. In front of 75,000 spectators, we were treated to a remarkable light show, with firecrackers going off all the time. The lights in the stadium were excellent for this day/night match and with rockets and thunder flashes exploding simultaneously, it was an amazing sight.

So we celebrated our first official international victory that night, at the end of a hectic five days' cricket, and we could take stock of how far we'd progressed. We knew the political significance of this tour, but fundamentally we just wanted to match ourselves against the world's best players. And I had just been bowling at one of them. When I got Sachin Tendulkar for one at New Delhi, I was delighted, because after a few deliveries at him in this short series, I knew how special he was. Sachin had been playing for India for two years, and yet he was still only eighteen. He looked a fabulous player. He got 62 in that first game in Calcutta – he and I shared the Man of the Match award – and after almost being run out for nought, he looked a class apart. We'd heard all about him modelling himself on Sunil Gavaskar, and he had the same neatness, the same time to spare, the same calmness – and a very heavy bat. He hits the ball so hard with apparently little effort. His shot selection is superb, he just lines you up and can make you look very silly. When Sachin scored a hundred at Lord's in 1998 in the Princess of Wales Memorial Match, it was as if he was having a net. He flicked one of my deliveries through midwicket from outside off stump at a rate of knots and I was daft enough to shout 'Catch it!' as the ball was rebounding off the boundary boards. That day, he just toyed with us, and I was so impressed I said, 'Good shot!' to that delivery, something I have never said to a batsman at any time in my career. Sachin Tendulkar's the best-looking batsman I've ever seen; everything is right in his technique and judgement. There isn't a fault there. He's also a lovely guy, and over the years I've enjoyed some interesting chats with him. I can't believe how much he suffers back home from the attentions of the public. He's virtually a prisoner in his home city of Bombay. He told me that if he wants to go out to the movies, he has to wear a wig or a false beard. What a life! I can't imagine me having to do that when I go out cycling in Bloemfontein or have a pint in the Dog and Duck in Harborne, near my Birmingham home, thank God!

So India in November 1991 was the start of a killing schedule of tours for South Africa. We had so much to make up, needing to learn what it was like in pressure situations against world-class players. Our ultra-competitive instinct would help us through some tough times, but there's no substitute for practical experience and we were about to embark on a series of tours which were designed to get us to the top of the international tree as soon as possible. The World Cup in Australia and New Zealand was next on the agenda in February/March 1992, followed by a short trip to the Caribbean, and our first Test match in Barbados. Before that, our national selectors had some hard choices ahead and the first of their deliberations caused a lot of controversy.

Clive Rice seemed almost certain to go to the World Cup as captain, but he was surprisingly dropped a month before the squad was announced. So was our opening batsman, Jimmy Cook. Both had served South African cricket brilliantly over the years, but Jimmy was 38, and the runs were drying up for him. He was also vulnerable in the field, and he could only be hidden at mid-off in one-day games. The Rice decision was very unpopular. At the age of 42, he wasn't in his prime, but he felt he still had enough left to get us through the World Cup and I must admit that, at the time, his experience would have been very valuable. But he didn't get on with the convenor of selectors, Peter van der Merwe, and it got a bit personal, I think. Clive was very bitter and there was a public outcry, but I could see the cricketing reasons for the decision to drop the captain and Jimmy Cook. Our fielding in India hadn't been up to the usual South African standards, partly because we were carrying a few players who were a little past their best, but good enough in their own specific disciplines, if you disregarded fielding. But you couldn't do that in a hectic, tiring competition like the World Cup and the selectors went for youthful mobility. One other decision caused another controversy, though – and it led to the selectors backing down. They originally dropped Peter Kirsten because they also felt he was over the top. That was wrong. Even though he was 36, Peter was still a brilliant fielder, and had scored runs consistently throughout the past decade whenever we came up against a 'rebel' side. His omission was greeted with howls of outrage throughout South Africa and eventually he was reinstated. Just as well he was – Peter was very impressive in the World Cup and fit enough to carry on playing for South Africa until 1995.

One of our selections for the World Cup absolutely delighted me. Omar Henry became the first non-white cricketer to play internationals for South Africa, and I was so proud for him when his name was read out. I happened to be in his house, watching a Currie Cup game on television, when our squad was announced and his wife climbed all over Omar in excitement, followed by me. He was ecstatic and proud, because it had taken a lot of bottle for Omar to throw in his lot to play for Western Province a few years back, when it was not the popular thing to do among black cricketers. He had elected to break away from cricket run by non-whites, because he felt he could better himself by playing in a higher grade of cricket, hoping that others would follow him. They did, and Omar became a role model for them. An accurate, left-arm spinner, an explosive batsman and a brilliant fielder who kept himself very fit, Omar Henry was picked on merit for that '92 World Cup. He started the line that led on to the likes of Paul Adams and Makhaya Ntini, and was a very deep thinker about the game. Omar later came to play with me at Free State and I was always impressed by his ideas about cricket. We are great friends and we've talked about the game for hours. It seems strange that he's now coaching in Namibia, when he should be used in South African cricket – on merit as a coach, quite apart from the inspiration he can give to non-white cricketers. I've told him so many times that he should offer some of his radical ideas to Bob Woolmer, the national side's coach, but he shies away from that. Somehow, I sense that Omar believes he was never given a fair crack of the whip when he played for South Africa, and that has influenced his decision not to push himself forward. Certainly, they did him no favours in the

'92 World Cup, playing him on the wrong pitches and not picking him in New Zealand, where the wickets were so slow. New Zealand would open the bowling with the off-spinner, Dipak Patel, but we wouldn't select Omar in conditions made for him. One night in Auckland, after he had missed out again, I was very upset for him, and he said 'Don't worry about it, these guys don't know what they're doing'. He was referring to our captain, Kepler Wessels and coach, Mike Procter and certainly I believe they could have got more out of him before age caught up with Omar.

Before we left for the World Cup, Free State had enjoyed a tremendous season, and to my relief, I had bowled well for them. So I hadn't left my best form behind in England this time. I was greatly helped by our overseas professional, Franklyn Stephenson, who was brilliant for us. Frankie was an early advocate of pinch-hitting in one-day games and would volunteer to go in and smash a few. He always wanted to bowl and his vast experience of county cricket for Nottinghamshire, then Sussex was tapped by all of us, especially our new young captain, Hansie Cronje, who soon showed great leadership qualities for such a young guy. Frankie was tremendously helpful in the nets, and he showed me to how to deliver the slower ball, his speciality. His method was to take the thumb off the ball when the arm comes down and over, so that the batsman doesn't see that. The trick was to bowl it at the same speed, with the thumb away at the last instant, and that used to fox so many batsmen. Years later, I got Graeme Hick out with the slower ball in the Leeds Test of '98, and it was all down to Franklyn Stephenson. We'd talked about Hick's tendency to move his feet slowly at the start of his innings, and that he was still keen on the front-foot drive whenever the ball was there for it. So I bowled him a slower one outside the off stump, he launched himself at it, got half a bat on it, and was caught at wide mid-off. Hick got a lot of stick for the stroke, but I honestly believe it was good bowling that outwitted him – and excellent tuition from Frankie in the Free State nets!

With the expertise and experience of Frankie, the ambitious captaincy of Hansie Cronje and some adventurous tactics, Free State won the one-day tournament, the Nissan Shield, and came second in the Currie Cup. The foundations for the successful Free State unit of subsequent years were laid in that 1991/92 season, and our new coach, Eddie Barlow must get a lot of credit for that as well. Eddie bullied us to new levels of fitness, and nobody could pull the wool over his eyes, because he knew all the tricks and kept telling us there were no short-cuts. Hard work was the only recipe. He had this thing about the way the Australians approached their cricket, that the game should be played at pace. We should bat at three runs per over minimum, and when we were in the field, don't try to bore the batsmen out by setting defensive fields. Our job was to bowl them out as quickly as possible. To a strike bowler like me, that was a great attitude. Eddie kept telling us that Free State would be the next Mean Machine, the nickname given to the great Transvaal side of the 1980s, and he was an inspirational guy, who did so much for our self-belief. Eddie was never shy of speaking his mind to the authorities and the media. So he never got on with the cricket hierarchy in South Africa, and when the job of national coach came up in 1994, it went to Bob Woolmer instead. Dr Ali Bacher asked my opinion, and I said that Eddie would have been a great number two to Bob, but I'm not sure if they would have gelled because of Eddie's outspoken nature. Still, he did a lot for me and Free State and I wish him well. He's still coaching in South African cricket at Griqualand West, still driving the boys on, and he might yet have an influential role to play in the future.

When we gathered to leave for the World Cup, the players were just as excited as a few months earlier, when we went to India. At the airport, Dr Bacher talked to us about our responsibilities, reminding us about the importance of representing a country that was looking positively to the future. He asked me if I was happy that I'd decided not to qualify for England and after I said, 'I was never serious about that, Doctor', we had a good laugh. Actually, I hadn't given that matter serious thought over the years, because I trusted Dr Bacher's judgement that we'd be reinstated with much of my career still to run. After Dr Bacher spoke, our new captain Kepler Wessels calmed us down by telling us we weren't just going for the experience, we were expected to do well. He wanted us to express ourselves and not be overawed by the occasion or the opposition, even though we were so inexperienced in high-pressure internationals. In effect, we were starting from scratch and would have to learn how to deal with tight situations without practical experience, but it was reasonable to expect the familiar South African competitiveness to help us get there. That's what happened, and to get to the World Cup semi-finals at the first time of asking was a great achievement in my book.

Australia is a fantastic place to play cricket and I was hugely impressed on this, my first trip. The practise facilities are wonderful, the hotels superb, the communications efficient and I love the aggressive way the Aussies play their cricket. That applies also to their media. When we practised in Sydney on the eve of our first game, a day-nighter against Australia, I was struck by the brash manner of the Aussie journalists when they asked questions. They wanted to know if we were going to stick it up the Aussies, and how we'd manage it. We were determined to be low-key in our responses, because we knew they were looking for some provocative headlines, and there was no doubt they were rooting for their own side. It all added spice to the occasion for us, and we played brilliantly to hammer them by nine wickets.

South Africa's performance at Sydney was a real eye-opener to the Australians, particularly the fielding of Jonty Rhodes. This was the first time he had been on the big international stage and he was determined to make an impression. He ran out David Boon with a spectacular swoop, and then did the same with an amazing dive, stop and throw to dismiss Craig McDermott. Jonty really imposed himself on that competition and yet I wasn't surprised. I'd first seen him play against Free State for South African Universities, and when he flicked a ball down to me at fine leg, took me on for the second run on my throw and absolutely cantered home, I thought 'Jeez, this guy's quick!' In that game, his fielding was stunning and he dominated the World Cup at the age of 22. The photographers loved his spectacular dives and speed over the ground and he was hugely popular because of his attractive personality. Jonty Rhodes is simply a lovely man, who sees it as a privilege to play for his country. He's a fantastic ambassador for South Africa, a guy who believes in putting a lot back on behalf of those not so lucky. He's a committed Christian who doesn't believe in ramming it down other people's throats, but he's also a very tough competitor. The way he fought his technical battles with his batting to get back into the side in later years underlines his steel and character. As for his fielding, he has been fantastic for me. To have a guy like that in your team is inspirational. You cannot fail to give your all with Jonty Rhodes encouraging you in the field, setting such an amazing example.

That Sydney victory really gave us a massive boost, particularly after a severe knock-back from the very first ball of the match. I had Geoff Marsh caught behind off the biggest nick you've ever seen; it was heading towards Kepler Wessels at first slip when Dave Richardson took it. Yet umpire Brian Aldridge gave Marsh not out. Our jaws dropped open and even though we South Africans aren't known for walking either, we couldn't believe he had the nerve to stand there. Kepler gave Marsh some dreadful verbals straight away, and for the next ten minutes, everybody else climbed in. It was almost like a rugby match out there for a time. I'd been very nervous when marking out my run-up, with my hands feeling numb, and that setback did nothing to help. My line was wayward in that first spell, and I struggled to concentrate after that amazing decision, but I was pleased to come back strongly and get three wickets in my second spell. With Kepler batting aggressively, we raced to victory and in the dressing-room afterwards, we were on a high after beating the holders on their home soil at the first time of asking. When the phone rang in the dressing-room, Hansie Cronje answered it. Somebody at the other end said it was President de Klerk calling to congratulate us. Hansie, thinking it was a wind-up, just laughed, but when the caller persisted, Hansie shouted over to our captain, 'Hey Kepler! Some guy here says he's the President!' and we all laughed. But it *was* the President, as Kepler discovered when he came to the phone. Hansie felt terrible about it, but we soon cheered him up!

In typically confident South African fashion, we now felt we could win the World Cup after just one great performance, and our large band of travelling supporters let us know they felt the same. A few days spent in New Zealand soon brought us down to earth. In Auckland, New Zealand hammered us with fifteen overs to spare, and we showed how tactically naive we were. We hadn't much of an idea how to play their slower bowlers on the dead pitch, with the off-spinner Dipak Patel taking one for 28 in his ten overs, after actually opening the bowling. There was no attempt to disrupt his line with the reverse sweep or the lap shot and when they batted, they showed the value of the pinch-hitter. This was a new one on us – a batter comes in and blazes away right from the off, chancing his arm, with most of the fielders having to be stationed inside the 30-metre ring for the first fifteen overs. So there were plenty of gaps if you were prepared to hit over the top and Mark Greatbatch certainly was. He hit Brian McMillan for a huge six, then deposited Adrian Kuiper straight out of the ground, over the rugby stand. It was awesome and we had no answer. Then Sri Lanka beat us in Wellington by three wickets. Again we didn't play their slower bowlers well. They took the pace off the ball on a slow wicket, and we just got frustrated.

Just a few days after the euphoria of Sydney, we were stuttering. We clearly weren't as innovative as other teams in the tournament, and our naivete was showing. Could we get by on the traditional South African qualities of hard work, team spirit and guts? Our captain, Kepler Wessels told us we could, as long as we played to our strengths. The next game, against West Indies at Christchurch would be vital. It was a surprisingly quick wicket and we hit them early, as we defended a total of just over 200. Meyrick Pringle bowled out of his socks, taking all the early wickets as we had them 19 for four. The ball was carrying high and fast and Kepler took some excellent slip catches. The back of their innings was broken and we ran out comfortable winners. It was a big win for us, beating them on a pitch that suited them and Peter Kirsten's gutsy 56 early on, when Curtly Ambrose was bowling brilliantly, must have given some thought to the selectors who had initially dropped him from this competition. That game was also a significant one in racial terms. We just weren't sure how a totally black team would relate to this totally white South African eleven, because it was the first time the West Indies had come up against us, after all those years of separate cricket. But they were fine about it, and there was a good atmosphere between us. It was much more strained whenever we played the New Zealanders because of our rugby heritage – we saw it as playing the All Blacks. The banners in the crowd underlined that point, and it was the same when we were up against Australia. That made victory all the sweeter.

That win over West Indies helped us build up a momentum that took us into the semi-finals. At Brisbane, we won a great game, beating the Pakistanis after rain had revised the target. It will always be remembered for one of the great cricket photographs of recent years, featuring – inevitably – Jonty Rhodes. Inzamam-ul-Haq was on strike, and he looked for a quick single off his pad, only to turn back and see his stumps demolished by a low-flying missile called

Rhodes. It was amazing. I was fielding at midwicket and had a great view of it. I could see Jonty's mind working – shall I throw the ball and risk overthrows if I miss? – and so he hung onto the ball and kept running. From backward point, he raced in and threw himself at the stumps. The batsman was out by a hair, a great decision by umpire Steve Bucknor. He didn't have the benefit in those days of a third umpire with all the replays available and he took the decision bravely on the naked eye. The incident was so spectacular that the sports goods manufacturers Adidas made Jonty a lot of money from that one moment. He endorsed their equipment, accompanied by that photo, but knowing Jonty, he wouldn't have kept much of the money for himself.

We were on a roll now, third in the table and really fancying ourselves to go all the way. We then beat Zimbabwe by seven wickets in Canberra, leaving us needing to beat India in Adelaide to get through to the last four. Peter Kirsten again batted brilliantly, and Cronje and Wessels saw us home. I've still got the photo at home of Hansie and Kepler with their arms aloft, smiling broadly at the winning runs. A great day for Grey College back in Bloemfontein as the two former pupils brought their country into the World Cup semi-finals. That victory over West Indies had given us so much self-belief after we'd faltered in New Zealand.

So it was to be England in the semi-finals at Sydney. What a prospect. Our supporters, and we players, were thrilled and excited at the prospect. We didn't care that England seemed to be the form team, after beating Australia and the West Indies. There was a sense of destiny about events. Yet, before we took the field at Sydney, something historic needed our attention. It was a matter that went beyond the barriers of sport, something vital to the future of South Africa. Back home, President de Klerk had announced plans for constitutional reform that would take South Africa away from the era of apartheid. There was to be an all-white referendum, and the President needed a two-thirds majority. It was a measure of the progress made towards democracy that, just two years after Nelson Mandela's release, the white population in South Africa was being asked to give up the basis of its supremacy, built up over many decades. It was an issue of fundamental importance and we sportsmen, who had suffered because of political matters, couldn't ignore it. Geoff Dakin, the President of the United Cricket Board of South Africa, was out in Australia with the team and he called a meeting. He outlined the significance of the referendum back home, and its impact on sporting matters and suggested we should send a statement, backing the constitutional reforms. We went further than that, stating that we would withdraw from the World Cup if the necessary two-thirds majority wasn't achieved. It was a very tense, sombre meeting, but everyone there knew the gravity of our decision. There was no dissent. The consensus was that it was the right thing to do, even though we could be sacrificing our chance of winning the World Cup. I felt that President de Klerk had been very brave and imaginative to broker a compromise with Nelson Mandela and that spirit of working together between the races was the only way forward for our country. High-profile sportsmen like us needed to take a stand. For my part, I wouldn't blame the other cricketing nations for again refusing to play against us if the referendum failed to usher in democratic methods. There was no point in moaning about the interference of politics in sport, that was a fact of life, and we needed to show that things were changing rapidly, and for the better in South Africa. It was a very worrying couple of days for us in Australia, waiting for the referendum result to come through, but we knew what we were doing. On the eve of the England match, we were told the good news – President de Klerk had his mandate and the reforms would go through. Two years later, Mr Mandela became our President, to worldwide approval. I hope the lead we took in Australia may have swayed a few voters back home, and I also hope that nobody forgets F. W. de Klerk's courageous leadership during this period.

A relieved South African team took the field at Sydney for the England match, only to be pulled up short by a sickening farce. It rained just at the wrong time for the match, and for us. The game had been bubbling up to a great finish, with our target 22 off 13 balls, and four wickets in hand. Dave Richardson had just carved Chris Lewis over extra cover for two boundaries in one over, and we were definitely back in the game, with the capable Brian McMillan out there as well. I looked out of the dressing-room and saw the rain falling. It got heavier and the players had to come off. It rained for precisely eight minutes, and then the regulations took over. The electronic scoreboard flashed up the news that the revised rate was 22 off seven balls, then a minute later, it was changed to 21 off a single delivery. I heard the crowd gasp in astonishment, and we were shattered. But we knew the rules before the competition started. There was no provision for a second day resumption, because the competition was geared to the demands of television, which had pumped in millions of dollars. You would have thought that the game could have been resumed in the normal way once the rain had stopped, but the TV schedules decreed the match had to be over at a certain time, and it couldn't be made up. That inflexibility led to an outcry for days afterwards, and we felt sorry for ourselves, but we knew the form before we bowled a ball in the competition. It was just a case of hoping for the best, while fearing the worst. We contributed to the farce, though. We just didn't bowl our overs quickly enough, losing five overs through a combination of no-balls, wides and taking too long to set the field. If we'd got through those overs quicker, the match would have been done and dusted before the rain came.

We performed a lap of honour around the SCG, and we got a sympathetic reception from everyone. Ours was definitely the hard-luck story, and the England boys were embarrassed. In their hearts, they shouldn't have been, because they had played great cricket throughout and could still have beaten us. It wasn't their fault we had been robbed of a classic finish. I can assure you that if the boot had been on the other foot, no South African cricketer would have moped around, feeling sorry for the opposition. Basically, we had to take some of the blame for the farcical finish, although we didn't see it that way in a dejected Sydney dressing-room. When we came back to Johannesburg, we were given an astonishing reception. There must have been a hundred thousand packing the streets as we paraded around on an open-topped bus. It was almost as if we had won the competition. All that was missing was the trophy. So the rain regulations that annoyed so many allowed us to return as heroes and our demanding sporting public could always fall back on the hard-luck story as comfort.

I watched the World Cup Final live at the Melbourne Cricket Ground, and I was so envious of the Pakistani and England players. I commentated on the match for M-Net Supersport, the South African sports channel, and the atmosphere was absolutely electric, with 87,000 inside the MCG. Wasim Akram bowled spectacularly, making the ball reverse swing brilliantly, and he inspired Pakistan to a great victory. I found night cricket in Australia an exhilarating experience. They led the way in the use of the white ball, coloured clothing and black sightscreen and on a warm evening, with the floodlights on, it's a unique atmosphere. I also loved the way Aussie TV gets right into the heart of the action, with some great close-ups and the use of the Super Slo-Mo camera. The World Cup of '92 was glamorous, hugely popular – watched by one billion people throughout the world – and tremendous fun for any cricketer who wants to prove himself on the big stage.

Three weeks after the World Cup ended, we were off on our travels again, this time to the West Indies for our first Test match and some one-day internationals. The honeymoon was soon over. We were thrashed by seven wickets, by 107 runs and by ten wickets in the three one-dayers, and we lost the Test by 52 runs when we should have won it. The West Indies players were up for our visit, after some adverse press criticism following their World Cup disappointments, and we took the flak for it. Our heads had been in the clouds after the World Cup and we copped a good hiding. That Test defeat remains one of the biggest disappointments of my career. The Barbados public boycotted the game, not because of the South African presence, but due to the omission of Malcolm Marshall and Carlisle Best from the World Cup party and Anderson Cummins from the Test. With no local players picked, there was no more than 6,000 at the whole game and that made for an eerie atmosphere, which surely should have helped us. Instead, we buckled when the pressure was on.

We made 345 in our first innings, and established a lead of 83 over them. Then we had them 196 for eight in their second innings, on the ropes and facing defeat. But we bowled badly at the tail, allowing Jimmy Adams to shepherd Patrick Patterson and Courtney Walsh to a total of 283. Patterson, an even worse batter than Walsh, came in at number eleven and added 62 with Adams, as we got increasingly frustrated. We should have bowled short of a length at the tail-enders, trying to intimidate them in West Indian fashion, but instead we pitched it up too much and they smashed us. Having said all that, we still should have won despite that poor bowling. We only needed 201 to win on a flat deck. Instead we put a rope around our necks and hung ourselves. On the final morning, we were 122 for two at the start, needing just another 79 to win. We were bowled out for 148 by Ambrose and Walsh. Kepler Wessels and Peter Kirsten, our two most experienced batsmen ought to have nailed down a comfortable victory, but Kepler was out in the first over of the day and we just folded. I got a 'pair' in my first Test and after losing, we then had to watch the whole West Indian side running round the boundary in triumph, hand-in-hand. What a sickener! Ambrose had given us an object lesson in hostility and accuracy – eight for 81 off 60.4 overs in the match – and the way he polished off our tail was awesome. But how did we lose that game?

I wasn't to know it at the time, but those batting frailties in Barbados have haunted us throughout our resumed Test career since 1992. Time and again, we have thrown away advantages won by the bowlers. The last two Tests in England on the '98 tour are obvious examples, but there are many more. This isn't the usual matter of a bowler having it in for the batters in the side, because we are all in it together, and I don't like divisions in a team. I'm always the first to put my hand up on behalf of the bowlers and admit we have let the side down. But since we came back to Test cricket, we've never been able to get the batting balance right. We veer from dogged defiance to rashness, there is no settled authority about our batting in the way the Australians seem to possess. Even England are more impressive than us in batting. I don't know if our problem is a lack of self-belief, or are we simply not as good as we think we are? The South African tradition is to chat ourselves up, and I do like a positive attitude, but we haven't proved our worth in batting since our return to Test cricket – and, as a result, we haven't won as many games and series as we expected. Our public and players are less self-effacing than England, we actually expect to win all the time, but it comes hard when that doesn't happen. I get the feeling in my time in the game that it's a pleasant surprise to the English when they win a series, despite the talent they undoubtedly possess. We are one great batter short in our line-up. If we had a Tendulkar, a Lara, a Steve Waugh, we could build around that sort of player. Darryl Cullinan has been the nearest, but too often he's been like a ticking time bomb and gets himself out when established. The great batsmen book in, as I know to my cost. All our established batsmen should have taken more responsibility. As a result, we have fallen short too many times, especially against the world's best, Australia.

That Barbados defeat certainly made us sit up. It came at the end of a draining six months of international cricket – playing in India, Australia, New Zealand and the Caribbean – and we were certainly jaded at the end of it all. There was much to learn about the mental toughness needed, as we started from base camp in November 1991. All the talking in the world doesn't prepare you for the actual experience of competing against the world's best players, when the pressure is full on. That was our short-term problem at the end of that first concentrated spell of international cricket. And that hectic first itinerary was the shape of things to come. Over the next few years, South African cricketers were to be worked very hard.

CHAPTER NINE

Learning to Win at Warwickshire

I n between international commitments, I was happily involved with a Warwickshire side that started to believe in itself. After a gradual pruning of the staff, and a revived youth policy, we developed into a handy unit in seasons 1992 and '93. Those two years established the disciplined framework and overall positive philosophy that led to spectacular success in later seasons. My only frustration was that my national duties meant I wasn't at Edgbaston as often as I'd have wished, to share in that success.

The '92 season saw us finish sixth in the championship and reach a place in the NatWest semis. We lost a close contest to Northants by three wickets, after battling hard to defend a total of just 149 on a quick pitch. With a little more luck, we would have squeezed home because we bowled well, and yet in a sense we needed to know such disappointment to harden us up. The key to it all was familiarity, knowing what to do in tense games like that one against Northants. Three years later, they were the opposition in the NatWest Final, and we kept our nerves better to win the trophy. In 1993, it was the same situation at Lord's, when we won a fantastic nail-biter against Sussex. We had learned over the previous seasons just how to react at key moments when tight matches are decided in just a couple of overs. Time and again, we would win games that seemed to be going against us, but we'd keep our nerve, sticking to our belief that a positive attitude was essential. If you go into your shell when the chips are down, you'll usually lose it – but you have to be able to rely on winning experiences that have stemmed from remaining calm and focused.

I was very happy with my bowling in the '92 championship season – 74 wickets at 22, with a wicket every 46 balls. I bowled particularly quickly at Guildford against Surrey, whistling out the first six batsmen on a slow pitch. I also hit Neil Searjeant hard on the jaw with a rapid bouncer, that forced him to retire. For me, that was just one of those things. I have never consciously set out to injure a batsman, but if he walks off the field with a broken finger, that's one less guy to get out. I just see it as the removal of an obstruction. When I get bounced when I'm at the crease, I understand the form and don't let it bother me. Ian Bishop bowled at the speed of light against me during that 1992 season, and I must admit I didn't get in line. The Derbyshire close fielders enjoyed it, though, saying to me 'Now you know what it's like to face you' and I must admit I wasn't too displeased when Bishop caught me off his own bowling! I realise now how important it is for South Africa to bat in depth, so I've worked hard at my batting in the nets. Bob Woolmer knows that because we lack a great batsman, we all need to chip in with runs all the way down the order, even numbers ten and eleven. If that means getting the sort of physical punishment I'm used to handing out, I've got to bite the bullet. We saw the other side of the coin in our recent series against the

West Indies when the opposition collapsed regularly after losing five or six wickets. On the other hand, we wouldn't give it away so easily, and that showed our mental resilience.

When the stick is flying from the fast bowlers, you just have to accept the situation when it's your turn. I do get annoyed though, when someone comes in to bat against me without a helmet. The West Indian captain, Richie Richardson did that against me in a one-day international in Cape Town, and I couldn't understand why. It was hardly a slow pitch at Newlands, yet he wandered in, wearing his trademark floppy sunhat, shades and a watch! That got my dander up, and my captain Kepler Wessels said 'Let him have it'. My first bouncer was mishooked just short of fine leg and the next, even quicker, went straight down the fielder's throat. Richie was a compulsive hooker, but I've no idea what got into him that day. The only top batsman not to wear a helmet against me was Viv Richards. He wasn't in his prime when I came up against him in county cricket, but he clearly felt that wearing a helmet would have been a psychological hit for any fast bowler. Certainly he never seemed ruffled by the short ball, as he relied on his amazingly sharp reactions and bat speed. Viv must have been a fantastic player at his best. He wasn't ever troubled much by me.

Warwickshire's progress towards becoming the best side in the country wasn't even halted by a change of captain. Near the end of the '92 season, Andy Lloyd was effectively sacked. He hadn't made many runs that summer, averaging just 25, although he did play many unselfish innings, going for quick runs. But he was also struggling in the field, and the key figures at the club wanted Dermot Reeve to replace him. For his part, Dermot made no secret that he wanted the job. I felt sorry for Andy that it all ended so messily for him, with two championship games to go before the end of the season, but the club was adamant that a change was necessary before the players dispersed that September. Andy did a hell of a lot to get Warwickshire along the right lines by approaching each day positively, and trying to get all the players gelling for each other. He was a great believer in the players enjoying each other's company away from the cricket. He used to stage karaoke parties at his house near Stratford-upon-Avon, when we'd bring along our partners, and they were great times, the ideal way to enjoy a day off from playing. We'd all make fools of ourselves on the karaoke machine – you should have seen my pathetic attempts at singing 'Summer Nights' with Tina – but we laughed along with each other and that helped forge our marvellous team spirit. Andy Lloyd also did a great deal to help me develop as a fast bowler, rationing my spells, helping me to understand opposition batsmen. He always captained me superbly.

So Dermot Reeve was to be the captain who lead us to cricket history a couple of years after taking the job. Although Dermot ruffled a few feathers with his ego, and his brash manner, he was the ideal successor to Andy Lloyd. When he took over, he talked openly and impressively about his aims and approach to the boys, and he was always excellent at articulating his thoughts. He gave every-one the freedom to express themselves, encouraging the young players especially, and he and Bob Woolmer were terrific at fostering a constructive, supportive atmosphere. Dermot wouldn't allow anybody to be slagged off for fail-ing, as long as the positive intent was there. His attitude was that it would come right next time, as long as the thinking was aggressive and dynamic. He wanted us to talk about our cricket, to express our aims without feeling inhibited, and that was just the way that Bob Woolmer saw it. They gelled straight away.

I loved Dermot's zest and dynamic approach. He was fearless. Dermot didn't mind about the opposition hating him for his cockiness and smart mouth, he saw it as a way of getting up their noses and putting them off their game. He backed himself, even when it was physically dangerous. I was batting with him against Northants on the day that Curtly Ambrose behaved disgracefully, sending down three beamers in a row. Dermot had just pulled him for four and Ambrose followed all the way down the wicket to say 'You'd better watch out'. The next three balls were fast, well-directed beamers that shocked the Northants fielders as much as Dermot and me. After the second, Dermot shouted at Ambrose, 'Look mate, I've got a wife and kid and if you hit me on the heart, then I'm dead', but he didn't show any fear. That made no difference to Ambrose, even after Geoff Humpage ran onto the pitch to give Dermot his chest protector, stopping off on the way back to tell Ambrose that he would 'break your f****** kneecaps' if he kept on bowling such dangerous stuff. At the non-striker's end, I was terrified, and relieved when suddenly Ambrose walked off the field, without stopping to tell his captain he was going. It was appalling behaviour from a world-class cricketer who knew exactly where he was aiming those three beamers, but I was knocked out by Dermot's bravery. He went on to score an unbeaten double-hundred, which surely says it all. I had some experience of his cockiness as an opponent when we came up against each other in the 1992 World Cup semi-final. Before the match, Dermot warned 'I'm going to be coming at you, Al' and he was as good as his word. He made 25 not out off just 14 balls at a key stage in their innings, taking 17 off one of my overs. He came down the wicket to me, hitting it over mid-on for six, a very big hit on the Sydney Cricket Ground. At close quarters, I could see how pumped up he was, yet still so calm. That is a fantastic quality to have in a cricketer, especially at crucial periods in one-day matches. No wonder Dermot was such an influential one-day player and captain. He simply relished the tight situation and the big occasion, and that huge self-confidence rubbed off on the rest of us.

Dermot's man-management was excellent when he became captain. He gave the players responsibility, told them the framework they should work inside, and backed them all the way. Somehow he managed to banish the fear of failure by relaxing the players. That refreshing attitude was at the heart of our remarkable victory in the 1993 NatWest Trophy Final against Sussex. We didn't seem to have a chance, chasing 322 in dreadful light, but we kept going, with Dermot in the forefront and Asif Din playing the innings of his life. He scored a hundred as we achieved the highest score to win a Lord's Final. Without that desire to win and huge self-belief that had been built up over the past couple of years, we would not have gone anywhere near to victory. It also set us up for subsequent seasons, because if we could win that Lord's Final, nothing was beyond us. It was a mould-breaking victory that hardly any other county at the time would have pulled off. I was particularly pleased for two of our batsmen, Asif Din and Paul Smith. Asif was due to be sacked at the end of the

'93 season, after a poor couple of seasons, and he just went for the bowling without fear. His luck came off, he became a hero in just a couple of hours, and he won a new contract and the promise of a benefit. A great guy, Asif Din. He'd been so genuine to me when I first came over to England and we used to have many chats indoors at Birmingham University, doing pre-season training. His gentle, amusing nature helped me get through the painful times in training. Paul Smith, who made a violent 60 in that Lord's Final, was another great mate of mine during his time at Edgbaston. A very funny man, with a sharp wit that put everyone down who tried to out-smart him, Paul was a genuine character who was misunderstood sometimes. He tended to drift in and out of matches when his concentration wandered but he was a very talented all-rounder, who could bowl genuinely fast at times, and could play classy, attacking innings. His great hero was Ian Botham, and they shared the same zest for life and belief in attacking cricket. Paul would often inspire me in the field with his quick mind. When he was bored, he'd ask me to translate a certain phrase into Afrikaans, and he'd repeat it over and over again, then laugh out loud as I was about to run in to bowl. I really enjoyed Paul's company – in dressing-room, bar and on the field.

Unfortunately, I couldn't share the excitement in person with the boys during that great day at Lord's. I had been called back by South Africa for training camp, then to Sri Lanka. It was the start of some frustrating times for me, when I've had to leave Warwickshire early because I had to represent my country. Each time, I've wanted to split myself in two and be in both places at once, but there has been no way round it and I understand the situation isn't ideal for anyone. But for me it has been hard, especially in

1993. I missed the last seven weeks of the season, playing in just nine championship games. We'd beaten Yorkshire in the NatWest quarter final at Headingley at the end of July, and I felt very down about it all as I drove back to Birmingham, knowing my county season was over. The boys staged a nice farewell party for me, which made me miss them even more when I flew home. By the time we'd got to the semi-final, at Taunton, I was in Colombo, playing in a day/night match, and I phoned Bob Woolmer as soon as I got back to the hotel. He gave me the good news that the lads had beaten Somerset, and I passed on best wishes for Lord's. A month later, I again put through a call from my hotel in Colombo, and spoke to Tina in Birmingham. As soon as we got through, she said 'Oh my God, Allan, Roger Twose has just hit the winning runs' and she then recounted to me what a fantastic effort it had been. So I took a chance and put a call through to Lord's. Luckily, someone was still there on the switchboard and I was put through to the Warwickshire dressing-room. I heard the guys screaming in triumph and singing and one by one, they all came on the phone for a quick word. That was a very expensive phone bill for me, but it was worth it. I desperately wanted to be there, but I was also very pleased I didn't have to bat in the dark in the closing overs. The 1989 Final hadn't been forgotten by me!

It was important for Roger Twose that he made the winning hit in the '93 Final. He had a poor season, but he still had the bottle to play the right shot off the final ball amid the unbelievable tension. Roger Twose was another key man in Warwickshire's revival. He was a very under-rated cricketer, who had scored a thousand runs in '92 with a sensible, no-frills approach. Roger had got himself very fit and he was also mentally strong in the manner of Dermot Reeve. Both Dermot and Bob Woolmer rated Roger very highly for his toughness under pressure and strong competitive instinct. Like Dermot, he wasn't bothered about being popular with the opposition, he liked to hand out the verbals on the field. He'd grab a team-mate by the scruff of the neck and demand to know why he wasn't giving his best. Roger worked very hard at his cricket and he had an excellent cricket brain. He asked me how to bowl quicker, because he didn't like people making light of his bowling. In the nets, he'd shout out to me 'If you bounce me, I'll hook you out of the park', and always tried to simulate match conditions. To Roger, a session in the nets was a competition between him and the bowlers, there was never a time when he would just coast. A solid, gritty character, he modelled himself on Dermot in his bowling – even down to the dirty looks, the smart remark, the change of pace, the double bluffs – and his batting won us many a tight game. But Roger was a very ambitious character and he wanted to play international cricket. His fiancee was from New Zealand and he eventually emigrated there in 1995, ending up a Test player by qualification. It hasn't worked out for him at international level, but he was an immense loss to Warwickshire when he left. I don't think we've replaced him adequately enough, with respect to the other all-rounders in the side. He was such a battler, his tenacity rubbed off on the others. With his sharp cricket brain and communication skills, he would have been a fine captain of Warwickshire, the nearest thing to Dermot Reeve.

So it was all gelling nicely for Warwickshire as I started to get used to zigzagging around the world with South

Africa. That Edgbaston dressing-room in the early 1990s was full of positive characters like Reeve, Twose, Lloyd and Paul Smith, plus deep thinkers like Munton, Neil Smith and Small with young, bouncy guys like Penney and Piper getting established, flourishing under a relaxed regime. Bob Woolmer was knitting it together, getting us all to talk more and more about cricket, adding his own vast technical knowledge without getting in the way of the captain. It was the model way to run a county side and soon we reaped the benefits of this enlightened approach. We were becoming ahead of the game in England, yet opposition sides weren't yet aware of that.

CHAPTER TEN

Climbing onto the Treadmill

After the initial euphoria about our international tour had worn off, it was time to get down to some hard work. That meant cramming as much big-match experience into the shortest possible period of time. I didn't believe we'd be able just to ease ourselves back into Test cricket and be as dominant as we were in 1970, the last time we had been involved. My time in county cricket over in England had given me an insight into the world-class players we would be up against when we played them at international level. There was a lot to do before we could establish ourselves in the top three, despite the rather blinkered attitude of some our supporters. We had to discover what it was like to play on spinners' pitches on the sub-continent, green wickets in England, bouncy ones in the Caribbean and then try to compete with the best side in the world, Australia. So we climbed aboard the international carousel, playing all round world for the next few years. It was a fantastic experience even though there were times when it was very hard work. But we had lost out on more than twenty years' invaluable experience of internationals, and the job had to be done.

First up – India, at home in a three-Test series and seven

one-day internationals. I've never quite known why our administrators are so keen on seven of those draining one-dayers. They can be very exhausting and mentally taxing, but I suppose they bring in the money. The amount of one-day internationals played by us since 1991 has also helped develop our skills in that particular region, especially in fielding and batting. It's helped establish us as one of the best one-day sides in world cricket and we have also been conscious of the need to generate money to benefit South African cricket at all levels. Dr Ali Bacher's Development Programme needs constant cash injections from the business community, but also from gate receipts. A proportion of the money that comes from ticket sales at home internationals and Tests goes to the Development Programme, so we can't really object to playing a few more one-dayers if it benefits such a good cause. But there are times when you need to remind yourself of that when you're on an early morning flight after a day/night match, with another due the next day, somewhere else in the country!

The one-day attendance figures were more impressive than those for the four-Test series – 160,000 for the one-dayers and less than 200,000 for the Tests – and that started a trend which has remained in South Africa. The day/night games are enormously popular, especially if the weather is good, while there are times when we struggle to get the public interested in a Test match. The crowds at the Wanderers in Johannesburg are good for the Tests – we had over 20,000 on the Saturday and Sunday against India in '92 – and Newlands in Cape Town hold up well enough. Yet we were surprised that only 30,000 attended the whole of the first Test, at Durban in '92. It was, after all, the first

Test in South Africa since 1970, and surely the large Indian community in Durban would come and support their team? Yet at no stage in that series did the Indians enjoy much support, which was surprising. I have to admit, though, that it was a boring series for the spectator. The wickets were slow, the rate of scoring usually about two runs per over, and neither side batted with much freedom. The Indians came with a shocking recent away record in Tests – not a single victory away in the last 25 Tests – and we were still feeling our way, relying on occupation of the crease. Perhaps we were too concerned about avoiding defeat by trying to post large scores, without looking at the wider issues like selling Test cricket to the public.

That first Test in Durban was a notable one in several aspects, though. My good friend, Omar Henry made his Test debut, the first non-white to play for South Africa. He'd been told the night before he was definitely playing, and I went to his room to congratulate him. Omar was on the phone to his wife, and they were both in tears. I was soon in the same state. When Omar finally walked onto the field as a fully-fledged Test cricketer, I looked over to him and saw him kiss his South African hat. It was a touching moment for him and I was very proud for the new South Africa as well. Omar may have been nearly 41, but he was still very fit and worth his place in the side. There was no tokenism involved, he was the best spinner available and his selection marked the way forward for our country. The aim now was to give cricketers of all races the best possible chance to see what they could do. No longer was it primarily a white man's game.

This was also the first series to feature television replays and a third umpire to adjudicate on close decisions, using the technology available. It seemed a sensible progression. There had been an increasing amount of dodgy decisions around the world, which didn't stand up to close inspection after a look at the television replays, so why not help the two umpires out in the middle, and aim for greater consistency? For now, the replays would only apply to hit-wicket, stumpings or run-outs. The first, historic decision involved Sachin Tendulkar, given run out from a Jonty Rhodes throw, by the third umpire, Cyril Mitchley. Soon we saw how much the umpires were going to rely on the third pair of eyes, even when there seemed no possible doubt. I threw out Mohammad Azharuddin from mid-wicket, and from the naked eye, he was clearly out. But the call went out to the third umpire, because the guys in the middle didn't want to be exposed, and would make doubly certain. As a result, the game has been held up over the subsequent years for apparently clear-cut decisions, but at least the option gives greater consistency and I'm sure the crowd likes the suspense involved.

The problem comes when the umpire doesn't call for the TV replay and gets caught out. That happened in the Johannesburg Test, when Jonty Rhodes was run out by at least six inches, but Steve Bucknor didn't involve the third umpire. Yet from sideways on, where we were sitting, Jonty was always struggling and the TV replay confirmed he was well out. Jonty was on 28 at the time, but went on to make 91. We all want the umpires to make the right decisions, but there's a problem when they run the risk of being exposed by not using an electronic aid. The fact that the TV replay is only available for stumpings, run-outs and hit-wicket only served to highlight what a poor decision Jimmy Cook got in the Durban Test. Jimmy became the first man to be given out first ball in his first Test when he edged one to Sachin Tendulkar at third slip. Jimmy wasn't sure it had bounced, stood his ground and was given out. He came into the dressing-room, sat down in his usual calm manner, and said 'I'm not sure if that one carried'. It hadn't. Jimmy was very unlucky. If the TV replay had been available for decisions such as that one, then Jimmy would rightly have been given the benefit of the doubt.

We managed to get the only win of this inaugural series at Port Elizabeth, when I took twelve wickets in the match. Kapil Dev got after me in the second innings, smashing me all over the shop for a scintillating hundred. They were 88 for seven at one stage, but Kapil hit the ball so sweetly. If I pitched it up, he drove beautifully and he got the angles right for the hook and the pull when I dropped short. But apart from his innings, the rest of the Indians didn't seem to want to hang around. Hansie Cronje scored his maiden Test hundred in this game, so it was a happy time for two Bloemfontein boys. He was 23 at the time, still a happy-go-lucky character. A year later, a tragic accident changed Hansie's life and his approach to cricket. While travelling through northern Natal, Hansie's car killed a little black girl as he passed through a village, late at night. Apparently the girl ran out from nowhere, and Hansie couldn't do a thing about it. He did stop at the scene of the accident while waiting for the ambulance and police to arrive, but it all got very ugly. About forty people emerged from nowhere, threatening Hansie and the child's grieving mother was screaming frantically. Hansie and our wicket-keeper, Roger Brown honestly thought they were going to be killed, as they were surrounded by the group, who were brandishing knives. Eventually Hansie and Roger were allowed to leave, and they were very shaken when they caught up with us at the team hotel. We later heard that there had been quite a few hit-and-runs in that particular area, and that nobody ever stopped, for fear of being murdered. But Hansie and Roger felt it was the right thing to do, and they got away with it. After that tragedy, Hansie changed his lifestyle and became a committed Christian. Before, he enjoyed a few beers and sometimes carried a bit of extra weight, but all that stopped. He worked very hard in the gym, became super-fit, and has stayed with this regime ever since. After taking counselling about the incident, Hansie committed himself to God, and became a very dignified person. He was already ideal leadership material once Kepler Wessels retired and his new, serious outlook on life gave him even greater stature.

That haul of wickets for me at Port Elizabeth was largely instrumental in me being named Man of the Series for taking 20 in the series at 19 apiece and I was pleased at my consistent speed. I didn't feel their batters were all that happy against pace, but I was also keen to be seen to do well at home, to banish further this idea that I only do well consistently for Warwickshire and come home shattered. My initial target as I came into this first series was to get to 50 Test wickets. I believe in personal targets because they help the team effort if they are channelled properly, and I'd seen all the statistics about those South African bowlers who had taken a hundred Test wickets. At the top of the tree was the great off-spinner from the 1950s, Hugh Tayfield, who had 170 wickets. I didn't allow myself to think that far and it's been a matter of great personal pride that I've been the first South African to get past the 200 mark.

That first home summer of international cricket wasn't just a case of learning how to play in high-pressure situations, but also how to be careful when the spotlight is on you. We were playing Pakistan in a one-day game at Verwoerdburg, near Pretoria when I became involved in something initially trivial that soon became worryingly significant. There was a big crowd in – around 20,000 – and the Pakistanis had a lot of support that day. That was fine by me, I like to see all the flags and hear the chants, that gees me up. But some of the Pakistani supporters around the boundary edge kept baiting me, saying that Waqar Younis was faster than me, with a few other tasteless comments thrown in. I reacted wrongly, turning round, making a gesture and adding a few choice words. Next day, there was a picture of me in an Asian newspaper, with the caption 'It's because of people like this that South Africa will never change'. The article didn't bother pointing out that I'd apologised soon after to those spectators, but I ought to have known better. Ali Bacher gave me a right rollicking, and I couldn't apologise enough. It may have looked a racist action by me, but it had nothing to do with the fact that those fans were Pakistanis – I was just fed up of getting some stick that I didn't really deserve. I learned my lesson that day, because I don't turn round anymore and react to the verbals. It leads to all sorts of misunderstandings.

In fact, there were a few flashpoints on the field during that international season. We were annoyed for some time at Sachin Tendulkar for not reprieving Jimmy Cook in that first Test at Durban, and we weren't at all bothered when he was given out for nought at Port Elizabeth, caught behind when it came off his thigh pad. In that same Test, Manoj Prabhakar was fined ten per cent of his match fee for dissent at being given out, and by the end of the tour, the Indians were complaining a lot. They looked demoralised and at odds with each other. The series had been marketed as 'The Friendship Tour', but there was little of that in the one-day international at Port Elizabeth, when Kapil Dev ran out Peter Kirsten at his end, after failing to deliver the ball. Kapil hadn't warned him about backing up too far, although he had done so three times earlier on the tour, and he obviously felt that was sufficient warning. When Cyril Mitchley gave Peter out, Kapil pointed him to the pavilion, which only inflamed Peter even more. He stormed into our dressing-room, his helmet bounced around the walls, and he stormed off to see the Indian tour manager. He told him, 'If you still think this is a f****** Friendship Tour, you've got it f****** wrong!' Next time Kapil and Peter faced each other out in the middle, Kapil was smacked a painful blow on the shins, as Peter turned at his end for another run. Kapil went down like a sack, the TV cameras didn't see the incident because they were following the ball on the way to the boundary, but there's no doubt Peter meant it. It wasn't in character, because Peter was a quiet sort of guy, but he had been enraged by Kapil. Eventually, Peter was fined fifty per cent of his match fee. Just because we were new to international cricket didn't mean that South Africans were going to be meek and mild on the field. Over the next few years, we clocked up a fair amount of meetings with various match referees.

I can understand how Dr Bacher and our other administrators were so keen to stress the positive aspects of our national side, and try to avoid flashpoints. It was important to bring the game to wider sections of the South African public than previous generations, to fall into line with the encouraging progress towards dismantling the old political order. Right from the start of our return to the international scene, the African National Congress was tremendously supportive. We needed them to demonstrate to the non-white community that cricket was trying to unite all the races in South Africa, and the lead given by Nelson Mandela and the sports spokesman, Steve Tshwete was brilliant. During the '92 World Cup, Steve was always in our dressing-room after the games, often in tears when we had won, and he made it quite clear he wanted the white guys to do it for his country. We all knew the harsh image of the ANC from our childhood days, when we were fed the party line from right-wingers, but their constructive stance to us when we returned to international cricket was inspirational. They've been great for us, they've lead the way in bringing sport to all sections of the South African community.

The ANC's support must have had something to do with the boom in attendances in South African cricket during that '92/93 season. Although the Test crowds were dis-appointing, the total attendances for all domestic matches doubled on the previous year, almost getting to 800,000. Almost a quarter of a million watched the floodlit Benson and Hedges Cup series, and the TV coverage started to reflect this massive interest in one-day cricket. Cricket in South Africa was starting a boom period, and it was mar-vellous to be in at the beginning of a bright new era for us. Just to make it a perfect season for me, Free State won the Currie Cup for the first time in its history. I was very proud that the province with the least amount of players available had triumphed, after we had built up our pool of players in recent years. The climax came when we beat

Western Province by 114 runs, after hundreds by Hansie Cronje and Omar Henry and five wickets from Omar. We were running neck and neck with Transvaal for the Shield in this last series of matches, and we were struggling to bowl out Western Province on a flat wicket. Just before tea, word came through to us that Transvaal had collapsed to Natal's Pat Symcox and Malcolm Marshall, and that if we could winkle out the remaining wickets, we were home and dry. With the second new ball, I had Gary Kirsten caught in the gully by Franklyn Stephenson, and that was the start of the slide. With six overs left, we needed just one final wicket. Meyrick Pringle came in, snicked one from Brad Player through the hands of Frankie for four, and the next delivery bowled him. There was a great newspaper photograph showing all eleven of us leaping into the air when Brad took that wicket, and the atmosphere around the ground was brilliant. News had spread through Bloemfontein that we were about to make history, and we were all carried shoulder-high off the field. Eddie Barlow, our coach and Hansie Cronje, our captain, had been saying for a few years that we could compete with the big boys and here was the vindication. They had pleaded with players not to go to other provinces that appeared more glamorous and were better payers, and loyalty was rewarded at last. Natal, Western Province and Transvaal have all made serious offers to me, but I'm so glad I stayed in Bloem. I love playing for my home state, to go back to Bloemfontein, knowing that each season we will be a force to reckon with. I know Hansie Cronje feels the same about being from a small community, stacking up against the big boys and doing well. Free State had only ever won the Currie Cup rugby shield once – in 1978, and I saw those games as a schoolboy – so to help bring the major cricket trophy home for the first time was so satisfying. We also picked up the one-day trophy, beating Eastern Province in front of large home crowd on a lovely hot day. Life was good if you played for Free State and South Africa that season.

A few months later, and our first Test series abroad, in Sri Lanka. This was a major test of character for our boys, quite apart from stretching us as cricketers. I've never experienced such humidity before, and it was so hard to keep going. We'd trained beforehand in Durban, the most humid of the South African cities, but there was no comparison when we got to Sri Lanka, you just can't prepare for something like that. I've always been very careful about the sun, but I was amazed at the effects of the heat and humidity, when the sun was never really out. On the first morning of the first Test, in Moratuwa, the heat was the most intense I've ever known. I lost about three kilos in weight that day. I'd be standing at fine leg, and the sweat would just pour out of me. In the Colombo Test, it was even more ridiculous – around 43 degrees heat and seventy per cent humidity. At one point the umpires discussed if we should stay out on the field, because they felt the conditions were endangering our health, but Kepler Wessels, our tough captain, wouldn't go off, because he wanted to win the match. Meanwhile, our twelfth man kept throwing buckets of water over me in the outfield! The best part of those days was going back to our superb hotel and feeling the cooling effects of the air-conditioning. Sheer bliss!

Considering the distress we all felt at times through the weather, I thought we did excellently to win the series. I was overshadowed by our fast left-arm bowler, Brett Schultz, who took 20 wickets at 16 apiece in the three

Tests. The highlight was the Colombo Test, when he took nine wickets on a fast, bouncy pitch to help us win by an innings. I was very impressed by the natural way that Brett adapted to Test cricket, bowling inswinging yorkers at a rapid pace. The Sri Lankans didn't like his aggression and folded against him more than once. Kepler was very impressed by the big man, forecasting a big future for him, alongside me as our fast-bowling spearhead, but he's had fitness problems since that tour, and his knees in particular have caused him a lot of problems.

If Brett Schultz was our trump card in winning the series, then Jonty Rhodes must get an honourable mention in saving the Moratuwa Test. He batted for more than four hours to keep out the off-spinner Muttiah Muralitharan, using his feet superbly, getting to the pitch of the ball, playing defensively with soft hands. With three hours left, and the ball turning sharply, we had only four wickets left, but Jonty batted so superbly with Pat Symcox and Clive Eksteen that we lost only one wicket after that. I can still remember sitting in our dressing-room for ages, waiting to bat, alongside Brett Schultz, each of us gripping one end of a cold towel. We were sweating so much that this was the only way we could keep our hands dry. It was also nerves on my part, because I don't think I would have lasted very long against Muralitharan ripping it square! He looked a remarkable bowler, and he's proved it since. On that tour, he spun it such a long way. He bowled Brian McMillan with one that spun so much that it went through his legs as he padded up. Only Hansie Cronje played with him any real assurance all series, taking a chance by sweeping him.

This series will always be remembered by Daryll Cullinan, who made his first Test hundred. He'd made his debut in the home series against India, and soon looked comfortable in the big time. Since he was at school, Daryll has been saddled with the tag of being the next Graeme Pollock, and although that's been a burden to him, he does have a commanding, relaxed air at the wicket. I think he has been South Africa's most naturally gifted batsman since we came back to international cricket. He's stylish, aggressive and rarely looks in difficulty when set. Fast bowling never seems to trouble him. But Daryll does get himself out rather too often, when he loses concentration or goes for the wrong shot. I'm worried that Daryll might be one of those guys who fall short at the highest level. I keep waiting for him to dominate a series, but he never quite gets there, making excellent fifties, but not enough hundreds. He's our version of Graeme Hick, I suppose. Daryll isn't the most popular guy in South African cricket, although I've always got on well with him. He's very opinionated and strong-minded, excellent in team meetings, where he's not shy about fingering those he considers to have been at fault. He talks very well in those meetings, offering some very good ideas when he feels like it. The trouble is that Daryll is very moody, and when he's not making runs he can be very quiet and withdrawn. I think he is captaincy material though, because he's not afraid to be unpopular, wouldn't get drawn into personal issues and is also worth his place in the side. He certainly wouldn't be fazed by the opposition, because he just doesn't believe in mixing with them. In fact, I've rarely seen Daryll go into the opposition dressing-room.

That Sri Lankan tour was important to toughen us up, because we had been spoilt in the West Indies and Australia, where the wickets are generally good, the crowds enthusiastic and the climate ideal if you're from South Africa. Dr Ali Bacher had some words of consolation after Sri Lanka: 'Don't worry, boys, the worst is yet to come' and he was right. He was preparing us for long tours to India and Pakistan, where many things are against you – like the climate, the umpiring, the practise facilities, the travelling and the different types of pitches – but you just have to get on with it. I think the South Africans have coped well with such challenges, because it's in our nature to grit our teeth and battle through. We have enough discipline to prepare ourselves mentally, telling ourselves it's going to be a hard tour, and then getting a pleasant surprise during the good sections of the trip. You have to make your own fun on the sub-continent, and stick together as a unit. That actually helps your cricket when you bond so closely, and we soon realised there was simply no point in moaning our way around India and Pakistan, when you're there for three months. Australia have the same positive attitude on the sub-continent, but I'm not so sure about England. After all, they've managed to avoid a Test series in Pakistan since 1987 and it's 1993 since they last played Tests in Sri Lanka and India.

If Sri Lanka was a test of character under trying conditions, our next encounter was bound to extend us fully. In 1994 we faced back-to-back series against Australia, the best side in the world, and that would be a true measure of how far we had progressed in a couple of years. We knew about the intensity the Australians bring to their cricket, and we were ready for them. It would be like the All Blacks against the Springboks in rugby, but there was always the extra ingredients of their proven class and

Above: Outside the family home in Bloemfontein, a toddler ready for action.

Right: As a five-year-old, my ears were rather prominent!

Below: Aged six (that's me, back row, fourth from the left) at President Brand Primary School, Bloemfontein.

The South African Schools side, at Cape Town, in 1984. I am second right, middle row and among the others who became Test colleagues are Clive Ekstee (extreme left, middle row) Darryl Cullinan (middle, front row) and Merryck Pringle (extreme right, front row).

With Roy Pienaar and (centre) General Jannie Geldenheys. Roy and I were then in the South African Defence Force, and became the only ones from that Force to play for South Africa.

Hugh Page becomes one of my wickets for Free State against Transvaal in 1993.

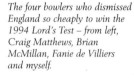

The four bowlers who dismissed England so cheaply to win the 1994 Lord's Test – from left, Craig Matthews, Brian McMillan, Fanie de Villiers and myself.

Bowling in my early days of Test cricket. I like the position of my arms – that right arm across the chest and high left arm means I'm following through properly.

The quartet from South Africa who have seen service at Edgbaston for Warwickshire – from left, English-born Bob Woolmer, the coach, Shaun Pollock, Brian McMillan and myself.

Dennis Amiss, a team-mate when I first played for Warwickshire, and now my boss at Edgbaston.

Brian Lara and I have always had a good personal relationship at Warwickshire, despite my disappointment at being passed over in his favour in 1996.

Above: Obliging the public at a Warwickshire Open Day, when we mingle with our supporters just before the season starts.

Right: Not sure if I got the verdict here. Do I really wear so much sun cream?!

Warwickshire joy. Neil Smith catches Min Patel off my bowling at Canterbury to seal the County Championship in 1995.

Celebrations on the Canterbury balcony with the Championship trophy. A few hours later, we were even less restrained.

With Dermot Reeve at a civic reception at the Birmingham Council House to commemorate winning the Championship and the NatWest Trophy in 1995.

Middlesex's Angus Fraser becomes one of my victims during Warwickshire's successful Sunday League campaign of 1997.

Batting at Lord's during the 1997 NatWest Trophy Final against Essex. The fact that I was out there with my bat only underlines what a desperate position we were in!

Taking the final wicket of the 1997 Sunday League season – Gloucestershire's Jonathan Lewis – to seal the trophy for us. A few seconds later, I was whisked onto the shoulders of some Warwickshire supporters and chaired off the field.

Sunday League champions, 1997 – seven trophies for us in five seasons. And the champer still tastes good once we stop pouring it over each other!

experience at international level, when we were still testing the water. So coming out of those two series with a couple of one-all draws was a good effort by us. On the first leg, in Australia, we relaxed subconsciously after winning a fantastic Test in Sydney. Before the final Test, in Adelaide, we had lost the one-day finals by 2–1 and their captain Allan Border told the media that we were there for the taking now, after being bowled out for just 69 on a ridiculous pitch in the one-dayer at Sydney. He was proved right, as we lost the Adelaide Test, when we really should have saved it. We'd gone off the boil on the tour, something that has happened to us rather too often for my liking . . . It happened on both tours to England, in '94 and '98, when it seemed hard to get motivated for the one-dayers at the end of the trip. That's something that shouldn't be needed.

At least we showed our mental bravery and guts by winning that Sydney Test. That's the greatest Test I've played in so far. The tension was amazing and what pleased me so much was that we hung in there, to bowl them out when they assumed they'd get the runs as a formality. They needed just 117 to win, but after Jonty Rhodes had added 36 with me for the final wicket, he told me as we walked off, 'I tell you, Allan, that's enough'. He'd been on at me throughout our partnership, about getting some runs. 'Every run we get now will be enough' he said after hitting Craig McDermott for a massive six, pulling him halfway up the first terrace on the long boundary on the SCG. Jonty, who batted almost four hours for his 76 not out, said the wicket was breaking up, that the cracks were there for the faster bowlers to exploit. I wanted to believe him, of course, but the key was to get some early wickets.

Right away, Fanie de Villiers hit the off stump of Michael

Slater with an absolute peach. Then I dropped David Boon off my own bowling, a dolly that came back too slowly, leaving me to grab at it. 'There goes the Test match', I thought – but then Boon chipped De Villiers hard and fast into the midriff of Gary Kirsten at short leg. The night-watchman, Tim May came and went first ball, then Fanie had Mark Taylor caught behind. That's when Mark Waugh started behaving a little arrogantly, saying to Hansie Cronje, 'Hey, Hansie! Put yourself on to bowl, mate, do us all a favour and we can finish it tonight!' That rankled with us and they were getting worried at the close, on a score of 63 for four. We had a team meeting then in the dressing-room and Kepler Wessels said 'We'll win this tomorrow because they won't fancy batting on this wicket. The ball's old, there'll be some reverse swing. Take no notice of their arrogance, they're worried. We've got to believe that tomorrow will be one of the biggest days in South African cricket'. Kepler wouldn't be able to captain us next day because of a broken finger, but he told me how I could get out Allan Border. He said I needed to bowl across the left-hander, line him up and then drag the next one in on him. It worked perfectly. After the first two balls went across him, allowing Border to give them the big leave, he shouldered arms to the next one, it reversed a little and clipped the off bail. I don't know who was more surprised – batsman or bowler – but that was a vital early breakthrough. Now we really could win.

I then got Mark Waugh lbw with a reverse, inswinging yorker, straight on his foot. After that, every batsman showed a great deal of tension. Damien Martyn scratched around for ages till I had him caught at cover at 110 for 8, and he had played into our hands. Craig McDermott had the right idea, trying to smash the game Australia's way. The last man, Glenn McGrath came in with seven needed, and even though I had four balls at him, he survived. He even took a single off me for the last ball, which amazed me. I couldn't believe McDermott would expose such a negligible number eleven to the whole of the next over and sure enough, McGrath popped one straight back to Fanie. We'd won. A famous victory, against all the odds, against a team who were highly fancied to get those runs. All the guys who weren't playing for us ran onto the field in joy, and Hansie carried Fanie off the field on his shoulders. Hansie had done an incredible job in the field, standing in for Kepler. He was cool, clearly in command and his run out of Shane Warne was inspiring. On that final morning, Pat Symcox had said to us 'Remember Headingley, fellas – these guys don't like chasing small totals, as they showed against Beefy Botham and Bob Willis in '81'.

Fanie de Villiers' success in that Sydney Test delighted us all. This was only his second Test, having come late into Test cricket and he loved every minute of it. Fanie always has a smile on his face and his family's like that. If you see Fanie's two kids, you just know who their father is. He was the life and soul of the South African dressing-room, full of fun and japes, a guy who would give you absolutely everything on the field, and then have a laugh and a beer afterwards. Fanie was a tough old boy, who surmounted many injuries to set a brilliant example. He was never short of ideas and suggestions. A brilliant man on tour, especially the tough ones, Fanie would be there with his video camera, getting fun and interest out of the hardest times.

After such a brilliant effort at Sydney, we ought to have avoided defeat in the Adelaide Test to win the series, but we blew it. It was partly our fault that we lost by 191 runs, as we ought to have batted out the final few hours comfortably enough. Yet the umpiring was disgraceful, doing us no favours at all. In the second innings, there were some shocking lbw decisions given, some of them the most disgraceful I've ever seen. We got the feeling that whenever the pad was hit, the finger would go up. Peter Kirsten was particularly livid after being given out lbw by Darryl Hair, so much so that he became the first player to be fined twice for separate dissent in a Test match. A Johannesburg radio station launched an appeal to pay his fine, so he didn't suffer financially, but the fact that Peter was so enraged was significant. He was usually the complete professional, better able than most to accept decisions that weren't correct, but this time, he really flipped. At the end of the Test, he stormed into the umpire's room and shouted 'That's one of the worst examples of umpiring I've seen in my life', which really wasn't like Peter Kirsten. After we had lost, I was standing outside our dressing-room, talking to a few of our supporters, unaware that the boys inside were trashing the room like rock stars. When I came back in, I saw glass all over the floor and holes in the cardboard walls, courtesy of a few bats hurled in anger. It wasn't nice, but in defence, we were so disappointed not to hang on for the draw, when the borderline decisions went against us that day. To be fair, at least Hair was impartial as the opposition copped one or two shockers as well. Steve Waugh was given out by umpire Terry Prue, adjudged caught down the legside by the wicket-keeper, even though the ball brushed only his thigh pad, and I offered only a half-hearted appeal. I was as stunned as Waugh that he was given out. It was so disappointing that a match of this importance should be spoiled by poor umpiring.

In fact there had been a few losses of temper in that first series and there were clearly a few scores due to be settled. Allan Border had been particularly cranky, probably because he knew he wasn't the same player as in the past. He was under pressure, perhaps feeling his age and he tried to take his frustrations out on us. In the Adelaide Test, Michael Slater took a great liking to me, smashing me for thirty-odd in my first five overs. In my second spell, I had him caught off a bouncer, and pointed him to the dressing-room. All fast bowlers do that at some stage in their frustration, after they've been hammered by the guy they've just got out, and I thought no more of it. In came Border, full of simmering anger. He got an inside edge to one from me that almost sneaked through him and I shouted 'Oh!' He shouted back 'Oh, that was f****** close, was it? You're going to get it mate – we'll see how f****** confident you are when you come into bat'. I rapped back 'You're obviously getting too old for this game, that's why you're whingeing so f****** much!' Pretty subtle stuff, you'll agree. When we played them in the one-day international at Brisbane, Border gave Jonty Rhodes some unnecessary verbals. Jonty had played a ball from Border back to the bowler and stood his ground for the appeal, thinking that the ball had hit the ground first. As soon as he was given out, Jonty was off – as he always is – but not before Border got stuck into him for justifiably standing there. Border, a tough man, was clearly rattled by our refusal to lie down and take all the verbals meekly and Brian McMillan decided to wade into him. He gave Border a taste of his own medicine, and exposed his weakness against the short ball. He started to bounce him out for a pastime, telling him he was past it and should get into his rocking chair. Border was 39 then and not as sharp as he was. He was grumpy because he'd been slipping from his very high standards and didn't like us telling him so. By the time he'd got to South Africa, word had got round that he didn't like it around his earholes anymore and that got to him. He didn't like being dominated and his crankiness got to the rest of the team. So there was bound to be some bad blood swirling around when the two sides faced up to each other so soon after the first tense series where we had rattled them.

So there was a legacy of dissatisfaction when we played hosts to Australia a month later. We won the First Test in Johannesburg, bowling them out, with the wickets shared. Throughout, the Aussies were very grumpy and Shane Warne and Merv Hughes had their match fees withheld by their own Board for shocking behaviour. Warne gave an astonishing display of bad temper towards Andrew Hudson when he dismissed him, racing down the wicket, giving him some awful abuse. He was clearly frustrated, having been kept out of the attack for the first 44 overs of that second innings, but why did he climb into Hudson? Andrew is a committed Christian, a quiet guy who never makes waves and he was astonished at the verbal assault that just continued. Luckily for Warne, Ian Healy spotted the bowler move towards square leg, where Hudson was walking, en route to the pavilion, and the wicket-keeper managed to restrain Warne. Otherwise it would have been ever nastier. When it came to appearing in front of the match referee, Warne walked through our dressing-room area and said to us 'This is it – suspension, I reckon' and he should have been. Instead he was only docked ten per cent of his match fee, when it ought to have been the full amount. Now I like Warney, but there was no excuse for that attack on Hudson. Merv Hughes was just as culpable. At the end of the match, after we had won, he hurled his bat into the crowd, hitting someone on the arm. No doubt he was getting some stick from the more boisterous of our supporters, but that's nothing big Merv couldn't handle. He'd also given Gary Kirsten a dreadful amount of sledging and it seemed most of the Aussies were in a foul mood that Test. Perhaps they weren't used to losing.

That was a great start for us, especially as we felt the Aussies might be a little down on themselves and vulnerable. It's always important to go one up in a three-Test series, to establish a bit of a psychological hold, and the next stage was to hammer home our advantage. That's where we failed again, losing straight away in Cape Town by nine wickets. It was a huge disappointment, losing on a great wicket, where all we had to do was just bat out. Yet we collapsed from 69 for one to 164 all out, with the wickets going to Steve Waugh, of all people. All he did was bowl straight, at medium pace, with a few slight variations, managing to skid the ball through. He had a golden spell, ending up with five for 28 – on a flat pitch! This after we'd scored 361 in our first innings. So they'd pulled it back straight away, when it really mattered. Shane Warne's value in that victory was also apparent. He took six for 116 in 77 overs in the match, on a wicket that didn't suit him at all. But he can still block an end up, even when there's nothing there for him in the pitch, whereas other leg-spinners might be expensive. Tactically, Warne was fantastic, with a great aura about him that overwhelmed so many top batsmen. His subtle little variations were just enough, and he had the accuracy to go with his powers of spin. He'd sit waiting patiently, just biding his time, letting you think he had you on toast. His attitude to his bowling was tremendous, and at his best, he was the complete bowler. I just hope for the good of cricket all around the world that he makes a complete recovery from his shoulder problems and keeps on giving everyone so much pleasure. When you see a guy like Shane Warne, it doesn't matter which country he plays for if you love cricket.

With Warne in the side, the Australians were always a force, even when they didn't play all that well – and for long periods in the Cape Town Test, they weren't on top. But they went for the jugular when we started to panic and never gave us a chance to recover. That's what we had to understand: never take your foot off the accelerator when you've got the chance. The Australians under Allan Border, then Mark Taylor have been brilliant at seeing the chance of victory very early and then pursuing it ruthlessly, exerting great pressure in the field. They've had top bowlers in my time – McGrath, McDermott and Warne – and some fine batters, but the main distinguishing feature of their cricket has been their flexibility and knack of creating a victory push through aggressive cricket. That's something South Africa needs to master. We have to be aware that games are often decided in a few overs, rather than just a session. It's not that we are the type to coast – I believe we have been very committed, intense and tough – but there have been times when we lacked concentration and subconsciously left it to others to take responsibility. You never see the Australians do that, they stand up to be counted all the time.

With the series all square, the two sides boxed themselves to a standstill at Durban. We were disappointingly passive, taking nearly fourteen hours to score 412, which used up far too much time. A draw was inevitable after just a couple of days. The wicket was too good, and by now I was struggling for rhythm and unable to raise much of a gallop. By the time we started the one-day internationals, I was out on my feet. I was dropped for the second one-dayer at Verwoerdburg, and rightly so. It was the first time I'd been dropped by South Africa, but nobody has a divine right to be an automatic choice and I didn't deserve to be picked. I came back for the next one-dayer, at Port Elizabeth, conceded 60 in ten overs and got the chop again, for the Durban game. For the final three games of the one-day series, I was out of it. I'd bowled a lot of overs in the Test series in South Africa, and for me, this was just a tournament too far. For the first time in my career I felt totally drained. I was aware that my legs felt very flat, that I had no spring in my leap at the crease, no conviction that I could generate any pace at all. When your brain feels tired, it affects the body and my ability to concentrate had gone. So had my balance at the crease, my alignment of the wrist. I was just a zombie and needed time out.

I discussed the situation with Mike Procter, our national coach, Peter Pollock, our chairman of selectors and Ali Bacher. They were all very understanding and as two former fast bowlers themselves, Pollock and Procter knew all about the dangers of burnout. I wasn't worried that I had lost the ability to bowl fast, but at the age of 27, I needed to understand more about long-term fitness and the avoidance of physical exhaustion. It was clear that I was at that stage because I asked to be excused for the final round of one-day internationals, and if I was to be any use at all to South Africa in the near future, I had to recharge those batteries, away from cricket. With the tour to England coming up in a couple of months, that necessity was obvious to all concerned. All of a sudden, our hectic international itinerary had caught up on me. Since our first one-day international in November 1991, I had played in 45 of South Africa's 54 matches, and in all fourteen Tests. I know Australia was playing a great amount of international cricket as well, but they were used to the gruelling itinerary. For the South Africans, it had all been a huge adventure, but eventually you need to draw on the experience of coping with the hard slog.

With 63 wickets in those 14 Tests, I was happy with my strike rate, but I knew I had to do something about my long-term fitness, to prolong my career. I didn't want to feel as jaded as I did in March 1994. That would be sorted later. In the early months of the English summer, I was back in Birmingham, working out in the University gym, topping up my fitness. An historic tour to England lay ahead.

CHAPTER ELEVEN

To England –
At Last!

Ever since our readmission to international cricket, we had talked about going on the England tour. We knew that South Africa hadn't been there since 1965, that the '70 trip had been called off late in the day because of the risk of political upheavals, and that many in England were very keen to see us again. After the election of Nelson Mandela to the Presidency in May 1994, we were even more welcome when we arrived in London a month earlier. It was to prove an emotional rollercoaster of a tour for the team and myself, as we lurched from the joy of victory at Lord's to humiliation at the Oval at the hands of Devon Malcolm, ending up one-all in the series. On the way to defeat at the Oval, I fell out with my captain, Kepler Wessels, a rift that wasn't repaired for four years, and I ended the tour genuinely worried about my future, due to a foot injury that led to my dispute with Kepler. I didn't play for another four months when we came back from England, as I hobbled around on crutches after the foot operation that led the surgeon to warn me that it was a tricky job and he couldn't guarantee success. At the age of 28, with so much cricket ahead of me, I had to face the prospect of a premature end. Yet Kepler didn't seem to grasp how serious the injury had been.

The problem was that Kepler was so wound up about this tour, so intent on beating England. I don't know whether it stemmed from having played county cricket for Sussex, or playing for Australia against England a decade earlier – but he kept on about his desire to take the series. I've never seen him so joyous than at Lord's, first when he got a hundred on the first day, then – more importantly – when we won on the fourth day. He was ecstatic, and Kepler isn't a demonstrative man. He is the original strong, silent type, the typical tough Afrikaaner – yet in our London hotel the night of the Lord's victory, he was beside himself with delight, allowing us to pour champagne all over his head. I have never seen Kepler Wessels the worse for wear until that night, and it was fascinating to see just how much that victory meant to him. He kept saying this was his last series before he retired, and that he had to go home the winning captain. That was the gist of his team talk to us on the eve of the Oval Test. We were still one-up, after drawing at Leeds, and he said this was our biggest Test match so far, and that we had to win it. Kepler was so committed to the prospect of victory that he seemed unaware of how much I was struggling with my foot injury. If he hadn't been so focused, our disagreement might not have happened, and we would have stayed on friendly terms.

The pain from my foot flared up during the Leeds Test. After the first day, I couldn't walk, yet I somehow bowled 29 overs. A doctor said I might have an infection and an injection was needed. When he pushed and poked at it, I nearly hit the roof. Two little bones on the ball of the foot were the problem and the doctor wondered if I actually had gout. He wanted to book me into hospital that night, but Dr Ali Bacher said I was going nowhere, and suggested the needle was infected. So I was caught between the opinions of two doctors, and in a great deal of pain. I batted with a runner, didn't bowl in the second innings and the tour management decided I'd just have to be patched up for the Oval Test, the series decider. Of course, I wanted to play, but knew I was taking a risk. I didn't do any bowling for the next ten days, and had a fitness test the day before the start. I was patched up, full of medication and worried about how I'd get on. I was right to be worried.

The flashpoint came just after I'd yorked Graeme Hick in their first innings. They were four down for around 140, and I found I could barely stand up. There was nothing left in my legs. Cramp had hit me due to the lack of exercise over the past ten days, as I tried to get patched up for the Oval. All of a sudden, the lack of proper physical preparation caught up with me. Hansie Cronje saw the distress I was in, and he told me I just had to bite the bullet. I tried, but couldn't manage to run in. I knew the importance of ramming home our advantage, of getting them out cheaply on the second day, but I felt helpless. Kepler was furious at me, telling me to 'F*** off' the field. I had an injection in my buttock to try to ease the cramp, and that coincided with the boys coming in for tea. Kepler came in, looking very threatening at me, swearing, kicking the pads around. I thought he was going to have a pop at me, and anyone who knows Kepler's fondness for boxing would have shared my concern. He clearly thought I was gutless, even more so when I came back onto the field after tea, and couldn't bowl again that day. You can imagine his mood at the close, after Darren Gough and Phil DeFreitas had hammered us around the park, to establish a precious lead. There was clearly no reasoning with him, and I was very hurt that he would imagine I'd pull the ladder up on him or the rest of the team. That has never been my way.

My captain was even more cold towards me in England's second innings, as they clattered us everywhere, rushing to a handsome victory. When Craig Matthews finally dismissed Graham Gooch, I ran up to congratulate Craig and join the rest of the boys for a chat, but Kepler cut me dead. He looked coldly at me and said, 'Just don't come anywhere near me'. I turned away, deeply hurt. It seemed as if the rest of the side shared Kepler's views, that I'd run away from the pressure. I had a spot of cramp, so what's the story? How could I explain to them the pain and frustration I was feeling? I had admired at first hand the high pain threshold of Kepler Wessels, the hardest cricketer I've ever seen, a man who just seemed never to acknowledge pain. During that Oval Test, he was hit hard on the elbow by Darren Gough, and he came into the dressing-room, crying with the pain. Yet he wouldn't discuss it or complain and he obviously felt I should have done the same. But I couldn't. It isn't a case of getting through the pain barrier when agonising cramp means you just can't run in to bowl.

After that Test, Kepler remained very distant with me for the rest of the tour. Right at the end, he insisted with great force that I should play in two matches at Scarborough, even though I was virtually a passenger, waiting for a worrying operation when I got back to South Africa. I didn't bat or bowl in the three-day game at Scarborough, so I wasn't sure of the point of being selected, other than to let me know I was still in the doghouse with him. I played in the one-dayer, to no great effect, but Kepler clearly felt he had made his point. Once we got back home, Kepler withdrew from my benefit game in Bloemfontein, which was a shame. I was still struggling with my foot injury, but a lot of fine players had agreed to play on my behalf and I felt honoured by their commitment. But Kepler sent me a fax, saying he couldn't make it, and that he was sorry about the incident at the Oval. I too felt sorry because he was a guy for whom I had so much respect. For the next four years, I brooded about Kepler's attitude to me at the Oval, and finally I plucked up enough courage to ask the view of Dave Richardson, South Africa's wicket-keeper at the time. Dave is a man I've always respected and now that he's retired from playing cricket, he could surely give me a different perspective on Kepler's opinion. Dave didn't duck the issue and told me straight: that Kepler felt I'd dipped out of a challenge when I was needed to go over the top for him. That hurt me greatly. I've always prided myself on my commitment and could offer many examples of that from all my captains. I'm still disappointed that Kepler felt that way, even though we are now talking to each other again. But I believe he treated me unfairly towards the end of that 1994 tour, because he was so obsessed with beating England. Kepler lost sight of the fact that human beings sometimes can't go the whole way because they aren't super-human, and their bodies tell them so. The idea that I bottled it at the Oval in '94 still angers me.

That tour of England was such a full-on, emotional time for us all that I can sympathise with Kepler Wessels and understand how he could get things out of proportion in his desire to bring home the kudos of a South African series victory. The burden of expectation from our people back home was enormous. We were besieged by faxes and phone calls wherever we went in England that summer, and had great support from so many who had decided to build their holiday abroad around this historic series. It didn't matter that the England side wasn't exactly at the highest level on the international ladder, we were going to the home of cricket, starting the Test series at Lord's. What more could we ask for? A win perhaps – and we were surprised how easy it came to us.

On that first morning, when Gary Kirsten and Andrew Hudson walked through the Long Room to open our innings, the reception from the crowd absolutely knocked us out. All those 'Welcome Back' banners around the ground looked marvellous as we surveyed the scene from the dressing-room balcony at Lord's. Kepler Wessels had said to us beforehand that Test cricket was about taking responsibility and we were all thrilled for him that he made a hundred. His ecstatic reaction from such a tough, single-minded man told us all what it meant to him. So much happened on and off the field during that Lord's Test. Archbishop Desmond Tutu was initially not allowed to enter the Lord's pavilion because he wasn't wearing a jacket and tie. Yet he was on his way up to our dressing-room to take prayers before we went out to bowl on the second day. Eventually commonsense prevailed, and the Archbishop was allowed in to conduct a moving few minutes when we all stood together in prayer. No wonder that we sprinted out of the Long Room onto the field like men possessed, we couldn't wait to get at the English! We also ran into the old-fashioned rule about flying flags at Lord's. We draped the new South African flag from our balcony on the first morning, because we were so proud to be back, certain that our new constitution and influence of President Mandela would make people in England realise that we genuinely wanted to put the bad old days behind us. Our new Vice-President, Thabo Mbeki was at the match and we were delighted that he gave such public support to the players, and, by extension, our country. I'd watched Nelson Mandela being sworn in as President from my home in Birmingham, while training for the tour, and I was knocked out by the warmth of the occasion. My brother was there in the crowd, as a personal bodyguard, and I felt a strong involvement in the historic ceremony as the most popular statesman in the world officially committed himself to leading my country. The pace of acceleration was amazing and we were all proud that a man who had been in prison just four years earlier could now be our Head of State. It was in that spirit that we wanted to show world cricket that we were thrilled to be back at Lord's, representing a new country. Yet the officials at Lord's told us to take down the flag. Our coach, Mike Procter went berserk, saying this wasn't a temple, it was only a cricket ground. We could have done without petty regulations like this on such an historic occasion, but Kepler did well to calm down Proccy, to keep the boys focused on the game. Not that we forgot the pettiness of the MCC. In the closing stages of the game, on the fourth afternoon, we looked up to our balcony to find our flag had mysteriously reappeared, draped on the balcony. Nobody tried to stop us that day!

Our victory at Lord's was comfortable. Bowling them out for 99 on a good wicket in the second innings was a terrific performance and when I took five for 74 in the first innings, I was delighted to see my name placed on the roll of honour, as one of those who've taken five in an innings or scored a hundred in a Lord's Test. I'd been told by those lucky enough to be on that board that I'd feel honoured, and that was certainly true. But our triumph didn't get the headlines it deserved because of the Dirt in the Pocket Affair, and Mike Atherton's punishment for dodging the issue initially. On the Saturday afternoon, when the TV cameras picked up Atherton applying dirt to the ball, we were amazed in our dressing-room. Mike Procter shouted 'He can't do that! That's not on!' and we couldn't believe he was doing something as blatant as it looked, in full view of the cameras. We started looking up the regulations. Was he trying to alter the condition of the ball? Was dirt an artificial substance? Procter said 'Now what are they going to do about this?' and there was no doubt he felt that the England captain had violated Law 42.5, but I wasn't so sure. To me, Athers was just trying to keep one side of the ball dry in humid, sweaty conditions and he didn't realise the full implication of applying dirt from his pocket. Some of our guys were sure he'd be sacked as captain as the row raged for 24 hours, but I didn't. I suffer from sweaty palms myself when bowling, and I could understand why he was trying to keep one side of the ball dry. If he was doing anything underhand, he wouldn't have been so obvious in his actions. It wasn't a good idea, though, to tell the match referee, Peter Burge initially that he had nothing in his pocket. When he had to come clean next day, he was bound to get a hefty fine, and that was fair enough. It all got a bit hysterical, but in the end commonsense came to the rescue.

We made no official complaint, and I'm glad we stayed out of it. But the controversy over Atherton took some of the gloss from a wonderful win. We bowled them out in 43 overs in their second innings, and that was a top effort, with the wickets shared around. When the final wicket went down, I was at fine leg at the Nursery End, and it took me a long time to race through the crowds to share the moment with the rest of the boys. That night, we had a great party in our hotel, with hundreds of our supporters crammed into the reception area. The management kindly ordered 20 cases of Castle Lager, our favourite tipple from back home, and we did justice to them alright. London is a great place to enjoy a day off when you've won at Lord's, and I really enjoyed my shopping trip the next day in the West End. Faxes from back home kept pouring into our hotel and it was a marvellous feeling to think we'd given so much pleasure and pride to all races in South Africa. That point was made very clear to us in our triumphant dressing-room by Vice-President Mbeki and Archbishop Desmond Tutu.

England stopped the rot at Leeds, on a turgid pitch which never looked like giving us a definite result. I had great respect for Atherton for his gritty 99, fighting back after he'd taken a real pasting from the press since Lord's. A tough customer, Atherton, as he proved at our expense eighteen months later to save the Johannesburg Test. We still felt, though, that we were a better side than England, with a harder attitude and better bowling. They weren't all as mentally strong as their captain. Yet when we folded at the Oval, it was our lack of spirit that undermined us. We were swept away by the most destructive piece of fast bowling I have ever seen, but our batsmen capitulated against Devon Malcolm's hostility, with just one exception – Darryl Cullinan.

That Oval Test was so dramatic in many ways. It was all over by lunch on the fourth day, on a pitch ideal for the strokemaker and the quick bowler. A brilliant cricket wicket, with runs coming at four per over throughout, and a wicket falling every 48 balls. If you blinked, you missed some drama in that Test. We thought that making 332 in the first innings would give us security, but we reckoned without the pace of the action, with the fortunes ebbing and flowing at such high speed. On the first day, Jonty Rhodes was taken to hospital after being hit on the head by Devon Malcolm. Some of our blokes blamed Devon for that, but I didn't, because Jonty ducked into a ball that kept lower than he anticipated. It could even have got Devon an lbw decision. We were all very worried about Jonty as he was carted off to hospital, because he suffers from a mild form of epilepsy. I hit him on the head once in a match in Durban, and he fell face first onto the turf. It looked bad and he wasn't well for a few days, but that was a chance that Jonty was prepared to take. He was detained in hospital overnight after that first day at the Oval and we were all relieved when he said he'd bat in the second innings. We hoped we wouldn't need him. Meanwhile, some resentment towards Devon Malcolm was simmering, which certainly didn't do us any favours on that historic third day.

When they batted first, Mike Atherton showed that he may be bright academically but lacks commonsense at times, after he was given out lbw first ball. He made it clear as he walked off slowly that he felt he'd nicked the ball onto his pad, and shook his head several times. We said as he walked off 'He's begging for another fine', especially as the match referee was the same one who had been led up the garden path at Lord's by Atherton. Peter Burge was obviously waiting for Athers to transgress again, and here he was, walking straight into another hefty fine. We couldn't believe he'd put his head on a plate for the match referee.

There was a lot of needle out in the middle in that Test, and we copped a lot of it from the England boys. That was fair enough, they were clearly down after that failure at Lord's and they came back very hard at us here. After I'd limped off with cramp in their first innings – much to the anger of my captain – England really tore into us, turning a poor position into equality in the space of an hour. It was remarkable. One minute they were 222 for seven, still 110 behind, and the next they were 292 for eight at the close, with Darren Gough and Phil DeFreitas panning us everywhere. They had the right attitude, taking on the short ball, putting pressure on us, and making us bowl badly. Next morning, we were still a bit ragged. When Devon Malcolm came in, Kepler was determined to make him pay for sending Jonty Rhodes to hospital, something I couldn't understand. He said to the bowler, Fanie de Villiers, 'Let him have it first ball – smack on the head', and Fanie duly obliged. Devon was smacked straight on the head, he never picked the ball up at all. A piece of foam padding flew off from Devon's helmet and Gary Kirsten, fielding at short leg, bent down to pick it up. Devon said to him 'F*** off, I'm going to kill you guys', and Gary just smiled back at him. The rest of the close fielders joined in to chirrup Devon, and he turned round to them, snarling 'You guys are f****** history'. Soon we were. At the end of the over, I came up from the outfield and asked if he was alright. I was genuine about it – I liked Devon, rated him as a fast bowler and thought he had been unfairly singled out over the Jonty Rhodes injury. Well Devon soon sent me on my way with a curse or two. He was very pumped up, and I wondered how he would bowl in this hostile frame of mind. I soon found out.

We made a rod for our own backs in the ten minutes before we went out again to bat in our second innings. Someone – Kepler or Proccy preferably – should have warned us about Malcolm, his state of mind, the fact that he was obviously raring to have a go back at us on a fast, bouncy pitch, absolutely ideal for him. We knew he was erratic, but dangerous on his day. Someone in authority ought to have said 'Look, this guy is obviously going to come at us big-time for the first five overs or so. We must see him off, take the sting out of it, wait till he gets mad and then he'll be expensive. But we've got to stand up to him'. No one said a word, though. It was almost as though we didn't consider Devon a threat. It was incredibly slap-dash. The first ball made us sit up. Devon almost cleaned up Gary Kirsten with a beauty that took off and made Steve Rhodes, their keeper, leap away to his left. I certainly sat up and took notice at that delivery. This guy meant business. In the first over, he caught and bowled Gary Kirsten, then he bowled Hansie Cronje, with Hansie not appearing to fancy it at all, leaving a big gap between bat and pad. Peter Kirsten then tried to take the bowler on, but was caught at fine leg. We were one for 3. Ridiculous. Our batters just didn't seem to stomach it. Even Kepler Wessels looked ill-at-ease. He played some very loose shots against Malcolm. After Devon went round the wicket to him, and threatened him with the short ball, Kepler looked rattled. He then wafted at a wide ball, outside the off-stump, and was caught behind. That was very uncharacter-istic of Kepler. The ball before – nearly hitting him on the nose, rearing up sharply – was the one that led to his dismissal, because he looked very uncomfortable. All of our batters seemed to lack the guts for the battle that day, and only Darryl Cullinan appeared to want to see it through. He sat there, in a deathly quiet dressing-room, with his bat between his pads, waiting for his turn to bat. I could tell he was angry at the way we were capitulating and when his time came, he slapped his bat on the ground and shouted 'You f****** watch me!' Darryl played beautifully, making it look so easy and putting our other frenetic batters to shame. He saw it early, played calmly, hooked the short one when necessary and looked in no trouble at all. The rest of us let him down. I confess I wasn't exactly in line when Devon bowled me off my pads, but I wasn't in the side for my batting. Apart from Darryl, there weren't enough brave boys out there. We'd talked the talk with our verbals, but couldn't handle the pressure when it was really on.

Devon took nine for 57 off just 99 balls, a great piece of hostile fast bowling. His rhythm was superb, his line perfect and we made him look awesome. I wish we'd had him in our side during our career, he'd have been treated far better than England managed. He'd bowl a different line to me, and we would have complemented each other very well, just as Franklyn Stephenson and I did for Free State for a couple of seasons. When Devon Malcolm got it right, he could be awesome, and it was the England management's fault that they never got the best out of him consistently, preferring to harp on about his expensive spells, rather than the fact that no batsman was ever sure how to play him. No other England fast bowler in my time has got anywhere near that display of Devon Malcolm's at the Oval. He would never have been out of our side if he'd been born a South African.

We were left crumpled after that Malcolm blitz and England really tore into us, going all out for the 204 needed for victory. They judged it right. Knowing we were demoralised, they went for our bowling and Gooch and Atherton took a particular fancy to me. They lashed me everywhere – one for 96 off just twelve overs tells its own story. I couldn't cope with the onslaught and we were blown away, hammered by eight wickets. That Oval Test was one of the most disappointing and unhappy experiences of my career for various reasons and the rest of the tour was very difficult for me. I could tell that all was not well between Mike Procter, Kepler Wessels and his vice-captain, Hansie Cronje as that tour slid away into anti-climax after the earlier triumph at Lord's. The vibes were no longer positive and Kepler and Proccy were struggling to get on the same wavelength by the last few weeks in England. Something had to give.

As soon as we got home, Ali Bacher sounded out various opinions and acted in his usual decisive manner. Mike Procter was sacked as coach. I think most of the senior players felt that was inevitable. Proccy had been in charge since we had returned to international cricket three years earlier, but he wasn't taking us very far. A great player in his time, he relied on setting a personal example when he was captain, but you need more from a coach than expecting you to give your all when you walk onto the pitch for your country. Proccy wasn't a great communicator, as we saw in the Oval dressing-room just before Devon

Malcolm's onslaught, and we needed some fresh ideas, more sophisticated coaching as we entered a more scientific age. Even though he had been a wonderful fast bowler, Proccy did very little for me, and I took to phoning up Bob Woolmer, either in England or in South Africa, whenever I was struggling. Proccy didn't mind that, but it was a bit of an indictment of his limitations as a coach.

Ali Bacher sent the senior players a form, canvassing our views on the best man for the job, asking for a scale of preferences for particular facets of the job. There were two fancied candidates, Eddie Barlow and Bob Woolmer. I had worked with them both and rated them very highly for their different assets. Yet Eddie could be a little dogmatic and abrupt, whereas Bob's man-management was superb. He was a great listener, absolutely bursting with progress-ive ideas and articulate enough to put them over clearly and calmly. He got my vote and in the end, Bob was the choice. I was amazed that the England hierarchy at Lord's didn't recognise his qualities and fast-track Bob onto a tour before we snapped him up. After coaching Warwickshire to that fantastic treble in 1994, he didn't even get an 'A' tour position, and that to me was an awful waste of talent. A few months later, Keith Fletcher was sacked as England's coach, and then Raymond Illingworth took over as sup-remo, with disastrous consequences. By the time he had finished with them, after the '96 World Cup, the whole set-up was a shambles and the morale of the players was very low. That would never have happened under Bob Woolmer – he was just too good at his job.

The South African players and public had no qualms about the top coaching job going to an Englishman. After all, he was married to a South African and the family home was in Cape Town. I told the lads that they were in for some exciting times and that first year was an eye-opener for all of them. Hansie Cronje was also appointed the new South African captain at the same time and it was good to make a fresh start. Hansie was very open-minded about what was needed to push us ahead and he and Bob ushered in an era of the scientific approach, where we would pride ourselves on a more dynamic approach. I needed Bob's input at first hand at that stage in my career. I had missed working hands-on with him since July, 1993 and I had become worried that my bowling was now rather one-dimensional. There was little subtlety about my bowling, no change of pace. It seemed as if every delivery from me was just designed to blast the batsman out. At the age of 28, there were only so many years left in me as a genuine, consistent fast bowler, and I needed to know how to develop greater variety. I had to widen my range technically and Bob Woolmer came back into my career at just the right time. Soon he was introducing me to the slower ball, the off-cutter and getting me to cut down my run-up, giving me greater control and stamina. Bob definitely made me a better bowler once he became South Africa's coach and his success in broadening the base of back-up staff – with advice on training, diet, stamina work from chosen special-ists – extended my career.

First, though, I had to get myself fit from my foot injury before I could really tap into Bob Woolmer's network of specialists. I was operated on as soon as I returned after the England tour, and the surgeon discovered I had a little cyst. He cut open my big toe, took out some bone and filled it again. He said he didn't want to take out the whole bone, which was on the ball of the foot, because sometimes the patient doesn't recover fully from such a move. It all stemmed from a lot of stud pressure, from heavy pounding on hard grounds. He showed me the tiny crack on the scan before the operation and made a point of not being too optimistic. He was right to do that. I knew that if the operation was a success, I would face weeks of frustration, hobbling around on crutches, and that the rehabilitation was vital. I would do serious damage to the foot if I rushed back too soon. I didn't need any further warning, because I was only too grateful that the operation was a success and my career saved. My return to the game would just have to wait. So I missed the home Test series against New Zealand and Pakistan. After my plaster came off, I rejoined the international squad for rehabilitation and further treatment. I was three weeks ahead of schedule and although the surgeon was delighted, we were both very cautious.

By January, the selectors were pushing me to play in the day/night final of the one-day tournament against Pakistan at the Wanderers, Johannesburg. I was sorely tempted, but worried about rushing back too soon. My surgeon insisted on watching me bowl in the nets, and when I told him I felt sharp pains in my foot, he told me it was just scar tissue and that it would soon pass. So he said I could play. You really have to be out of top-class sport for a time to appreciate what it means to you. When I had the ball in my hand for my first over, and I heard the voice on the public address system saying 'And now – bowling from the Golf Course End – Allan Donald!', I was floating on air. The crowd reaction was so positive and supportive that it lifted me. The stadium seemed to erupt and that support got me through my nervous start. I was nowhere near fully fit, a few kilos overweight, and operating off my short run, so I didn't expect to bruise the wicket-keeper's hands, but I did alright. I took three for 25 and they were good wickets – Salim Malik, Inzamam and Rashid Latif – and it was good to get through the initial pain that I had been told to expect. After that game, I played in the next Test against the Pakistanis, still not at my physical best, but I picked up four wickets. It was wonderful to be back, after a worrying four months. It's been the only serious injury of my career so far, and it made me realise what it must be like for those unlucky enough to be dogged by injury. Perhaps they should follow my recipe for preventative injuries – hard work in the gym, plus Castle Lager and some excellent Pinotage wine!

Having been reassured about my career, and hugely relieved that the operation had been a success, I travelled to New Zealand for a Test series, determined to make up for lost time, looking forward to working closely with Bob Woolmer. Yet I was about to need Bob's support after some shock news from Edgbaston. It seemed I was no longer wanted. Again.

CHAPTER TWELVE

In Lara's Shadow

During the English summer of '94, I popped into Edgbaston whenever my duties on the South African tour allowed. I was on the edge, seeing a remarkable triumph by Warwickshire, but still wanted to share it with the boys. Warwickshire created history, winning three trophies out of four and coming second in the fourth, the NatWest Trophy, when the toss of the coin helped determine the result. It was an amazing effort, the culmination of hard work behind the scenes in recent years, a brilliant team spirit and imaginative leadership by Dermot Reeve and Bob Woolmer. I've never seen a more positive, vibrant bunch of cricketers than Warwickshire in '94, and I was torn between pleasure for them and professional envy. I wanted to be part of that again. They thought they'd win every game and it was great to pop in now and then to savour how well my friends were doing. I was desperate to share that team success again as the overseas player. But Brian Lara was in the way.

Brian had a fantastic season in '94, scoring more than 2,000 championship runs at a run a ball, and his presence and performances had much to do with the positive cricket played by our guys. I saw him now and again during that summer, had a few cheerful chats, and congratulated him on a marvellous season. To me, he was just passing through Edgbaston for just one season, keeping the seat warm for me until I returned after my South African tour. I was the long-term overseas player, while Brian was the fill-in, a spectacularly successful one, but not one for the future. His difficult relationship with our captain didn't suggest he'd be around after the '94 season, either. He and Dermot Reeve simply didn't get on and Brian clearly had no respect for him. Every time I dropped into Edgbaston, one of the players would say, 'Have you heard the latest about Brian and Dermot?' There always seemed to be some strife over Brian's time-keeping, or his niggling injuries or his blatant personality clashes with Dermot. I thought Dermot was quite right to try to be hard on Brian, because he was the captain – and an excellent one – and he had done much to create that marvellous team spirit in our dressing-room. Just because Brian was our star player that year didn't entitle him to upset the cart. I got the impression from chats with Dermot and the players that the hierarchy at Edgbaston were just papering it all over until the end of the season. Then Brian would go, and everything would be perfect for the captain with me back in the side. I could understand that with so much success coming from the appointment of Lara, it made sense not to rock the boat, especially as he had never given any hint that he saw his long-term future in county cricket. In fact, he made it quite clear at times in that historic season, that he found many aspects of county cricket a chore.

So I didn't have any worries about how I'd fit in at Edgbaston from '95 onwards. South Africa weren't due back in England until the summer of '98, and I looked forward to a few more years of playing with my friends in a supportive, positive atmosphere. But in September '94, with the South Africa tour over, I started to have a few niggles at the back of my mind. When I popped into Edgbaston, one or two members would sidle up to me and say, 'Have you heard that Brian might be staying on?' I couldn't believe that, and my team-mates were just as sceptical. They knew that Lara wasn't the type of guy who'd relish playing so much cricket. I thought of raising the matter with the club, but left it. If they had something important to say to me about my future, surely the chairman, M.J.K. Smith or the chief executive, Dennis Amiss would have pulled me into the office before I left the country?

I'll never forget the day, the time and the place when Warwickshire shattered me. It was early in the evening, in Hamilton, New Zealand, on 18 February 1995. I had just returned to our hotel after playing in a one-day international, and the phone call came through from Dennis Amiss. Initially, it was to Bob Woolmer and he came to my door, saying Dennis was on the line. Dennis got straight to the point: 'Al, I know this isn't what you want to hear, but the committee have decided to sign Brian Lara for three years'. I went dead quiet. I saw my whole Warwickshire career flashing past me in just a few seconds. What was I going to do? I just said 'OK' and handed the phone back to Bob Woolmer. He proceeded to give Dennis Amiss a volley. Later on, I asked Bob if he knew already that there was a possibility that I'd be bounced out in favour of Lara, and he admitted that he had discussed it with Dennis. They had been big pals for years and I wasn't surprised that Dennis had floated the idea with Bob. But Bob told me that he'd stuck out for me, that he insisted that Lara would be bad for Warwickshire, because he wouldn't give them three disciplined years. I was deeply shocked at that. Bob should have given me a nudge, to prepare me for this devastating blow.

After he left my room, I sat in my bath for ages, brooding. The implications started to sink in. I had one more year left on my contract, and after that, Warwickshire didn't want me. In effect, I'd been sacked. I had to find another county if I wanted to stay in the professional game in England. I had my living to earn, so I would have to do that. It would mean starting all over again with another county, getting used to the new dressing-room atmosphere, moving house, hoping that Tina would settle wherever we went. All because Brian Lara had decided he would like a few more years of county cricket, despite showing little enthusiasm for it from halfway through the '94 season. It made little cricket sense to me, because Warwickshire knew that I had the ability to bowl sides out, and Brian's marvellous talent would mean no opposition side would set us a decent target for the fourth innings, because with this guy in our team, anything was possible. It was clear to me that I was being booted out for commercial reasons. They thought that Brian would put more bums on seats than me. I felt very hurt by that, because the club and I had been good for each other and my commitment to them would always be deeper than that of Brian Lara. I wondered if the commercial and marketing people at Edgbaston were more concerned with finance rather than on the field matters.

It was my room-mate, Paddy Upton who snapped me out of my depression that night in Hamilton. Paddy, our fitness trainer, had some subtle advice for me – 'No sense in sitting here all night, Al, come and get pissed'. I told my team-mates in the bar that I'd been sacked and they couldn't believe it. Strangely, though, my mind cleared very quickly after that. I said to the boys, 'When I get back to Warwickshire, I'm going to be ultra-positive, not show them I'm disappointed. I'm going to take a hundred championship wickets and then we'll see who's the more valuable overseas player'. There'd be no sulking. As far as I was concerned it was third time unlucky. I'd seen off Tony Merrick and Tom Moody but Brian Lara's challenge had been too much for me. So it would have to be another county. I'd put myself in the market place with a great season. I was going to win trophies as well in that '95 season, letting Warwickshire know what they were missing in letting me go. There would be nothing personal between me and Brian Lara. We had always got on well, and I wasn't going to let myself be distracted by the personal issues. There would be no bleating by me to the press, I'd let my performances out on the field do the talking for me.

I was in turmoil over who were my allies when I returned to Edgbaston in April '95. I was certain, though, that Dermot Reeve was in my camp, and he was tremendously supportive to me when we met. He said he wanted me, rather than Lara, that we all had to hang together in the dressing-room that season, and prove the cricket committee wrong. Andy Lloyd, my former captain, who was now on the cricket committee said 'Bowlers win matches, Al', and I had to agree with him. I would be strong out on the park, and let influential journalists write about the decision and its merits.

I'm very proud of my 88 wickets in the '95 championship season, that helped Warwickshire retain the title. That was one ambition of mine realised, because I had been envious of the boys the year before. When we picked up the NatWest Trophy in September, that crowned a great season for me. We were in fantastic form that summer, winning fourteen out of seventeen championship matches, and I hadn't bowled better consistently in my career. I bowled 511 championship overs, with Tim Munton the nearest of the seamers to that with 353, and Neil Smith the only other bowler to come near to me with 400 overs. My strike rate was one wicket every six overs, and I headed the national averages. If Adam Hollioake hadn't broken my toe when I batted against Surrey, I'm sure I'd have taken a hundred wickets. Every morning, I'd wake up feeling terrific. It felt so right in the warm-ups and then out in the middle. I was really up for it, I needed no extra motivation other than personal pride, to prove the cricket committee wrong for sacking me. It was a brilliant atmosphere in our dressing-room and Dermot Reeve regained his all-round form after injuries and preoccupation with Lara the year before. As a result, he captained the side superbly, guiding us through so many tight finishes – particularly the NatWest Final when he kept his nerve with the bat. The vibes were so positive that young players like Dougie Brown and Ashley Giles could be absorbed into our team pattern, and do well right from the off, without needing time to bed in. Nick Knight, a very strong, bubbly character, was a great signing from Essex. A fine motivator, very imaginative about tactics and opponents, Nick spoke very well in team meetings and he gave us even more drive and confidence. We had some very good cricket brains in the dressing-room that season – Munton, Twose, Neil Smith, Knight and of course, Reeve. Every session was important for us, we were full-on all the time and we couldn't wait to get at the opposition. Dermot seemed to take the right tactical option every time, he read situations brilliantly. At Canterbury, when we won the championship, he opened the bowling in the second innings with our spinner, Ashley Giles and myself. He felt that the wicket was damp enough to make the ball grip, so why not use a spinner when the seam was large enough for Ashley to grip? It worked. Dermot was superb at making an immediate assessment after looking at the pitch, and he had the courage to go for it plus the personality and intelligence to bring the boys along with him in that decision.

The run-in to the championship was marvellously satisfying. In the penultimate game, at Edgbaston, we needed to beat Derbyshire to stay ahead of Middlesex. The weather was very iffy and there was no time to waste. On the third evening, Dermot declared, just over a hundred ahead and before we came off, he said to me in the dressing-room, 'Al, I want you to get loose. I'll give you twenty minutes before I declare. I need you really firing, because we need wickets tonight'. I love a challenge like that and from the first ball, I felt just right. I took three wickets in eight balls, and the boys said it was the fastest I'd bowled since I'd been at the club. Afterwards, it was a great feeling to walk into the Members' Bar to get a standing ovation. The members realised the importance of that short period of play and many of them said to me, 'We'll win the championship on Monday'. We didn't, though. It was put on ice because Middlesex won off the last ball at Uxbridge, beating Leicestershire. We had polished off Derbyshire, with five wickets for me, so after a long afternoon waiting for the Uxbridge result, it was off to Canterbury. By now,

I was feeling tired after a long season, but we just had to get ourselves up for one final push. We played brilliantly to win by an innings inside three days, and to my great joy, I took the wicket that clinched the championship. I was bowling at Min Patel, and at the start of that over, I said to myself, 'I've got to do it in this over – I want to be the bowler who does it'. Neil Smith took the edge at slip and I sank to my knees in joy and relief. It was one of the most wonderful moments of my career. All the goals I had set for myself at the start of the season had been achieved. I'd given everything to the side, the boys had been brilliant to me, and the members were fantastically supportive as well. Personal pride had spurred me on, improving my performances. I wasn't going to let down my team-mates by sulking over the Lara decision, and I wanted to ram it back down the throats of those on the cricket committee who had voted against me. If I'd had a moderate season, they could have said 'Told you so, he wasn't interested anymore, Lara's the man for the future'. No chance of giving them that opportunity. I wanted so badly for us to win the championship again, and for me to play an influential part in it. The script couldn't have been written more beautifully for me and that night at Canterbury, I was a very fulfilled man as we celebrated. Our wives and girl-friends were all with us, sharing in our triumph and I was so glad for all the players and our supporters. The feelings of those on the cricket committee were of no interest to me. I felt vindicated. It was the most satisfying season I have enjoyed at Edgbaston, because so much else was involved, other than just playing.

On top of all that, South Africa won the Rugby World Cup! We were playing Yorkshire at home on that June

Saturday, and I was desperate for us to wrap up the match before the start. We were playing the All Blacks in the Final, and all week I had been having a go about the result at Roger Twose, who was engaged to a New Zealand girl, and looking to emigrate out there at the end of the season. Roger was just as convinced that the All Blacks, the favourites, would beat us, and it all added extra spice to the occasion. But first we had to roll over Yorkshire. I'd already broken Martyn Moxon's thumb, then had David Byas taken in the gully, a stinging catch to Dominic Ostler. Dougie Brown then got the ball to swing, they lost their last seven wickets for six runs in five overs and we were all sat in front of the dressing-room television for the big kick-off at two o'clock. Perfect! And we beat the All Blacks! This despite Roger Twose doing the hakka in front of me. This is the ceremonial dance of the All Blacks, designed to throw down the gauntlet of defiance against the opposition and Roger was never shy of performing it in restaurants or bars when the mood took him. This time, he really meant it, doing all the actions, grabbing me by the shirt, getting in my face. He was wearing just his jock-strap (never a pretty sight), and the gist of his message was, 'Let's see who the real men are'. We found out a couple of hours later. Near the end, the winning points came for us when Joel Stransky dropped a goal and I just screamed my head off. Roger had tears in his eyes, although he did shake hands at the final whistle. What an afternoon! I couldn't believe it when President Mandela walked onto the pitch, wearing François Pienaar's number six shirt and when Pienaar sank to his knees at the final whistle to offer a prayer of thanks, I was overwhelmed. Some of my teammates in the South African side were there that day, and they all said it was the most unbelievable atmosphere they've ever experienced. That was a memorable weekend for me. We beat Yorkshire twice, in the championship and the Sunday League, when I took six for 15. They were bowled out for just 56, I bowled very fast and they kept nicking it. Sometimes professional sport can appear very simple!

It wasn't just self-motivation and pride in performance that helped me bowl so well in that '95 season. Bob Woolmer's coaching back in South Africa the previous few months was very influential. With the aid of videos and stopwatches, Bob helped streamline my run-up. It was just a matter of taking three quarters of a second longer to get to the crease, but it worked. In 1994, Bob had spotted that I was rushing in, that I wasn't quite balanced enough at the crease. I was getting there too quickly. He timed me, and discovered that there was quite a difference between when I was bowling well and struggling for rhythm. He worked out that I was racing through from the time of hitting my mark, running in to bowl and actually releasing it. By getting me to slow down just a fraction in that process, he hit on the time of 4.11 seconds as the best duration to arrive at the crease in the best balanced position. At times, I'd say, 'Bob, I'm not getting to the crease in time' and he'd say 'Then re-mark your run-up' and I'd be amazed to find that I was sometimes a yard too long. I'd forget that when the adrenalin flows, you tend to walk back too quickly in measuring out your run-up, and take too big a stride. So the run-up is then too long, and an extra yard makes a huge difference to a fast bowler. When I was bowling well, Bob would put the stopwatch on me and worked out the perfect time was 4.11 seconds from when

I was actually flat out on my way to the crease. It's like a golf swing, it has to be grooved. If your rhythm is right, you can rely on the basics, then work out the best way actually to bowl. It's such an elusive thing, and you try to hang onto it, but lack of rhythm is the one thing that's let me down over the years. It's been easier to find and maintain since 1995, thanks to the Woolmer stopwatch. He also used to tell the Warwickshire fielders to listen to the sound of my feet as I approached the crease, because that was another way of telling if my rhythm was good. If I was hanging in the air too long, that meant I wasn't being explosive enough at the crease, and failing to generate real pace. Bob felt there had to be a 'Bang! Bang! Bang!' of my feet on the ground in that instant before I delivered the ball. He'd point to Wasim Akram as an example, and he was right. Whenever I listened to the stump microphone on TV as Wasim started to deliver the ball, the banging sound of his feet showed he really meant business, and he delivered the ball at high speed. So from 1995 onwards, I used to rely on the Warwickshire mid-off or mid-on to tell me how my feet sounded as I wound up at delivery. If they were loud, I was motoring.

Bob Woolmer also encouraged me to experiment with a shortened run-up at specific times and at last I tried it during the 1995 season with Warwickshire. He felt that there were times when it made sense to cut down my pace on a slow wicket, and try to swing the ball, rather than blast out the batsmen. I'd tried a shortened run in the Edgbaston nets several times and wondered how it would go out in the middle, but wasn't sure how my team-mates would react. Finally, I gave it a go in the Northants game at the end of July. It felt fine right from the start, and after

I'd peppered Kevin Curran with the short ball for a time, I begged Dermot Reeve for another over. He agreed and I had Curran caught at slip off the slower ball. That spell was sixteen overs on the trot, in very hot conditions, and I felt very happy with my control and ability to swing the ball. Since then, my short run-up has remained at fourteen paces, while my long one is fifteen paces, after going back a yard or two and sprinting into the marker. It has definitely improved my bowling, giving me better control and helping the outswinger and it has prolonged my career. It means I can conserve my energy while still keeping my accuracy. I use it often in one-day cricket and in the longer games, when I feel the wicket isn't conducive to high pace. In the last two Tests on the England tour in '98, I operated all the time off my short run, and I think I kept the batters on their toes at Trent Bridge and Leeds. I think Mike Atherton would agree!

That '95 season also saw me use reverse swing for the first time with any consistency. I'd marvelled at the way Wasim Akram and Waqar Younis had outclassed batsmen for so long with reverse swing and I wanted to add that to my bowling. The hot summer meant that conditions were ideal for reverse swing – dry, dusty, the ball getting worn fairly quickly. After about thirty overs, the ball was in an ideal shape for reverse swing. Basically the idea is to fox the batsman by swinging the ball in to the right-hander when he expects it to go the other way, or even straight on. Batsmen at first-class level have good enough eyesight to spot the position of the seam in your hand as you are running in, or when you are about to deliver it, and they adjust accordingly to the outswinger or the inswinger. Wasim, though, is clever enough to conceal the ball in his hand until the last instant. He's also got such a fast arm that the ball is on you before you can react. He's the greatest reverse swing bowler I've ever seen.

Learning his trade on those dry Pakistan wickets, he had to learn to swing the ball late and to look after the ball. That is the key. You must keep one side of the ball shiny when it's around thirty overs old, and soak the other side with perspiration. That soaked side has to be as heavy as possible, so that it reacts against the shiny side in the air. Traditionally, to bowl the outswinger, you hold the shiny side to leg and the basic aerodynamics makes it go away from the right-hander. With reverse swing, you hold the ball as you normally would for the outswinger, but the heavy, soaked side tugs against it in the air and sends it to the legside. With the batsman expecting the outswinger, he can get an unpleasant surprise when his leg stump is pinged. It's important to get the angle of the wrist right. The traditional method of getting the wrist behind the ball doesn't apply. You have to slant the wrist towards legside to give the ball the necessary angle, so that it doesn't come down with a straight seam. Bowlers like Waqar, Darren Gough and Craig White have the perfect actions for reverse swing – slingy actions, with the arm not brushing the right hip in the traditional manner, but delivered more front-on to the batsman. That allows the ball to move later towards legside in the air. I tend to come a little wider of the crease to create the necessary angle. It needs to be bowled as full as possible, so that it has a chance of swinging late. I aim for the off stump, hoping it'll go late towards middle and leg, but it's a very fine dividing line between devastating late inswing and half-volleys that are meat and drink to a class batsman. So it can be expensive, and can easily go wrong if everything isn't in full working order.

At the start of the '95 season, I was excited about the potential of reverse swing and I discussed when I should try it with Dermot Reeve. The dry weather was perfect for us, and Dermot, Tim Munton, Dougie Brown and myself got a lot of wickets on dry, brown pitches – especially at Cardiff, Ilford, Southampton and Canterbury in the first innings. We were ahead of other counties in that mode of bowling, yet we still had our detractors, despite winning so many championship matches. People said the Edgbaston wickets were tailor-made for our experienced seamers, even though Munton, Donald and Small operated together as a unit just once at Edgbaston that season, through injuries – and that turned out to be a draw, against Sussex, because of rain. We won six games away from home, and our percentage of championship victories, 82%, was the highest ever in any championship season. Yet we still got labelled a side that relied on favourable home pitches. Our morale was so high, though, that we didn't let the carping bother us. We'd just look at the championship table.

The Lara setback undoubtedly made me a better cricketer and stronger person. It taught me how to handle setbacks and turn them into a positive. I was able to achieve much more, now that I had proved to myself that I could surmount serious knockbacks. Reacting positively to disappointment, tapping into my own pride, meant I could handle the responsibility better of having to bowl out a side. I'd been able to deal professionally with the Lara disappointment through the help of a guy called Alan Jones, whom I'd met in Australia the year before. He used to be the Wallabies rugby union coach, then became a sports psychologist, and now he runs a radio talk show in Sydney, where he upsets a lot of people with his strong-minded views. He's a dynamic, challenging character and I was very impressed by him when Kepler Wessels invited him to come and talk to the South African squad when we toured Australia. He was very good also at dealing on an individual basis, watching you out of the corner of the eye, seeing how you reacted to pressure situations. He noticed that I tended to drop my shoulders when things didn't go my way. Alan wanted to get through to me that I had to show leadership when I had the ball in my hand, that my personal responsibility meant there would be no ducking of the issue. He taught me that when the strike bowler is in a negative mood, that then applies to the rest of the side.

Since 1994, I've called Alan Jones at various times in the year, he does the same to me and we meet up whenever I'm in Australia. I was delighted when he called me after the 1998 tour to England, complimenting me on my attitude more than my success. He told me that it now seemed as if I didn't feel the pressure anymore, that it looked as if I was stimulated by it, and I guess that was the case. Hansie Cronje calls me the leader of the side, and I relish that role. You simply have to get on with the job, don't look for excuses, and deliver. Since 1994, Alan has been of great benefit to me psychologically. A lot of what he says is commonsense but he unclutters my mind, by bringing out something that was in my subconscious and getting it into sharper focus. His basic message is that you must embrace the responsibility, rather than be inhibited by it. I never thought he was spouting mumbo-jumbo when he sat in on our team meetings in 1994, then gave his thoughts. It was inspiring.

He said to me in private, 'Kepler says you're going to become one of the great fast bowlers in the world' and my response was that such a goal was years ahead, if I was lucky and stayed fit. Alan cut through all that. 'What you have to do is think about now', he said. 'You have the potential to perform consistently well at the highest level, but the quicker you realise that you can join the elite of fast bowlers the more chance you've got. Isn't that what you really want?' I told him that was true, but that I hadn't really thought about it, but Alan continued to pepper me with positives. He said that 'responsibility' was a better word than 'pressure', that all I was doing was my job, just like any other person in other professions. So don't whinge about your problems. Now, when people interview me about my career, and ask about the pressures, I reply that it's a challenge when the captain throws me the new ball, that I want to discharge my personal responsibility. There must be no hiding place. Injury worries or technical problems mustn't seep into your psyche and drain you.

Before I met Alan Jones, I'd show how disgusted I was with myself if I bowled a bad ball and got smashed away. That would give the batsman a plus over you, by seeing that you were disconcerted and feeling negative. Alan pointed out that Steve Waugh doesn't let on to the bowler that he's fretting when he can't hit you off the square. If you shout 'f*** it' when he's hit you for a boundary, that's points in his corner. Steve Waugh is the most mentally resilient cricketer I've played against, you never know what he's thinking. He has proved over the years that it isn't just a matter of natural talent, it's also a case of applying it and delivering the goods when your side really needs it. I'm now a great believer in being strong-minded and ultra-positive. I get very annoyed at some of my team-mates when I think they're shirking responsibility. I believe some of the South African boys ducked out of it during the last two Tests in England in 1998, when we allowed the opposition back into the series after almost burying them. With a stronger mental attitude we would have won the series, despite the umpiring lapses that went against us at Trent Bridge and Leeds. When there are players who are doubtful about their form and their steadiness under pressure, that seeps away at the team's efficiency and potential. The word 'if' is now banned from my vocabulary – I prefer 'when'. And it's up to the most talented players to set the right example, to take the others with you down the road to success. There's a responsibility when you're one of the best players, you must show you want to keep coming back for more and not coast, leaving it to others.

In 1995, Warwickshire were the most consistently positive side I'd yet played for. Dermot Reeve was marvellous at getting us up for each session in the championship. He'd have clever phrases like 'it's about controlling the controllables' and 'in one-day cricket, every ball's an event'. Dermot was straight out of the Alan Jones manual, and he made sure our minds were right for each day. It was a great feeling to be part of such a memorable season for Warwickshire. I was beginning to get there as a fast bowler, approaching the standards Alan Jones and Kepler Wessels had expected of me when we first talked in 1994. Kepler said 'In Test cricket, the fast bowler shouldn't be worried about spells one and two, but spells three to five near the end of the day. They are the important ones, when you're looking to strike back'. On that basis, I was developing well, because in 1995, I bowled consistently fast and for longer spells than at any other stage in my career up till then. And the tactical developments I'd picked up under

Bob Woolmer had made me a more subtle bowler, far superior to the regimented, unimaginative fast bowler that Gooch and Atherton had plundered at the Oval the previous year.

That mental clarity I'd developed with the help of Alan Jones helped me bounce back quickly after being told I was to be sacked by Warwickshire and it also allowed me to dig my heels in later, when they decided they did want me after all. By then, I had hardened up mentally and I wasn't going to be pushed around by anybody anymore, especially after I had shown what I could do throughout the 1995 season. So when Brian Lara told me that he wanted out of his three-year contract, I was determined not to make it easy for the club. I got wind of Lara's change of heart in August 1995 when Gladstone Small came to me to set up a meeting with Brian. It was at the end of the West Indies tour to England, and Lara had been in some trouble with the management and the captain Richie Richardson after walking out of the tour at one stage in the final month. Brian told me he was exhausted from all the pressures, and that he didn't want to play for Warwickshire in 1996, but needed time away from the game. None of that surprised me, because his financial advisors had worked him very hard in the previous year and he had shown that the grind of an English county season wouldn't suit him. That made Warwickshire's decision to go for him rather than me even more hurtful, but I was now over that. Brian said he'd talk to Dennis Amiss about transferring his contract to me for 1996, but by this stage in the summer, I wasn't sure if I wanted to play next season at all.

During the months since the Lara decision, the South African Board had been very sympathetic towards me. Ali

Bacher, the managing director spent a lot of time on the phone to me, checking my morale was good, encouraging me all the way, telling me how important I was to South Africa, even if Warwickshire didn't seem to share the same opinion of me. Dr Bacher felt I now needed to ration my time in English cricket. We had a big home season coming up, with England the visitors, then it was off to India and Pakistan for the World Cup and within the next twelve months, there were one-day tournaments in Sharjah and Nairobi, plus Test series at home and away against India, followed by a home series against Australia, plus the usual one-day internationals. That looked like a killing schedule, especially for a fast bowler. Ali was genuinely concerned about me suffering from burnout and looking at that itinerary, I could see his point.

After Brian Lara requested his release from his Warwickshire contract in August 1995, the club officially asked me to replace him. I had meetings with Dennis Amiss, M.J.K.Smith and John Whitehouse, the chairman of cricket, but we didn't get very far. I was in no hurry to snap their hands off because recent events had toughened me up, and I was determined to do what was best for me. A lot of other counties were now sniffing around me, but I was more swayed by the need to recharge my batteries. I told Warwickshire that Ali Bacher and his Board colleagues weren't keen for me to play county cricket in 1996, and that I was giving the matter serious thought. I wasn't thinking of revenge, I was influenced by the faith the South African Board were showing me, giving me the confidence to plan a long international career as I neared thirty. I needed that feeling of security after being deeply hurt by Warwickshire. Negotiations dragged on for three months, as I talked with my family, with Bob Woolmer and Ali Bacher in South Africa. Finally, I decided to opt out of the 1996 season. I'm convinced it was the best decision for me, because it gave me time to think more deeply about fitness and stamina. That summer sabbatical helped prolong my career.

So in a sense, Warwickshire's initial decision to go with Brian Lara ended up favouring me. It tested my new, tougher mental resilience, stretched me sufficiently to bowl better than ever in 1995, and gave me the necessary steel to think clearly about where my career was going, making me think deeper about how to stay fit for longer periods. With a heavy international workload coming up, I was going to need all that input to keep going.

CHAPTER THIRTEEN

Falling at the Crucial Hurdle

In the space of two months at the start of 1996, South Africa showed its international strength, then its fallibility. With us, it's been a case of two steps forward, then one back ever since we returned to international cricket in 1991, and that's still the same. We win the majority of our international games, then fall down at the vital stage, when we really need to be strong. In 1996, the crucial hurdle was the World Cup. We were set up for that, after beating England at home in both the Test and the one-day series. By the quarter-final stage of the World Cup, we were the form team of the tournament, having won ten games in a row against England at home and then in the World Cup qualifying stages. We were absolutely flying. Then we came a cropper, losing to West Indies in Karachi. It was a shattering blow and, for me, it was even worse. I was dropped for that West Indies game, and I have to admit I cried my eyes out. It was the biggest disappointment of my career and it still is. What made the whole thing so bad was that all our hard work and optimism that had built up over the past few months seemed to be wasted. When the heat was on, we couldn't handle it.

By the time we squared up to England in the 1995/96

Test series, we were ready for them. We'd limbered up nicely by beating Zimbabwe by seven wickets in a one-off Test in Harare, where I returned the best figures of my Test career. Operating off a shortened run-up, I managed to hit a slight ridge consistently and took eight for 71 in their second innings, to give me eleven for the match. My pace wasn't affected by my short run-up, and I couldn't have been in better shape or form for the England series. It seemed the whole country was up for the England visit. We wanted to set the record straight after our humiliation at the Oval at Devon Malcolm's hands. We were better prepared than England, with Bob Woolmer's scientific approach starting to bear fruit. He had recommended Professor Tim Noakes from the Sports Institute in Cape Town to oversee the scientific programme and it was a very impressive initiative. Bob Woolmer had convinced our Cricket Board that science was the way forward and so we had specialists in all physical areas – eyes, backs, feet, shoulders, the whole range. Any player with an injury now had to refer it to Professor Noakes, and we felt very comfortable with the new system. Bob Woolmer also introduced us to his video gadgets, enabling us to watch technical things in close-up. His room became like a studio, and he would play back something relevant whenever you wanted. He had a complete data bank of statistics available for those who were interested in such things, but the real aid for me was to study where opposition batsmen play their shots. We spent hours doing our homework on the England batsmen in the 1995/96 series and as a result, we were miles ahead of them in planning and attention to detail. After spending some productive weeks in training camp, we couldn't have been better prepared for that series against England. Over the next couple of months their approach under Raymond Illingworth looked very staid and old-fashioned in comparison.

The first Test, at Centurion Park, began in a blaze of publicity with so many reminders of the historic nature of this Test, the first against England at home since 1965. But after two days, that was it. It rained and rained and the thunderstorms were spectacular. As far as we were concerned, there was no advantage to either side, but England tried to talk themselves up after their first innings score of 381 for nine, saying it was a great platform for victory. I couldn't see how they could say that, when you consider it was a flat wicket and they'd taken two days out of five to score only 381. We would have had to bat very badly indeed to give them even a sniff of a chance, with just three days left. The most significant part of this Test for us came just before the start when Brett Schultz declared himself fit. He'd been struggling with a buttock injury and there was a doubt that he would play. Brett was my roomie in that Test and I kept saying to him, 'Look mate, you've got to be sure that you're right, otherwise they'll really come down hard on you if you pull up during the game'. That's exactly what happened. On the first morning, he still didn't look right during our warm-ups. Bob Woolmer shouted over to him, 'Are you OK?' and Brett assured him he was fit. He was trusted, but then tore a buttock muscle in his first over. There were understandable repercussions. Ali Bacher was very unhappy and our physio, Craig Smith, was given a rollicking. So was Bob Woolmer. Craig was told that in future he should concentrate on just treating injuries and that our army of specialists were available for diagnosis in cases like the Schultz one. That was a bit harsh on Craig, because there's only so much a physio can do when a player assures him he's fit for a five-day Test. Basically Brett took a big chance on his fitness in his eagerness to play in a such an historic game.

If England were talking themselves up after that first Test, you can imagine how much they made of the Great Escape after the next Test in Johannesburg. They banged on about the turn of the tide, that we'd be down after failing to nail down the win. But the only reason we didn't win in Johannesburg was because Mike Atherton saved them with his 185 not out. That was a brilliant effort from him, a gutsy innings, with good support from Mr Scruffy himself, Jack Russell. But if Gary Kirsten had caught Atherton at short leg off me when he was on 99, that would have been game, set and match to us. Then Meyrick Pringle dropped Russell off an easy caught and bowled early on, and if he had gone, not even Atherton would have saved England, because one end would have been open.

Atherton is an annoying batsman to bowl at, because he rarely misjudges a ball. He's a great leaver of the ball, very easy and steady at the wicket, and he has that priceless knack of saving his energy by switching off at the right times. A lot of other batters like Robin Smith chatter away to themselves and dance around between each delivery but Atherton just relaxes, and gears himself up for the next ball. He seems to have amazing powers of concentration. Sometimes he gets out on the hook because he likes the shot and sees it as a productive stroke for him, but there aren't many weaknesses in his game. He's very disciplined, leaving well on the bounce and doesn't get drawn into areas where he doesn't want to play. You can pull some batters across their stumps and then do them with a straight ball, but not Athers. You've got to be very tight with him and make him play, because he won't go outside the area that he's marked out. Athers rarely gets into the ball, apart from driving a full length, and there are times when he's a candidate for lbw because he can get planted at the crease. In other words, the guy has a great Test match game. You've got to earn his wicket, bowl him out, because he rarely gives it away with a misjudgement. After Johannesburg, I was very pleased with the way I bowled at Atherton for the rest of the series. I got him twice with the new ball at Cape Town and at Durban, when we worked out that he was a candidate for a catch in the gully to a ball of extra bounce. Over the years, I have really enjoyed my battles with Mike Atherton, because he stretches you as a bowler.

Had we missed our chance in Johannesburg? That was the talk, with England suggesting we had. I didn't see it that way. We'd bowled them out for 200 in the first innings at Jo'Burg, on the best pitch of the series, and it was only Atherton's defiance in the second innings that saved them. We'd outplayed them for most of the game, so all we had to do was keep playing to our strengths. England didn't look integrated and their morale appeared low under Illingworth's dogmatic style of management. I thought they were there for the taking. In the next Test, at Durban, rain again ruined the game, but I felt that we would have had the better of it if we'd had more play. We only managed 225 on a dry, brown surface and when the rains came they were 152 for five. But they were really six down, because John Crawley had torn a hamstring and was out of the reckoning for the rest of the Test. We were also encouraged to think that we'd worked out Atherton. Hansie Cronje reckoned that he liked to play a short ball through gully, with soft hands, so he brought Andrew Hudson closer in for the dab shot. It worked, and we were all pleased with the dismissal. With Atherton out of the way early, we always fancied our chances ... It would have been nice, though, to get on the park for any period of time. So far in the series, we'd only had ten days out of fifteen in the three Tests in what was turning out to be a very rainy summer.

The fourth Test in Port Elizabeth was dull, with neither side preparing to risk much on a dreadfully slow wicket. There was no pace or zip to the pitch, and when England started the final day needing 308 to win, Hansie Cronje set defensive fields and they didn't seem interested in the chase. So they ended up 169 for three and everybody was bored. With four Tests now gone, it felt as if the series had just started. The most memorable aspect of that Port Elizabeth Test was the debut of Paul Adams, the Cape coloured spinner. He'd bowled England out at Kimberley earlier in the tour, with Alec Stewart and Graham Thorpe looking particularly bewildered by his amazing action. It was freakish the way he contorted his body to deliver the ball, and it looked as if he wasn't looking down the pitch when he released it. His selection was a big story for South Africa because he became the second non-white after Omar Henry to play a Test for us. Ali Bacher had been pushing all series for Adams, and the ANC were very keen to see a non-white in the side. After his efforts in Kimberley, he was fairly selected on merit and bowled well. But I'm not sure he's made good enough progress since then. He's worked hard on his flipper and he is destructive against the tail, because he bowls quickly at them and they can't get after him. He needs more variety, though. Paul seems to value accuracy more than the unplayable delivery that gets out the best players. I'm also not sure how much he's prepared to learn, how much real drive he has. Paul is an easy-going lad, who likes to party and enjoys life to the full. He can be a little lazy and has the potential to balloon up in weight unless he works harder at his fitness.

Paul's a lovely guy, who gets on very well with all of us in the South African squad, but the next year or so will show just how far he will go. Certainly that unique action puts a lot of demand on his shins, back and shoulder.

We won the series in the final game at Cape Town by ten wickets. It will always be known as the Test lost by Devon Malcolm – well that's the propaganda that was put about by Raymond Illingworth and his captain, Mike Atherton. Devon was blamed for not being able to knock over our last-wicket pair of Dave Richardson and Paul Adams, when he was armed with the second new ball. But Devon was only given three overs, and he wasn't the only bowler to be panned about. They all got stick in that last-wicket partnership, which brought us a valuable lead of 91. Devon should have been picked for Durban, and due to the management being so short-sighted, he hadn't played a game for a month. Yet he was expected to bowl at his best after kicking his heels for so long. I thought it was disgraceful of Atherton to point the finger at Devon in his press conference after the game. I was surprised at the captain's tactless comments about one of his team. As for Ray Illingworth, I remember him giving Devon some awful stick in Bloemfontein, when he shouted at him in the nets about his technical shortcomings. 'Devon, you're not doing it right!' he shouted, 'Your left arm is going the wrong way!' It was pathetic the way he talked to a bowler who had frightened the life out of us just over a year earlier at the Oval. For Illingworth to talk about changing his action during an England tour was just ridiculous. And it was disgraceful to make him twelfth man in a one-dayer against Western Province a few days after that Test. It seemed as if it was designed to teach Devon a lesson. I wondered if Atherton had stood up for him? The whole thing was an object lesson in bad man-management.

England lost for different reasons other than three way-ward overs from Devon Malcolm. They picked the wrong team for a start. Batting Jack Russell at number six wasn't a good plan, and they were a batsman short. I couldn't work out why they'd given up on Mark Ramprakash after Johannesburg. It must have been a blow to him to be passed over at Port Elizabeth in favour of Jason Gallian, who had been drafted into the tour party once John Crawley pulled his hamstring. I was more than happy to see Gallian play ahead of Ramprakash, because I felt he moves all over his crease and has an inferior technique. He didn't trouble us at all. The main reason why they lost in Cape Town was because they were bowled out for 157 and 153, but Atherton and Illingworth didn't want to focus too much on that. Devon was just a smokescreen. They were very down on themselves when they batted again after Richardson and Adams had demoralised them. That was our best chance of victory and we grabbed them by the throat. I got Atherton out early, caught behind on the second evening and they were rolled over the next day.

I was surprised at the way England buckled. Their morale appeared very low, and when I went into their dressing-room at the end of the game, I saw some very depressed faces. Jack Russell, a great fighter, looked utterly drained. The tour had boiled over for them at the wrong time, and they lacked the stomach for the fight. A few days later, Devon's version of his treatment by Illingworth appeared in the papers in England. His story was relayed to the South African papers, and the morale of their squad dipped even further. I knew then that they'd be also-rans in the World Cup, and I sympathised with guys like Dermot Reeve, Neil Smith and Neil Fairbrother, joining them for the one-day series immediately after the Cape Town Test. They were joining a sinking ship, and it was no surprise when we hammered them 6–1. Their fielding fell apart, and they looked a demoralised lot by the end of the tour. I gave them no chance of regrouping in time for the World Cup.

In contrast, we felt we had a great chance of winning the World Cup. The country was alive with excitement about the prospect. We'd just won the African Nations Soccer Trophy, to set alongside the Rugby World Cup and this was a fantastic time to be a South African sports fan. Publicly, the players didn't get involved in all the hype, but we were very confident privately. The pitches on the sub-continent would be good, and we'd played well over there on previous tours. We'd got on a roll by thrashing England and felt we could maintain the momentum. That made the disappointment of missing out even harder to take.

We got off the mark by hammering the United Arab Emirates in the first game. That was the only time I thought I'd seriously injured a batsman. Their captain, Sultan Hirwani came out wearing a sunhat and me ready to bowl at him. I was baffled that he wasn't wearing a helmet. Pat Symcox, ever the man for the provocative word, said 'Come on Al, knock some sense in to him. He's got money, a Ferrari, so what's he doing, wearing a sunhat?' I told him the best thing to do was just block his stumps, because he was only playing because he was so wealthy. Jonty Rhodes agreed, but Simmo persisted. 'Come on Al, hit him on the head first ball'. So I decided on the bouncer, just to shut up Simmo and it turned out to be a peach. It hit the Sultan at the top of his left temple. I'd meant to bowl it over his head, but unfortunately it was just in the right area. His hat flew off, his hair stood on end and I thought he was in serious trouble. Steve Bucknor, one of the umpires told me, 'This bloke's only playing because he's rich. He's funding the team, so go easy on him'. Meanwhile Simmo was standing over him, being his usual charming self. 'I don't care how much money you've got, mate – this is a real game, pal'. But he still wouldn't put on a helmet, and thankfully he was out soon afterwards. It was a worrying few minutes.

The next match was more serious. We beat New Zealand by five wickets in Faisalabad, and Bob Woolmer described it as our best all-round performance in one-day cricket since he'd been in charge. There were three brilliant run-outs, and we played their slow-medium bowlers very well. Victory with twelve overs to spare capped a great performance. The next performance was even more impressive, as we beat the holders, Pakistan by five wickets. I wasn't all that impressive, though, going for 50 off eight overs. I felt tired, lacking zip and got panned. I wasn't much better in the following game, against Holland, but I wasn't prepared for the next event. We were due to face West Indies in Karachi, but a few days on, I could sense some negative vibes about me. Hansie Cronje, the vice-captain Craig

Matthews and Bob Woolmer just weren't communicating with me. In the days before the game, I was told to bowl at the later batsmen, rather than at the top-order players. At the time I thought little of that, believing that they were trying to get me motivated and angry. On the eve of the match, Hansie came to my room, looking serious, and I said, 'Forget it, don't tell me'. When I was on my own, I cried my eyes out. Bob Woolmer came to see me later and said he didn't realise I felt so strongly about being omitted. He said they wanted to take the pace off the ball, that they were going for two spinners on a slow pitch to frustrate the batsmen, and that I'd be back for the semi-final. I understood the reasoning, but it still hurt like hell. Curtly Ambrose, Ian Bishop and Courtney Walsh all played for West Indies in that game, so they stayed with their best bowlers. Admittedly, I wasn't bowling all that well, but I felt I'd get it back. I was also worried that if we lost, my chance of playing in a World Cup Final would have gone for good. There was no guarantee I'd be fit enough or in form for the next World Cup, four years away. All that positive stuff I'd picked up from Alan Jones over the previous two years went straight out of the window. I've never felt more disappointed in my career. Later on, Fanie de Villiers poured me a beer to cheer me up, but I still felt let down. Why didn't the management just tell me I hadn't been bowling well, rather than go on about 'taking the pace off the ball'?

And then we lost the next day. It was no consolation to me that my hotel was deluged with sympathetic faxes for me from South Africa. I wanted us to win despite being dropped, there was no element of grim satisfaction in our defeat. We allowed Jimmy Adams too much respect when he bowled tightly at us, and despite a typical piece of hitting by Pat Symcox, we couldn't get near enough to their total of 264 for eight, and we lost by nineteen runs. In the dressing-room afterwards, we were very quiet and despondent. We knew we'd stuffed up after playing such excellent one-day cricket in the tournament up to this day. But we chose the wrong day to be under par. It's not that we were over-confident going into the match, more a case of not being able to deliver when we really had to. I won't call it 'pressure', more 'reacting to responsibility in the right way'. That was to become a theme for us in key matches. As for me, the Karachi experience was a lesson in life. Get on with it, and swallow your disappointment. It was hard to see it that way at the time.

CHAPTER FOURTEEN

Time Out

M issing out on the 1996 season with Warwickshire was the best thing I could have done at that stage in my career. In a sense, the club's dilemma over Brain Lara worked out well for me. The whole thing dragged on so long that I had come to the conclusion that I needed some time off the treadmill to avoid prolonged lethargy. At the same time I wanted to know more about the methods of achieving and maintaining greater fitness. So I kept my hand in at the weekend by playing league cricket up in Lancashire for Rishton, while working as a fitness advisor for Warwickshire during the week. So I felt rejuvenated when I returned to international action towards the end of 1996, and my knowledge of what was involved in keeping my fitness was greatly enhanced.

Once Warwickshire had signed Shaun Pollock as their overseas player for the season, they approached me to be their fitness advisor. I was surprised because I had little practical knowledge of the subject, but I set to work with Paddy Upton, South Africa's fitness trainer. He put me in touch with the Sports Science Institute at Cape Town, who organised programmes for individual disciplines. By the time I met up with the Warwickshire boys for pre-season training in Cape Town, I was full of ideas and looking forward to the new challenge. I told them all about shuttle runs, stretching exercises and training with light weights, and some of them looked sceptically at me. They knew that I liked my red wine, my beer and the occasional burger or curry and wondered what I was banging on about. They soon found out I meant business and I really put them through it. When we returned to England, I spoke to some fitness training experts at Birmingham University and they helped me focus on the need to prevent injuries.

I was introduced to the principle of Biokinetics, which is all about how to get the best out of your body, pushing it to the maximum. The basis of this is correct stretching exercises. You start from scratch every morning, stretching the body properly and patiently. There are no half-measures, you have to do them properly – for example, with a straight back when doing a hamstring stretch. The first thing to do on a morning when I'm playing is a pro-longed stretch. At least twenty minutes, whether or not I'm due to have a bowl. This is before nets or throwdowns and it's designed to prevent injuries. So many English county professionals get injuries because they're more worried about getting through a season, rather than being aware of suppleness. They turn up at the ground at 9.30, hit a few balls, then go back to the dressing-room for a coffee. That's not the way to train anymore. Stamina work isn't enough. I'd learned from Professor Tim Noakes about the need for suppleness, to make sure that South Africa had the fittest group of players around. That was the brief given to him by our Cricket Board, because they realised that with the amount of international cricket due to be played, we would need to be consistently fit. So the deal is that they look after us with specialists for all areas of the body while we put in the work. That's what the Warwickshire lads needed to grasp. I wasn't going to be soft on them just because they were my mates.

I introduced fielding drills to be done at close of play, which led to some good-natured grumbling. Probably because it kept us out of the bar for an extra half-hour! I'd make them do eight shuttle runs in a straight line, ending with throws, and then I'd move back the line and make them do it again. It was done to improve suppleness and throwing. We'd pick a winner and the guys really concentrated hard on it, once they got into the idea. I used to bitch like a baby when Paddy Upton introduced this exercise into the South African routine, but it helped us. I think you'll find that the South African fast bowlers all have good throws, and that's not just because we are blessed with natural flexibility, it's because we work at it.

The 'bleep' test was another important aid to greater fitness. Everybody dreads this cardiovascular exercise, including me, but it really pushes up stamina and flexibility levels, and the ability to recover quickly from an explosive burst of physical activity. The 'bleep' test involves shuttle runs that go up to certain levels, getting quicker all the time, with less recovery time allowed. You must run on a good, even surface over a distance of 22 yards, with eight of the runs constituting one 'bleep'. When you've done one 'bleep', you go on to stage two, which is quicker. By level eleven, your legs are starting to hurt and the lungs are heaving. A good standard of fitness is thirteen. I've managed that, but I'm no fitness paragon. Dermot Reeve used to be very good, Jonty Rhodes has got up to fifteen, while Hansie Cronje has managed a phenomenal seventeen. Nick

Knight and Dougie Brown have both done fifteen. Batsmen like Nick and Nasser Hussain have definitely become better players because they are very fit. They concentrate hard all day, run quickly between the wickets and they're both very agile and sharp in the field. They prove that when you're fit, your concentration levels are very high. I look at some county cricketers and they're clearly not working on their bodies. They turn up and go through the motions. When a side's not doing well, they ought to work even harder but some English players just let it go.

I'm no fitness fanatic, far from it. I moan just as much as anybody else when there's hard work to be done but I realise it's simply a case of getting on with it. There's nothing I like more than a game of golf, then a few beers, but that comes after I've been to the gym in the morning. Paddy Upton's programme that he organised for me in 1995 helps me enjoy myself after I've done the hard work. At close of play, I'll do some shuttle runs over a 40-metre area – six in a row multiplied by ten, with a rest in between of about two minutes. I sprint the last quarter after going at good pace for the majority of the 40 metres. Next day, it'll be up to 60 of these shuttles, back and forth, with little rest in between. The day after, I'll have to do 20 minutes of strengthening work on my stomach, back, legs and ankles – on the ground, not in the gym, and this after my shuttles work. The gym comes once a week, when some serious work is involved. There'll be 40 minutes' work on the bike, then I'll test the buttocks, groin, shoulders, and legs with light weights of around fifteen kilos. The key is light weight, repeated often, so that the heartbeat is up. I'll go for the bench press, with a 30kg weight – eight of those, multiplied three times. Push up onto the chest, then raise the weight nice and easy. Repetition is more important than going through the pain barrier. I'll do all this gym work at any stage of the year, although I'll do a bit less during the off-season, whenever that is for a South African cricketer who also plays county cricket!

The key to the gym work is quality time. There is a danger in doing too much for your particular discipline. Hansie Cronje, for example, concentrates more on getting physically stronger than me. I aim for suppleness, preferring repetitions on light weights. Jonty Rhodes had troubles with his thigh muscles and hamstrings for a time, but after Paddy Upton designed him a specific programme, he worked himself very hard on his vulnerable areas. He became a very strong guy, who can hurl himself about in the field, throw strongly off-balance and also hit the ball very hard with his powerful forearms. For me, it's a case of stretching every day, that is the most important area of my training. Without suppleness, I'd struggle to bowl fast. It's a case of marrying up the morning warm-ups and stretching with the strengthening exercises. The stomach and back muscles must be strong for a fast bowler, and that means you need to train every day during a tour or county season. In the close season, back in Bloemfontein, I'll do fitness work with the local rugby club, but that will involve touch rugby. That helps speed up my reactions by learning about the best time to sprint and how to find space when surrounded by a few rugby players intent on crashing you to the ground. Basically, you never give up on training, whatever the time of the year, you just learn to taper off when necessary. The principle remains the same, though – no pain, no gain.

This professional approach has certainly kept the South

African cricketers on the park. When you consider the amount of cricket we play, all around the world, I think it's remarkable how few of our players break down. Between October 1997 and August 1998, we played 16 Tests and 27 one-day internationals, and yet we only had to have one operation, on Lance Klusener's broken bone in his foot, that cut short his England tour. We lost Brett Schultz from the tour to Pakistan, because he tore a tendon under his left arm doing throwing practice. Brett is a very strong guy – fourteen in the 'bleep' test – but he has a bad throwing technique in fielding drills, and the day before the first Test, he didn't let on that he had a sore arm. He was throwing 70 yards from the boundary, but his arm was eventually black from the ruptured tendon. He had to return home for treatment, and our captain, Hansie Cronje wasn't impressed. So Brett had fallen foul again of the back-up team after he was selected for the first Test against England in 1995 despite carrying an injury. His injury this time helped the rest of us, though. The Sports Institute hired a baseball pitcher to look at our throwing techniques and helped improve a few of us. It also improved our chances of avoiding an arm injury by throwing in from the deep. Attention to detail – very important.

With South Africa, it's simply a case of getting on with the hard work. Every international squad complains at some stage about their workload, but I do believe that we are more phlegmatic about it than most of the others. Dr Ali Bacher tells us that it's a huge honour to be representing our country, that many great players missed out during the wilderness years between 1970 and 1991, and we shouldn't dwell on fatigue, but think of national pride and personal satisfaction. He is, of course, absolutely right to see it that way, and I honestly feel that South African players of the modern era are keen to play as much as possible. I couldn't believe that England failed to send a decent rugby union squad to Australia in 1998. That's something we'd never sanction, no matter how tired our top players were feeling. It was the same for the Commonwealth Games in Kuala Lumpar in September 1998 when England pleaded county commitments for their failure to compete in cricket. I was one of those who didn't go with the South African squad because of my ankle injury that needed an operation, but I know how proud Shaun Pollock was to captain us to the gold medal. You can't think to achieve glory like that when you've retired, it's a matter of gritting your teeth on long, draining tours and getting used to the routine of airport/hotel/ground and disruption of your body clock when it's a day/night match and you're off to the airport the following morning. Of course we play too much international cricket, but I honestly think we are better at gritting our teeth than others – including England.

I now realise that if I hadn't taken stock of myself during the English summer of 1996 that I might easily have faded away as a fast bowler. I was approaching thirty, with many ambitions left, but there was no point in looking to achieve them if I kept dipping out of important spells later in the day, when hostility and aggression were needed. Getting the chance to nag away at the Warwickshire boys as their fitness advisor also gave me time to assess where I was going in my career. That time away from the middle rejuvenated me.

CHAPTER FIFTEEN

A Hard Slog

Between 1996 and 1998, we South African cricketers saw a lot of passport controls, hotels and cricket grounds all over the world. It was the most concentrated period of cricket we had experienced since we'd become accepted again in 1991. I'm amazed at the amount we played during that period. From September 1996 to April 1998, we toured Kenya, India, Pakistan and Australia, then hosted home Test and one-day series against India, Zimbabwe, Australia, Sri Lanka and Pakistan. A total of 49 one-day internationals and 20 Tests. And just a month after all that lot finished, we were off to England for a full Test series, then a triangular one-day tournament that also involved Sri Lanka before we got home in August 1998. No wonder we looked rather jaded in those last one-dayers – I reckon we all felt we were subconsciously on the plane when England and Sri Lanka were smashing us all over the park.

I'm very glad that I took that 1996 season off from Warwickshire duty, because I wouldn't have got through that killing itinerary unless I'd been fully rested and raring to go. I was delighted with my form, taking 99 international wickets during the 1996/97 South African season – 41 in

Tests, 58 in the one-dayers. My stamina had improved greatly, and the various tours around the world were definitely expanding my bowling skills. Over the next eighteen months, I was to learn a lot about variety by bowling on the dusty pitches of the sub-continent. It all gelled for me right from the start, in Kenya, where we played a one-day tournament against Sri Lanka and Pakistan, in September 1996. I remember getting Pakistan's Ijaz Ahmed with a slower ball, which pleased me greatly because I'd worked hard on it in the nets. The pitches in Kenya were very flat and in the hot, dusty conditions, you couldn't expect to bowl flat out, trying to blast out the batters. Some ingenuity was needed. To get 14 wickets in four matches in that series, and to be voted Man of the Series was a great boost for me at the start of such a hectic itinerary.

India was our next stop, and although I had to go home early after the second Test to rest a bruised heel, I felt I learned a lot. It's probably the worst country to tour from the point of view of your health – you never know when illness is going to strike you down – but from a cricketing perspective, it's a great challenge. I learned more about reverse swing, what precise length to bowl on those flat pitches and the right time to bowl the short one. The former Australian batsman, David Hookes once told me that his skill levels improved by thirty per cent after touring India. On turning wickets he learned to be more selective against the spinners, more patient in defence. I could see what he meant. It applied to my bowling. In India, you need to adapt for every match, because no wicket is the same. In the two Tests I played, I took a wicket every six overs and I felt in control of my bowling, able to reverse swing at Ahmedebad on a brown, dusty pitch. I felt loose, fit and in control of my game. That tour of India made me aware how much England's fast bowlers have missed by not touring the sub-continent regularly. They haven't played a Test series in Pakistan since 1987, nor one in India or Sri Lanka since 1993, and I'm convinced their international standard has suffered as a result. The fast bowlers would learn more about their craft, how to think the batsmen out on dead pitches, how to look after the ball, and their batsmen would develop better techniques against the spinners. When you saw how poorly they played the leg-spinner Stuart McGill in the recent Ashes series, it was clear that the English guys were a long way behind other countries in practical experience of combating high-class spin. That's England's own fault – they should have told the players they had to tour the sub-continent on a regular basis, even though they didn't fancy it. If you want to be the best in the world, you travel the world to broaden your knowledge. It's very hard work, as we South Africans know only too well, but it's worth it. England's players have had it too soft – if it was up to them, they'd just like to tour South Africa, West Indies, New Zealand and Australia on a rota basis. But there are three other countries who play Test cricket.

By the time we staged the return series against India a few weeks later, I was fully fit again and raring to go. It was a great series for us, winning 2–0, and for me, taking 20 wickets, bowling quickly against Indian batsmen who generally didn't appear to fancy it. They moaned a lot about the itinerary, and looked an unhappy squad. They certainly appeared to be there for the taking, and we were ruthless. After the wickets had favoured them in their country, we had told them to watch out when they got to our place. Durban was a particularly quick pitch. We had them 7 for three in their first innings, all of them to me, and the atmosphere as I tore into them was inspirational, the noise really lifted me. They were bowled out for 100 and 66, and I took nine wickets, loving the pace and bounce of the surface, making the Indians hop around. One of those wickets was the prized one of the little maestro, Sachin Tendulkar, and it remains the best delivery I've ever bowled to a world-class batsman. Off the first two deliveries after lunch, he creamed me through the covers for two boundaries. They were awesome shots, he just seemed to block the ball, and it sped away. So I told myself that I was bowling it a little too full, that I had to pull it back a shade. The next ball nipped back through a tiny gap between bat and pad, knocking over his off stump, sending it cartwheeling out of the ground. I was fired up because I was backing myself against one of the greats, and I couldn't stop myself from running down the pitch, with my arms spread out wide in exhilaration. It didn't do me any harm, though, because I got a decent sponsorship deal from South African Airways, using the photograph. Fly with Allan Donald!

Tendulkar got some revenge in the next Test, at Cape Town, even though we won it easily enough. He made 169, and with Mohammad Azharuddin, added 222 at five an over. It was an astonishing exhibition from these two, and they clearly decided they'd had enough of being bullied by the fast bowlers, so they handed out the treatment. I was hammered everywhere, 'Azza' specialising in the cut and the pull until he ran himself out for 115, and Sachin just dominating. It was a fabulous innings by the little man, so certain in his strokeplay, so correct and balanced. It's not often a fast bowler with his tail up can detach himself from all the emotion of bowling in a Test match, to appreciate an opposition batsman, but you just had to on this day in Cape Town. It took an absolutely remarkable catch by Adam Bacher to get him out. Tendulkar smashed a ball to the mid-wicket boundary, and it looked a certain six, but Bacher dived to take it one-handed near the rope. Sachin was stunned and so were the rest of us, but something like that was needed to end a great innings.

Throughout that three-Test series, there was a tremendous atmosphere, generated by large crowds. More than 193,000 came to the Tests, a new record for a three-Test series in South Africa, and I'm sure the noisy support we enjoyed disconcerted some of the Indian players, even though it was good to see many from the Indian community come to the Cape Town and Durban Tests. The same fervent atmosphere inspired us during the one-day series, when we won six in a row against Zimbabwe and India and when we got to the final in Durban, against India, our big-match experience got us home in a tight finish by 16 runs in a rain-reduced match. We needed to defend 252 off 40 overs and after I got an early wicket, we were hammered by Sachin Tendulkar and Rahul Dravid. It was in the middle of a noisy, partisan atmosphere, with the final in the balance, that I got involved in an incident that has since caused me a lot of grief, leading to accusations that I am a racist.

I was really pumped up by the time Tendulkar and Dravid came together, but they soon got after me. Tendulkar pulled me for a flat six over midwicket, a wonderful shot. I could handle that sort of treatment from a great player, but when Dravid smashed me for six and four, I got carried away in typical fast bowler's fashion. I walked right up to him, face to face, and snarled, 'This isn't such a f****** easy game' and the TV cameras had me in close-up, with everyone lip-reading my words. Dravid's eyes lit up when he saw me standing so close, and the Durban crowd absolutely loved it. I've done something similar many times in tense games like this one, and I'm sure there were many South Africans watching at home, shouting at the television set, 'That's more like it, get stuck in!' That was certainly the gist of what my captain was saying on the field. As I eye-balled Dravid, Hansie Cronje shouted behind me 'That's it, f****** give it to him!', and he climbed into Dravid as well. A few of the other boys in the field picked up the aggressive vibes and they started to mouth off. It worked, because it revived us when it looked as if we were going to cop a hammering, and the crowd got behind us as well. That sort of confrontation goes down very well in South African sport and some of the Indian cricketers didn't like it.

In the end, Tendulkar got himself out, flicking one to midwicket for 84, and we were right back in the game, after going for around eight an over. In came Azharuddin, who told Cronje that what I'd said to Dravid was out of order. Hansie told him to shut his mouth and get on with the game. I believe his precise words were 'Go f****** cry somewhere else' and after that we all climbed into Azza and gave him some fearful stick. In the end, they folded, we won the Final after looking out of it, and I thought no more about it, to me it was just a high-octane period of a match that we desperately wanted to win, and we did because we had the bottle to do so. Straight afterwards, I went to Dravid and told him my words weren't meant to be personal, that it was all in the heat of the moment, it should stay out in the middle and shouldn't be a problem between us. He gave me a hard look, and left it at that. I thought no more of it until I got back to the team hotel afterwards. Then I really had a shock.

A letter had been placed under my door that was full of the most unbelievable comments. It came from an Indian who accused me of being blatantly racist towards Dravid, that my white skin disgusted the writer and that I was basically the scum of the earth. I wish I'd kept the letter instead of tearing it up in anger, because it was absolutely disgraceful. But it didn't stop there. I had various phone calls from him after that, calling me all sorts of names and each time he'd slam the phone down on me. Hansie Cronje had similar treatment from him. Somehow he got my home phone number in Bloemfontein, and abused me. One day, at home, Tina was opening my mail and she handed a letter to me, saying, 'Allan, here's your first racist letter'. It was him again. I've had several more disgusting letters from him. The whole thing really upset me. The guy just didn't understand the competitive edge that's involved in playing top-class sport, the need to dominate an opponent before he does the same to you. It had absolutely nothing to do with race, it was a matter of testing out Dravid with verbals, to see if he could fight back at me. If he couldn't take it in the heat of battle, then he shouldn't be out there. There's no way I'd ever get involved in racist comments. I'm simply not like that.

I believe the issue was about the Indians being less confrontational than us, and getting disconcerted by some typical South African verbal bullying. That's got nothing to do with racism. The Pakistanis are much stronger mentally than the Indians. Take their wicket-keeper, Moin Khan.

He really is a fiery little character and I like that. Once in a Test against Pakistan, he hit me away for runs, and as he passed me at the bowler's end, he swung the bat just past me. I wondered if he'd meant to hit me. Next ball, I found out. He went for more runs, lashed out with his bat and caught me a really hard blow on the shin. I jumped up in pain and shouted 'I suppose you f****** didn't mean to do that!' and he rapped back 'I'd never f****** do that – now f*** off!' I had to smile at that, admiring Moin's competitiveness, and I never thought he was being racist by whacking me on the shin.

If the weakness of the Indian opposition had given us a false sense of our own superiority, the Australians soon dispelled that notion when they came to South Africa, early in 1997. They beat us 2–1 in the Test series and 4–3 in the one-dayers, and we were made aware of just what's needed to be the number-one side in the world. They had that extra mental edge over us, and it was a choker for South Africans to have to admit that the opposition were even more competitive than us. The Test series had been hyped up as the unofficial championship of the world, a cricketing version of the Springboks against the Wallabies, but I thought that was rubbish. We just had to see how we measured up against the best, and we pulled up short. It was a difficult experience for us all.

In the first Test at Johannesburg, they kept us out in the field for two-and-a-half days. Steve Waugh and Greg Blewett batted an entire day without getting out, an unbelievable effort, even though it was a flat deck and the sun was out. That mental durability was so obvious, they had no intention of giving it away and they just ground us down. We were left to bat for a day and a half to save the

Test and we couldn't manage it. Michael Bevan's left-arm spin did the damage, while Glenn McGrath made the early inroads. McGrath had become a top bowler since I'd first seen him in '94. He'd worked out the angles, knew where to pitch the ball, aware that just a little deviation was enough to get the edge. Bowling very close to the stumps, running it away from the left-handers by going around the wicket, he also had an excellent, fast bouncer that he used sparingly, for surprise. McGrath was now a remorseless bowler, world-class.

One-down in the series, we lost again at Port Elizabeth through our own fault. That's not to deny the brilliant effort by the Australians to get home by two wickets, keeping their nerve. Our batting in the second innings was disgraceful – slapdash, careless, as if the batters thought the game was won. It would have been if we'd got another fifty runs. We'd bowled them out for 108 in the first innings, giving us a lead of 101, so all we had to do was bat them out of the game. At 83 for nought, a lead of 184, it was all going to plan, but then we were tumbled out for 168. Jason Gillespie bowled really well, but our shot selection was awful, and nobody seemed able to concentrate. So we'd let them back in with a chance – 270 to win, with two-and-a-half days to go, when they ought to have been dead and buried. Mark Waugh then came in to play what he called his best innings in Test cricket, and although he played and missed a few times, I could see what he meant. He gave the Australians stability, the belief that they could win it, and despite a late wobble, when they went from 256 for five to 265 for eight, that's what they did. Ian Healy took charge, realising that Gillespie and McGrath wouldn't be up to getting the runs. So he slapped a six over long leg to win the Test. A great effort from the Aussies. They showed their resilience by hauling themselves back in the game when they bowled us out cheaply, then batting relentlessly towards the target. When they wobbled late on, a bold approach by Healy did it. For me, it was one of the most disappointing Tests I've ever been involved in. I bowled so well in their second innings, beating the bat time and again, yet finished up with nought for 75, but it was even more important that we lost the Test. We just threw it away, and the memory of it still hurts. We South Africans thought we were the tops when it came to guts and competitiveness, but we were being out-gunned in front of our own fans by a superior outfit. Now we faced a 3–0 series hammering.

We pulled ourselves together at last in the final Test at Centurion Park. After bowling them out cheaply for 227 in the first innings, we established a big lead, then the wicket got quicker and we peppered them in the second innings, dismissing them for 185, to win by eight wickets. I bowled fast and well in that second innings, particularly early on when the big crowd got behind me. The atmosphere was electric, like a rugby international, as I had Mark Taylor caught behind and had Matt Elliott lbw. I then had a terrific duel with a batsman I admire greatly – Steve Waugh. He isn't the most stylish player in the world, but there's no one braver. At Centurion Park, I really put him through the mixer. In one particular over, I hit him five times out of six, on the gloves, the forearm, and finally just below the heart and he never flinched. After I hit him on the chest, he dropped his gloves, took off his helmet, waited for the physio to come on, then took his time to recover. I knew I'd hurt him, but he just wouldn't give me the satisfaction of showing it. In that Test, he batted over seven hours for 67 and 60 not out, and at no time did he ever look like giving it away. He was unlucky to be given out in the first innings, caught down the legside by the keeper, Dave Richardson, when he was nowhere near it. After a half-hearted appeal by Richardson, the umpire gave Waugh out. We were a little embarrassed, although not that much, when you consider the calibre of the man sent packing. The umpire was Merv Kitchen. Sadly, Trent Bridge '98 wasn't the first Test in which I'd seen Merv give a poor decision.

So we'd avoided a 3–0 thrashing, but we were inferior to Australia, and they proved that in the one-day series as well. That was hard for the South African public to take, because they don't like losing. When it doesn't go well for the national side, the South African sporting public can be very unforgiving, and they weren't slow to tell us so at the end of our international summer in April '97. Bob Woolmer was criticised for making too many excuses, which was hard on him, because he would just give straight answers to straight questions and not look to hide. The truth was that we had failed to cut it when it was needed, while the Aussies out-fought us. Our batting wasn't grinding down the opposition, none of the batters was taking responsibility to play a major innings, they were leaving it to each other. Statistics showed that we were one of the top three sides in Test cricket, but although we hadn't lost many Tests since our readmission, we weren't doing it when it came to the crunch. This Australian series had been billed as our biggest challenge yet, and we couldn't rise to it. On top of losing out in the '96 World Cup, it was a case of going back to the drawing board, and rediscovering our nerve. We had to learn how to get through the tight situations, like the Australians. For the first time since we came back to international cricket, our players and administrators were being asked pointed questions by the media and the public. They were perfectly justified in doing so. We had to learn how to win when up against it.

Meanwhile, as the inquests raged back in South Africa, I was playing again for Warwickshire. Just ten days after the last one-dayer, in Bloemfontein, I was running in to bowl at Cardiff, against Glamorgan. It was good to be back with the lads again on the field, after my summer off, and I had a good season, taking 60 championship wickets at a rate of one every 39 balls. I missed four championship matches after pulling an intercostal muscle at Canterbury, in a Benson and Hedges Cup game. I was gasping for air, and just had to leave the field. It was a very painful injury, and three weeks' rest was the only solution.

We suffered from a lot of injuries in the '97 season – no Tim Munton all summer, long absences for Nick Knight, Andy Moles and Keith Piper, plus my rib injury – and with three captains in charge at various stages, we did very well to be in contention for two trophies. One of them, the NatWest Trophy was decided by the toss of the coin, and it was very disappointing for all concerned to have the showpiece game again ruined. When we saw the Lord's wicket on the morning of the match, it was damp, and yet the day before had been beautiful. After Nick Knight was out third ball, we never had a chance of posting a big score on a pitch where the ball was seaming around so much. Essex needed just 171 to win, and when they batted, the sun came out and we never had a chance, getting thrashed by nine wickets. For the eleventh time in the last twelve

Finals, the side batting first had lost. I can't work out why the ball jags all over the place at Lord's on a September morning, unless it's because we start too early, with the dew still lying around. Far better to reduce the Final to 50 overs a side, and start half-an-hour later, when the pitch will be drier. Lord's is a great place to play, especially in front of a packed crowd in a one-day Final, but we need wickets that help the batsmen. These matches should be about large scores on a good pitch, and a tight finish when it's getting dark – just like the '93 Final between Warwickshire and Sussex.

We ended the season on a high note a week later, winning the Sunday League in front of our home fans. That was a great day, and a fine effort after losing the first three games of the campaign. Gladstone Small and I were used in the middle of the innings throughout the Sunday season, and that suited me, because that was the role I was used in by South Africa. Graeme Welch and Dougie Brown would start off, then 'Glad' and myself would use our experience to curtail the batters when they were looking to accelerate. It worked a treat. On the final Sunday of the season, we beat Gloucestershire by 71 runs, and I took the final wicket. I was bowling from the Pavilion End, and as I saw Keith Piper running towards me in delight, I knew I wasn't going to turn around in time and get to the dressing-room before the crowd got to me. I was grabbed, thrown into the air and chaired off the pitch. It was a fabulous feeling, one that summed up my relationship with the Edgbaston crowd, and the reception they gave me that evening in the Members' Bar overwhelmed me. I was very touched by their appreciation and warmth. Neil Smith, our acting captain, had been very thoughtful earlier, insisting that Tim Munton and myself should go forward to collect the trophy on the pavilion balcony, in front of our roaring supporters. That's a gesture and a memory that won't fade. Later Neil told the press that I had been the best overseas player on and off the field in the English game for the past decade, and that meant an awful lot to me. Neil's a very thoughtful character, who weighs his words carefully, and I've always respected his cricketing judgement greatly. Coming from him, that was a tremendous compliment that I'll treasure.

Just a few weeks after those Edgbaston celebrations, I was doing more of the same in Faisalabad, after we had managed to win a Test series in Pakistan for the first time. I was delighted for Bob Woolmer, who had taken a fair amount of stick earlier in the year, but had kept his head down, working out a strategy to combat the Pakistani spinners on their home pitches. Bob decided we had to be more aggressive against Mushtaq Ahmed and Saqlain Mushtaq and it worked. We did well against the spinners in our warm-up games and when the Tests started, our batters continued to use their feet and weren't afraid to hit over the top. The wicket at Rawalpindi was too good, though, and it rained for most of the time at Sheikhpura, so the Faisalabad Test turned out to be the decider. Straight away, our backs were up after hearing that Wasim Akram and Mushtaq had been bowling the day before on the actual strip. That was against the ICC regulations, because prior knowledge of the wicket would obviously influence the final shape of their side next morning. Our protest was sent to the ICC, but we've heard no more about it, which isn't surprising. Anyway, that incident really fired us up, and we were itching for a fight when the Test started.

No one was better for us in this sort of situation than

Pat Symcox and he played the game of his life for us. As well as taking valuable wickets with his off-breaks, Simmo belted the ball a long way to make 81 and 55, vital runs in a low-scoring match. He kept hitting Mushtaq straight and when Waqar Younis came on, he pulled him a long way time and again. We bowled them out for 92, to win by 53 runs, and I took the catch to win the game off Simmo, holding Moin Khan at deep midwicket. As the ball came towards me, I said to myself 'Do not drop this' and I couldn't wait to join the lads in the middle, who were hugging each other. Typically, Simmo was flat on his back in the middle of the wicket, shouting his head off.

Pat Symcox has been a fantastic competitor for South Africa, and I have thought at times that he ought to have played more Tests. He's an absolute dog on the field, a great scrapper who never gives in. Whatever it takes to get a win for his country, he's there for it. He was the one who reminded us about Leeds '81 at Sydney in 1994, before we went out to win so memorably by five runs. He's a very upfront character out in the middle, who never hesitates to tell a batsman he's rubbish. He gave Matthew Hayden a terrible time in the Centurion Park Test of '97, when Hayden was coming to the end of a miserable series for him, averaging around twelve. He hadn't been picked for the subsequent one-day series, so was going home to Australia after this Test. Simmo chided him mercilessly: 'Now don't forget Don Bradman also got a duck in his last Test, so don't f*** it up here. It's a shame you're not staying on for the one-dayers, but that Qantas flight number 235 to Perth will be calling out your name tonight in just a few hours' time – so don't f*** up your last chance'. He did – Hayden out for nought. He was then dropped for the tour to England a few months later. I wonder how much Simmo had got to him? Mind you, that sort of chirrup is subtle compared to some of the stuff we get from the Aussies!

For some reason, Simmo took a dislike to Adam Hollioake on the '98 tour of England, and whenever he came in to bat in the one-day series, Simmo really handed it out. Simmo's a great mate of Ian Botham – they have the same philosophy about social life – and he didn't believe that Hollioake deserved to be considered as an England all-rounder, when you judge the performances of Botham in that role. He also wasn't impressed by the smart boots Adam was wearing, with cushioned pimples on the sole. So when Hollioake came out to bat, he was greeted by this Symcox tirade: 'Well, look who's here – Mr f****** Ian Botham himself. My f****** arse! Look at those bubbles on his shoes – aren't they pretty? AD, aren't these shoes pretty? Ian Botham? My arse!' All delivered straight into Adam Hollioake's face. Simmo's the sort of guy you'd rather have on your side, rather than in the opposition camp.

He was very influential in keeping everyone's spirits up on that tour of Pakistan, and winning the one-day series that also featured West Indies was another fine team effort. So much is against you in Pakistan if you let it get to you. Running in to bowl during a day/night game can be very hazardous, because the moths get attracted to the lights and you sometimes end up swallowing one of them on the way to the wicket. When we played in Sheikhpura, we had to go by bus from Lahore every morning, because there were no hotels there, so that meant a round trip of three hours a day. The lights in some of the dressing-rooms never really worked, and nothing was ever finished at any of the grounds, there was always something missing. You couldn't go out at night because of safety reasons, apart from Lahore, where the American Club provided sanctuary and a beer. But we knew what was in store after talking to the Australians about it. We had to make our own entertainment at night in the team room, and we had some generous sponsors who sent us out beers, videos and sweets. We knew that flights would be late or cancelled, that practise facilities wouldn't often be available, but we just had to get on with it. Pakistan is a very big psychological test for any visiting cricketer, but a great place to learn cricket skills. If you're winning out there, it binds the team together even stronger and it becomes a triumph of character. Winning that series ranks only slightly below that wonderful narrow victory in Sydney in 1994.

Next stop – Australia. It was ridiculously hyped as the Revenge Series, after their victory earlier in the year, but we weren't bothered about that, we just wanted to compete more strongly against them. The first Test, at Melbourne, was a fantastic experience. On the first day, Boxing Day, the crowd was 73,812 and we were lifted by the marvellous atmosphere. When the national anthems were sung just before the start, we were really fired up, and we stayed out there, waiting to take the field, bonding like a rugby side. Australia batted slowly, in a really tense atmosphere, and we did well to restrict them to 309 all out. When we batted, Shane Warne again dictated to us – my fears confirmed, despite our encouraging efforts in Pakistan. He bowled 42 overs to take three for 64, and his feud with Darryl Cullinan simmered to the boil. Darryl had decided he wasn't going to be psychologically intimidated by Warne and was upset to read comments from Warne to the effect that he'd love to bowl at him all the time, because he was Warne's bunny. So Darryl sledged him unmercifully when he came out to bat, going on about Warne's weight and his spreading stomach. When I had him caught in the gully in the first innings, Darryl shouted after him, 'Save some lunch for me, you fat f****', which wasn't a very clever thing to say. One of the banners at the MCG said, 'Don't worry, Warney – it's only five minutes to lunch!' and presumably that was Darryl's inspiration for the jibe. Well, that fired up Warne, and when he dismissed Darryl for nought in the second innings, he was given a massive send-off. Darryl underestimated Warne's competitive instinct, that he thrives on such a challenge. It was also a mistake to get under the skin of such a great bowler. For the rest of that series, Warne was on top of Cullinan.

That Melbourne Test was a milestone for me. When I had Mike Kasprowicz taken at point, I passed Hugh Tayfield's South African record of 170 Test wickets. It was a great feeling to be my country's top wicket-taker, and I immediately revised my targets to 200, then 250. I also bowled quickly in that second innings, to take six wickets, and we had a chance of victory before the Australian tail rallied and batted them back into contention. That left us a day and a half to hang on for a draw and we did that. That was a start at least.

We didn't capitalise, though, losing at Sydney by an innings and plenty, with Warne taking eleven wickets. We just didn't get enough runs in the first innings, making 287 when we needed at least 400 and Mark Taylor was right to criticise us for batting too slowly. They showed us how to play on that pitch when they batted, getting 421 in quick time, to give them enough room to bowl us out again. The Waugh twins got important runs at good pace, but not before I'd had a hugely enjoyable spell at them with the second new ball. I knew it was make-or-break, that they had to be dislodged and I gave it everything. It was one of the fastest spells I've ever bowled at two top batsmen. In a six-over spell, I hit them both on shoulders and arms, but they weathered it. I didn't get a wicket, but had the satisfaction of peppering two top batters and making them grit their teeth. But again, two Aussies showed how to tough it out, and I had to admire them.

Before the final Test in Adelaide, we again screwed up in the one-day series. We won the first of the three finals by six runs, an absolutely cracking game, but then fell apart in the next two. It was so frustrating. We were beginning to follow a predictable one-day pattern of winning the preliminary games, then folding when the pressure was really on. That had appeared the case ever since the World Cup in 1996. So that Adelaide Test was going to be a big test of our character and the Aussie press was happy to stoke up the hype. One newspaper headline said, 'And Now For Two Nil', and the Aussie players appeared to believe that as well. It was time for us to stand up and be counted.

I couldn't play, having strained a buttock muscle throwing the ball in one of the finals, and it was heartbreaking to see us come so close. We made good runs at good pace, then Shaun Pollock stuck his hand up and bowled sensationally in sapping heat to take seven for 89 in 41 overs, a fantastic effort. Hansie Cronje's declaration set them a target of 361 in 109 overs. He was convinced it was enough, that we could bowl them out, and we nearly did so. We got two early wickets, but then dropped Mark

Waugh four times. Then, in the seventh over of the final hour, Mark Waugh was even luckier. Pollock hit him on the elbow, the ball went to gully, where it was scooped up by Pat Symcox, who appealed for the catch. The batsman turned away, and as he did so, his bat dislodged the bails. We appealed for hit-wicket. The matter was referred to the third umpire, Steve Davis, who ruled that Waugh wasn't out, because the bails weren't dislodged in the act of taking a run or facing a ball. There was disagreement in the Channel Nine commentary box – Richie Benaud agreeing with the decision, Bill Lawry saying he was out – but the crucial element was that the sequence of play wasn't over when the bail was dislodged. The ball was still in the air, on its way to gully, when the bail was dislodged. We were shown endless TV replays in slow motion, but only one at normal speed. That was from sideways on and it looked as if everything had happened simultaneously. But we never saw that replay again. Why, I wonder? Was Channel Nine being rather too patriotic in its selection of replays? Hansie Cronje initially asked the umpire, Steve Randell to bring on the match referee, but he thought better of it. Mark Waugh said he didn't know if he was out or not, that his arm just went dead and he knew nothing else. Yet on the TV replays, you see him throwing back his head as if to say 'What have I done?' There was no doubt in my mind that Waugh was out, and the absence of that replay at normal speed made me even more suspicious.

They hung on for a draw after that, and when we came off the field, Hansie was furious. He walked past the umpire's door, and smashed a hole in it with a stump. I tried to calm him down, but he told me to 'F*** off'. And to make matters worse, Dave Richardson announced his retirement in the dressing-room. Dave had been with us since the start of our international comeback and he'd been very influential in my Test career. So no more 'Caught Richardson, bowled Donald' and there were a few tears shed in that dressing-room.

The bottom line about that Adelaide draw was that we dropped too many catches. Mark Waugh should have been out long before that controversial incident. Why were we not ramming home the advantage against Australia when we had them on the ropes? It was maddening. Steve Waugh had said before the three one-day Finals that he thought we were 'chokers', lacking the bottle to stay in the contest, and I was beginning to wonder if he had a point. I'd like to sit all of our guys down and ask why we don't handle the pressure consistently against Australia. Are we in awe of them? Are they just better than us and we know it subconsciously? Are they harder competitors? I wish I knew. We couldn't lay claim to any sort of high international standing until we could match Australia, blow for blow. I wonder if we are too full-on with our commitment, that we run out of steam. We are fit, disciplined and yet we fall at the big hurdle.

We were more than a match for Pakistan and Sri Lanka in a couple of short Test series at home after that Australian disappointment. Shaun Pollock emerged as a genuine Test all-rounder, and I bowled well against the Pakistanis at Port Elizabeth, when we won to square the series. They just disintegrated after winning a close Test at Durban by 29 runs. They seemed to stop playing once Wasim Akram was flown out after being earlier sacked as captain, then as a player. They clearly had morale problems, and we hammered them at Port Elizabeth. Against the Sri Lankans,

I took sixteen wickets in the two Tests, which were both won by us. I took my 200th Test wicket at Centurion Park, when Sanath Jayasuriya dragged one on. It was a marvellously fulfilling moment for me, because I rate Jayasuriya very highly, and it was a very nice feeling to look up to the South African dressing-room and see Bob Woolmer and all the boys applauding me. Now for another hundred more!

So we ended another hectic season of international cricket on a high note. I was certainly tired and a little worried about my ankle that I'd turned over in the footholds in the Sydney Test at the start of the year. It was to bother me for the rest of 1998. As for our status in world cricket – it was high, but ought to have been higher. We had picked up some invaluable experience over the past eighteen months of playing on different pitches, but a total of eleven Tests in the past six months was a lot, plus all the other one-dayers. Victory in Pakistan was the highlight, but at the back of my mind was the nagging feeling that we still weren't mentally strong enough. The next task was to start beating the big boys. The forthcoming England tour was the next stage in that process. It was to be a cruel reminder of our mental frailties.

CHAPTER SIXTEEN

Failure Against England

Losing the 1998 Test series 2–1 in England after being 1–0 up earlier ranks as one of the biggest disappointments of my career. Once again, we failed to carry the day when the chips were down. We could justifiably claim to have had the wrong end of some crucial umpiring decisions in the last two Tests that we lost, but I feel that the umpiring was a red herring. You get bad decisions wherever you play Test cricket, and the strong guys rise above them, and focus on what they can do to influence the match. We should have finished England off at Old Trafford in the third Test, but they escaped with a draw and after that they were rejuvenated, reprieved – and they played more positively than us. Once again, our batting failed when the pressure was on. Judged by the highest standards, we failed in England and no amount of bleating about bad luck can alter that fact. The hope was that we would eventually learn from that painful experience.

I began the series hoping to take at least 25 wickets. I reckoned that would mean at least a couple of five-wicket hauls in an innings, and therefore that could mean victories for us. I finished up with 33 wickets, and added to my reputation, but it didn't mean all that much to me because my team lost the series. We were all really up for victory in England. Just because England wasn't high in the international rankings didn't mean we would undervalue beating them. It was known as the home of cricket, but we felt that there was a lot of arrogance about the guys who run English cricket, who still think they have a major say in how world cricket is run. We love playing at Lord's, because it has a special atmosphere, but we don't think much of being told what to wear at Lord's, and that we can't fly our national flag over the dressing-room balcony. There was a huge desire to beat England, even though we get on very well with the players – it's English cricket that we wanted to beat, with all its stuffy conventions. It's on a par with beating Australia.

When we arrived in May, I thought it was the most focused South African tour party of my experience. We seemed to have got the Australian disappointment out of our system, and I sensed a collective desire to get at England straight away. At our last meeting in Johannesburg, the strategy had been talked through and it was made clear that the batsmen had to approach the series the Australian way. We had to score at around three an over, get 500 hundred if possible and expect to bat only once per Test. So the opposition bowlers had to be ground down, and then we needed to accelerate when they were demoralised. Every batsman was told his role. No one was to leave it subconsciously to the others, he had to want to play the major innings of the match. Darryl Cullinan was told to go out there and play his natural game, and so was Gerry Liebenberg – and, given Gerry's failures, it'll surprise many English fans that he is a naturally forcing batsman for Free State. Gary Kirsten was given licence to stay out there as the opener, gutsing it out while the others played with freedom. Everyone was told that he had to contribute with the bat, because the margin of victory or defeat could be just a handful of runs. That's what made our subsequent decline so hard to take. It came from our batting frailties, and it's not as if we hadn't talked and talked about our batting before the tour even started.

We also had some great technological aids available on that England tour, to help us study the opposition and eradicate any of our own technical faults. Bob Woolmer, our coach, has always been a fan of video aids, and on this tour he had it down to a fine art. Every night on tour, anyone could go to Bob's hotel room and look at the Super Slo-Mo on the video machine, where Bob would stop the action and point something out. He could say things like, 'That's why you're getting out – look at the angle of your bat' or 'Your foot's in the wrong position at the moment of delivery' and it was a very professional tool to have at our disposal. I remember being very grateful for it after the Old Trafford Test, when I'd been pleased at the way I'd bowled Graham Thorpe, operating around the wicket to the left-hander. I wanted to check my wrist action, because I'd got it right with that delivery. It was important to me to be able to check what I was doing right, so that I could maintain that standard for the rest of the series. So Bob Woolmer's video library was there to help you keep up the standard, as well as eradicate faults.

The Woolmer video machine certainly helped me out after the first Test, at Edgbaston where I bowled badly. There was a lot of talk during that Test that I was trying too hard on my home ground in England, and that's why my rhythm was poor, but I don't buy that. In fact, I felt very calm on that first morning, yet I sprayed it around all over the shop. I was either too short or too full in length, never in control of myself. I was subconsciously concerned about the ankle that I had damaged earlier in the year at Sydney, and perhaps that contributed to my feeling that I was off-balance. After that first day at Edgbaston, Barry Richards said I was flat at the crease, even though I'd been running in hard, while Bob Woolmer thought I was tearing in too quickly. I asked Bob for the tapes, so that I could watch them at home, just a couple of miles from the Edgbaston ground. Straight away, I saw how tired I looked, and my legs looked very heavy, without any spring. Tina watched it with me, and she said 'Have you thought about what the last heavy year has done to you?' I hadn't really, I thought I'd managed to recharge the batteries before this tour had begun. But clearly my body wasn't responding on that first day. I would have to be careful about maintaining my strength for the rest of this tour. Next morning, I got Mike Atherton with a beauty straight away, and my rhythm felt good for a time, but then I was horrible in the second innings, getting slapped by Alec Stewart, after bowling him too many half-volleys. There was work to be done before the next Test, at Lord's.

That Edgbaston Test was ruined by the weather on the last day, when either side had a chance of victory. For some reason, the England camp believed that the last day washout had saved South Africa from defeat, but I couldn't see why. We knew they were going to declare overnight, asking us to get around 290 in the day. A rate of just three an over was well within our sights, on what was still a good pitch, and they were a bowler short, after I'd broken Darren Gough's hand in the first innings. So why were

England favourites? I think that bluff was a sign of the new, positive England under Alec Stewart's captaincy. He had just taken over from Mike Atherton and was determined to fight fire with fire against us, even when it came to peddling a few distortions about how lucky we were that it rained at Edgbaston on that final day. We were fairly sure that we would soon have the measure of England, and it came in the next Test at Lord's.

We arrived at Lord's in a very positive frame of mind. We had an excellent team meeting in Nottingham, where everyone spoke frankly and positively. I admitted that not only had I bowled badly at Edgbaston, but the bowlers generally had let the side down. Darryl Cullinan thought I should have had more bowling out in the middle before Edgbaston, and he had a point. I certainly felt rusty as well as heavy-legged. But a session or two in front of the Woolmer video machine had helped sharpen up my mind, and I felt good. We were pleasantly surprised that England had picked Steve James to replace the injured Mark Butcher, because Lord's was a very difficult place for an England player to win his first cap, because the visitors are often inspired by the occasion and play above themselves. At our team meeting the night before, I said to the boys 'Steve James will be filling his pants. He's come out of the blue at short notice, he's in unfamiliar territory with all the pressure on him. What's more, he likes the ball on legside, and also wide on the off. We've got to be at him all the time, and deny him his favourite scoring areas'. That's exactly what we did, and the poor bloke looked out of his class.

Our batting really did us proud at Lord's, after a poor start. From 40 for four, Hansie Cronje and Jonty Rhodes rallied to make our best partnership of the tour, playing with aggression and bravery. Jonty made a hundred to add to his ninety-odd at Edgbaston, and his batting was a revelation. He had been out of the side for a year after a string of low scores, but he had the humility and intelligence to go back to school and work out where he was going wrong. Barry Richards worked with him in their home city of Durban, and the difference in Jonty was amazing. His weight transfer was suddenly so much better, so that he was getting into line far more quickly, enabling him to pull good-length balls. Jonty used to get caught on the crease, a real lbw candidate, and he was bowled far too often. I must admit I thought he was gone as a Test batsman, but he worked unbelievably hard at his new technique, capitalising on his quick footwork and fast hands. When he came to England, Jonty was very focused and pumped up, and I noticed how well he was playing in the nets. He was playing straighter than ever and giving the ball a real thump. I couldn't have been more pleased at the rehabilitation of Jonty Rhodes in this England series. He's a wonderful man, as good a bloke as he appears to all the autograph-hunters he always obliges. He puts us to shame the way he always helps people out, never complaining. He'll help unpack the kit from the team bus, because he hates to see people having to work on their own, he believes in helping anyone. That's an element of his Christianity, but he never talks about his beliefs, he just does kind things and sets a great example. He's wonderful with kids, a really caring man. On the field, he's not just a fantastic fielder, but a great team-man, never done shouting encouragement. Jonty Rhodes is the kind of guy who gives cricketers a good name. We were pleased that he soon became so popular in England, because he deserves that, he gives so much of himself to the game and to the fans all over the world.

After Jonty and Hansie had got us to a competitive total, I was bubbling over like a child and I couldn't wait to get out there to bowl. On the Friday night, I felt awesome, full of fire, overflowing with adrenalin. We had them 30 for three overnight, on a pitch that was quickening up, with good carry to the wicket-keeper. The conditions on the Saturday morning were perfect for us. It was overcast, yet muggy, so the ball swung as well as seamed around. We had some luck – a freak catch at short leg by Adam Bacher to get Graham Thorpe, and Mark Ramprakash looked to have got the wrong decision when he was adjudged caught at the wicket off me. Afterwards, Ramps got into trouble for a comment he made to the umpire, Darryl Hair when he was given out, and I can understand his frustration, although it's always a good idea to count to ten if you can. When the incident happened, I thought it was a clear edge and saw no problem with the decision. It definitely touched something, and in the heat of a Test match, you go up for the appeal. Later, watching the TV replays, it looked as if Ramps was unlucky, that the ball clipped his arm. I said as much that night in the press conference. It wasn't a case of me having a go at Darryl Hair, more a recognition that these things happen, but Dr Ali Bacher wasn't pleased at my comments. He rang me up at the hotel next morning, told me to avoid criticising any umpires and to leave all such comments to the captain in private, in his match report. I honestly wasn't trying to undermine the umpire, merely pointing out to the press that we're all human beings and prone to mistakes, but Dr Bacher was very touchy.

On the way to taking five wickets for South Africa in the one-day international against India, Calcutta 1991 – our first appearance back in international cricket after a gap of 21 years.

Sydney, 1992, and the World Cup semi-final against England. What a way to go out, courtesy of that rain regulation!

The historic Test match at Barbados, 1992. Our first Test since 1970 and we should have won it.

Fitness work at the Kensington Oval, Barbados, 1992.

Three influential men of South African cricket – from left, Dr Ali Bacher, Clive Rice and Mike Procter.

Celebrating our 1994 Lord's Test victory with one of the great characters I have known, Fanie de Villiers.

South Africa v United Arab Emirates, World Cup 1996, Rawalpindi – and the moment I thought I'd killed their captain, Sultan Zarawani. He should have worn a helmet, though.

The fifth Test, England v South Africa, Cape Town, 1996, and the victorious South African side that has just beaten England to take the series.

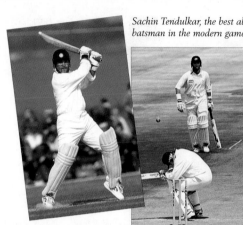

Sachin Tendulkar, the best all-round batsman in the modern game.

Giving Australia's Mark Taylor the treatment at Centurion Park, 1997.

Bowling Steve Waugh in one-day international at Bloemfontein, 1997. My joyous reaction tells you how much I respect this particular batsman.

A mixture of emotions in the South African players' area during the Brisbane Test of 1998.

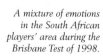

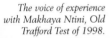

*onty Rhodes – spectacular
ut also brilliant. He has
een marvellous for my
areer.*

*The voice of experience
with Makhaya Ntini, Old
Trafford Test of 1998.*

*With Darryl Cullinan and
Hansie Cronje as we bond
during the South African
national anthem.*

*I'm in need of running repairs on
my knee during the 1998 Edgbaston Test.
Throughout my career, touch wood,
I've been free from serious injury.*

My mother, Francina, dad Stewart, daughter Hannah and my sister, Melloney.

My wife, Tina has been a rock during my career after we met on my very first day in Birmingham, way back in 1987.

Steve Tshwete, South African Sports Minister, looks on as our President, Nelson Mandela presents me with a medal to acknowledge my contribution to South African sport, August 1997.

The Edgbaston Test of 1998, and I get one over on a great opponent, Mike Atherton. I always had to earn his wicket.

England v South Africa, second Test, Lord's 1998, and I'm very close to dissent after registering my dismay that Nasser Hussain had survived an appeal for caught behind. I was out of order here in my reactions.

Getting a lucky lbw decision against Mike Atherton in the 1998 Leeds Test, when he got a big inside edge onto his pad.

I'm ecstatic after capturing Brian Lara's wicket in the first Test against West Indies, November 1998.

A disastrous run out in the final over means that Australia are through to the final of the 1999 World Cup at our expense. I dropped my bat and had no hope of regaining the crease.

Bowling Mike Atherton for nought in the first over of the 1999/2000 series at The Wanderers. His was the wicket I prized the most.

Explaining to the cameras why I'd decided to continue my international career.

Little did he realise that a few weeks later, we'd be even more provoked by umpiring errors. But I could see Dr Bacher's point. He's very passionate about South Africa doing well, has always supported me greatly, but likes our image to be right as well. Dr Bacher is not the sort of man to upset, so I took my bollocking from him, and then got on with the job of bowling England out a few hours later.

Everything went our way on that Sunday, and we bowled them out cheaply, to win by ten wickets. The atmosphere on the field was very tense and competitive, something I'd noticed from day one of the series. Alec Stewart had made it quite clear that under his captaincy, England would be more aggressive than under Mike Atherton and would give as good as they got on the field. So tempers were in danger of boiling over at various stages throughout the series. That was fine by us, we South Africans thrive on adrenalin and being over-competitive, but it was obvious that England were more inclined to that than in our last series against them. So there was a lot going on out there in the middle at Lord's, when we were chipping away at their batsmen. I almost boiled over when I was convinced that Nasser Hussain had been caught behind. I admit I made a fuss, and the tension and state of the match can't be offered by me as excuses. I just lost it for a moment, and by the standards of recent fines by the ICC, it was a clear case of dissent, liable to a fine. I got away with it, though, possibly because I apologised right away to the umpire, and did the same again at lunchtime. It may also be that my previous record had saved me, because I haven't been known as someone who throws all the toys out of the cot when a decision goes against me. Later, Alec Stewart was also guilty of dissent, because after he was given out, caught behind, he stood at the crease, looking amazed, then walked slowly off, shaking his head. I was at cover, heard a clear nick, and couldn't understand why he was so annoyed at the decision. On the way back to the pavilion, he paused several times to look at the replay on the giant screen, each time shaking his head. If that wasn't dissent, I don't know what is. There's a big difference between disappointment and dissent, and here he was prolonging his public disagreement with the decision, undermining the umpire's authority. But he got away with it, whereas Ramprakash got punished for a spontaneous outburst, offered in the heat of the moment.

Anyway, we weren't bothered about Stewart's attitude. He was out, and soon the rest of them fell apart, as we blew them away on an ideal wicket for our seam attack. We'd beaten them by ten wickets, having scored just 360 in our first innings. It was the second time in a row that we'd won the Lord's Test, always a special feeling in front of so many knowledgeable cricket lovers. There's no doubt that the opposition raises its game at Lord's, because the support for England is muted. It's almost like going to the theatre at Lord's, because the crowd are mainly experts, lovers of the game who are there to see good cricket, whoever plays it. So the England players feel they don't get the support they need and I can sympathise with them. You'd get really partisan home support at Newlands, Johannesburg or the Sydney Cricket Ground, whereas England only get it at certain grounds like Edgbaston or Headingley. So we had a definite advantage playing at Lord's, and it showed in our positive display, especially after starting so badly in our first innings. So we were absolutely flying as a unit after going 1–0 up in the series, and I was beginning to believe that we were gelling together nicely. Looking back, that was the high spot of the tour for us. The rest was an anti-climax, leading to bitter disappointment.

We really should have killed off England in the next Test, at Old Trafford. They were there for the taking after three days. We'd batted first, racked up a big score, and had them seven down for very little on the Saturday night. They'd batted badly, with little heart, and looked out for the count, certain to follow on. With two days left, there seemed no escape for England. The England supporters booed their players on that Saturday night, and although that's not something you really want to hear – there ought to be some respect for an international cricketer – we knew that sort of reception could demoralise England. To be fair to England's players, they showed a lot of guts in their second innings, to blunt our attack, and they got away with it on the final evening, with Angus Fraser blocking out my final over. Fair play to Gus, he was his usual gutsy, determined self, even if he had little idea where the ball was going, but we should have wrapped it up long before that.

There were certain factors at Old Trafford that told against us. Shaun Pollock missed the Test through injury, and Lance Klusener broke down with ankle ligament trouble that put him out of the tour. Klusener had impressed with his pace and aggression so far in the series, and I'm convinced that he would have kept his fire when they followed on, and would have been the ideal foil for me. Jacques Kallis, who also had bowled well so far, tweaked a hamstring, and couldn't operate at full throttle on that final afternoon, so we were down to the bare bones – myself, Makhaya Ntini, who was just a rookie paceman, and Paul

Adams, whose left-arm spin was negated by the slow pitch. That wicket was desperately slow, unsuited to Test cricket. Before the match, I thought it would break up, and England obviously thought so, because they played two spinners, Robert Croft and Ashley Giles. But the sun never really came out over the five days, and the pitch didn't deteriorate at all.

Afterwards, we were criticised for scoring our runs too slowly over the first couple of days, and for not being attacking enough in the field. I could concede the first point, we did occupy the crease until the third morning, when perhaps the Australians would have cracked on late on the second day, with a view to having a bowl at the opposition before the second day was out. As for the field-placing, Hansie Cronje had three slips in for most of Saturday, and he ended up with seven cheap wickets, enforcing the follow-on next morning. Perhaps we were subconsciously sure that it would come our way when they followed on, because they looked demoralised. We got two quick wickets, and even though we were held up a long time by Mike Atherton and Alec Stewart, victory would surely be ours sometime on the final day. On that Sunday night, Hansie was besieged by phone calls from back home from people he knew in the game, giving him advice on field-settings, and I could tell he was getting fed up with guys who were sat in front of the television sets, unaware of the subtleties involved. It didn't help Hansie's peace of mind when Clive Rice came into our dressing-room that evening to give his views on the field-placing. I know for a fact that Ricey would not have stood for that if he'd been captain, and he ought to have kept his thoughts to himself unless asked for them, even though he was one of our selectors. There is a time and a place for such things.

Yet it all seemed to be going our way on the final morning when Atherton, of all people, got himself out, mishooking to long leg. That was a major obstacle removed, because we were concerned about a repeat of Johannesburg '95. Now we thought that Mark Ramprakash was the only remaining problem, even though Stewart was playing so well. Stewart is such a free player that even though he can cane any attack, he still gives you a chance, whereas Ramprakash has a tight Test Match game, and the best technique of all the English batters, with the temperament to bat for long periods. Yet Stewart was still there at lunch, clearly intent on saving his side, and keeping them in the series. We didn't want another Captain Courageous effort, to deny us a Test victory we deserved. During the interval, Pat Symcox said to me, 'Why don't you start niggling at Stewart? Tell him if he plays one silly hook shot, that's the end of England and the whole series. Get under his skin, keep chirping at him!' Typical Symcox, but it made sense. Stewart's not the sort of character like Atherton, who just smiles and keeps chugging along. Stewart would mix it, he wouldn't turn the other cheek. So we gave him some stick after lunch. I said to him, 'Now there's a man out for the hook, don't f*** it up now!' and he answered 'Sorry – can you speak up?', so I said 'You heard me – don't f*** it up!' That was encouraging, we were getting a reaction from him, his concentration would surely be wavering after being at the crease for so long. Lance Klusener, who loves a chirrup, shouted 'Ah! That's nice to hear! The captain of England can actually say something!' and a few of the other boys started to join in. 'Careful, Stewie – the whole country depends on you – but there's no pressure on you!' Stewart wouldn't duck the confrontation and was happy to answer back. I went round the wicket to him, giving him the bait of the short ball, knowing he'd go for it at some stage, as we got under his skin. Finally, he fetched a wide one around to deep square leg and we had him. A few of our guys shouted at him, 'Thanks very much – you've just lost the match and the series' and you could see his anguish as he walked away. It appeared as if he agreed with us. That was a great passage of play, full of challenge and tension and we had come out on top.

The verbal aggression didn't work so well with Ramprakash, try as I might. Every time he played a defensive stroke, I'd shout 'Great block!', but he wasn't riled. Finally, I had him lbw second ball after tea, and then I got the injured Thorpe out quickly, unable to play defensively because of his bad back. Dominic Cork and Ashley Giles came and went quickly, and then at the start of my last spell, I had Darren Gough fending a short one to short leg. That left Robert Croft and Angus Fraser standing between us and victory. Croft doesn't fancy the short ball, as Australia's Glenn McGrath proved the previous year, and surely it was just a matter of time. Hansie Cronje came to me for one last heave: 'I hate to do this to you again, I know you're tired, but I have to push on your button'. I really was gone. The absence of Klusener and Kallis from our attack meant I had far exceeded my quota of overs and my tank was running on empty. It was such a flat, dead wicket that it was a huge effort to flog some life out of it. Also, my ankle was troubling me again. I had to switch ends, and bowl into the breeze, because the footholds were better at that end, but it wasn't ideal and I was struggling. But I gave it my all, and that made the last few minutes even more shattering.

I was to bowl the last over at Gus Fraser, and the equation was simple. Hansie said, 'You've got six balls to win us the match. He'll be looking to block you by going forward'. For the first few deliveries, I pitched it short and hit him on the forearm guard, the gloves and the chest, but couldn't get the fend-off to the close field. For the fifth ball, I decided on the yorker, even though I knew he'd be ready for it. Now in the first innings, Gus had been given out, lbw, when the ball was clearly going down legside. It was a shocking decision, the sort the number eleven batsman often gets, because the umpire wants to get off the field for a time, and you just know a front-line batsman wouldn't get one like that. So when I whistled the yorker through Gus' forward prod in that last over, I thought, 'That'll do', and roared out the appeal. Not out. I couldn't believe it. If he was out first innings, he was definitely out second time around. Looking at the TV replay later, it was a good decision, but I didn't think it at the time. My heart sank to my toes. I felt so deflated as we crawled off the pitch. Three days of blood and guts in the field, and nothing to show for it.

When that umpire's decision went Fraser's way, I looked up at the England balcony and saw Alec Stewart dancing around with joy, punching the air, and that made it worse. He then ran onto the pitch and hugged Croft and Fraser as if they'd won the match. The noise and celebrations coming out of the England dressing-room were totally out of proportion, when you consider we had outplayed them for the entire Test. Credit to them for showing the guts to crawl out of the hole, but you were only talking about five of their guys – Stewart, Atherton, Ramprakash, Croft and Fraser. The rest of their eleven ought to have been taking a long, hard look at their efforts. I felt so angry that we hadn't won. I grabbed a beer in the dressing-room, and said to Shaun Pollock 'Isn't this horribly familiar?' For Old Trafford '98, read Johannesburg '95, and for that matter, Adelaide '98, when Mark Waugh escaped that hit-wicket decision and Australia scraped a draw. It was happening too often for comfort. Shaun said, 'Thank God it wasn't Atherton again', but to me it was worse – we were defied by two tail-enders. I had six balls at Fraser and couldn't finish him off. I wouldn't offer my fatigue and the dead pitch as an excuse. I had failed. On the coach back to our hotel, I said to our wicket-keeper, Mark Boucher, 'I just hope we don't live to regret this, because so far we've got very little to show on this tour for working our butts off'. Prophetic words, as it turned out. That Old Trafford draw bugged me every single day for the rest of the tour. I'm convinced that if we had won there, then England would have slipped down the plughole, and we might have won the series 4–0. Instead we lost it 2–1.

So we came to Trent Bridge for the fourth Test, determined to make amends, and encouraged by the wholesale changes made by England. I couldn't believe they'd made four changes, to me that didn't exactly encourage stability, it was almost as if the selectors were agreeing that they'd been lucky to escape with a draw after playing badly. That's how we saw it. We were surprised they gave a first cap in the circumstances to Andy Flintoff. Obviously they were taking a chance that he'd play a dominating innings, because he was a big hitter, but he was very inexperienced. I thought Ben Hollioake would be a better selection, even though he was out of form, because he had more class. The return of Graeme Hick made sense. He was making runs for Worcestershire, and we couldn't work out why he wasn't in the side, especially when you recall how he hammered us in that hundred at Centurion Park at the start of the 1995/96 series. When he's going well, Hicky blocks it hard off the middle of the bat and it pings away to the boundary. A very dangerous player, but too often you can tell from his facial expression and body language that he's scared of getting out. If England had told him to go out at Trent Bridge and just look to dominate, then we could be in for some punishment from Hicky. They'd also brought back Ian Salisbury, the leg-spinner, into a team that was full of attacking intent, reflecting the desperate position England found themselves in the series. Yet we weren't worried about Salisbury, because we felt he bowls at least two bad ones per over. Our batters would just wait for them and pick him off. Hansie Cronje had come out very well from his recent duels with Shane Warne and Muttiah Muralitharan, so he was unlikely to be bothered about Salisbury. As it turned out, Hansie got a hundred at Trent Bridge and his premeditated assault on Salisbury put him out of the England tour to Australia later in the year.

We had a very positive team meeting on the eve of the Trent Bridge Test, in which we all agreed that we had made it difficult for ourselves by failing to win at Old Trafford, and that we just had to go and do the hard work all over again. Yet I had a nagging feeling about our mental strength. I like to look around a room and try to assess who fancies the pressure. I can usually tell by looking into the fellow's eyes, seeing if there's any doubt, and I was worried that some doubts were beginning to creep in, and whether there were going to be some negative vibes over the next few days. Quite rightly, Alec Stewart was working hard to talk up England's great escape in his media statements, saying that we were now the side under pressure, because we knew we should have nailed them down. In our case, we'd have done the same and Stewart was justified in trying to out-psyche us. He was far better at all that stuff than Atherton, his bristling aggression was just what England needed at the time. It was time for some 'up-and-at-'em' stuff from England and he was the ideal captain for that. Yet we should have seen them off, we allowed ourselves to get sucked into some very careless cricket at Trent Bridge.

We should have made more than 374, after being put in on a slow wicket. Angus Fraser bowled really well, hitting the indentations on the pitch, making it go sideways, but apart from him, the England attack wasn't exactly threatening. After Hansie had made an excellent hundred, somebody ought to have organised the lower order batting and given us a total of around five hundred, but too many bottled out, getting themselves out sloppily. Then England did well to get to within 38 of our first innings score. That's what they needed to do, so that they could put pressure on us when we batted again, and it worked for them. Mark Ramprakash blocked for a long time, while wickets fell at the other end, but when he was left with the tail, he played some good shots. That's what we needed from one of our batters. When we went in again, our batsmen queued up to get themselves out. Hansie Cronje chased a wide one, Darryl Cullinan clipped to square leg, Shaun Pollock played a poor shot and Steve Elworthy also got himself out when playing well. It was almost as if the batters thought someone else would come in and play the innings to save the game for us, but England just plugged away in the field, waiting for us to get out. It was diabolical. Jonty Rhodes got the worst decision of the series when he was adjudged caught behind. He was nowhere near it, and to make it worse, he copped a big send-off from Stewart, Mark Butcher and Dominic Cork when he left the crease. Jonty said when he came into the dressing-room that he had deliberately played late at the ball, in case he'd got a little scratch on it, and he was astonished to be given out. I could then see the nerves start to prey on some of our guys. Gloves were being thrown around in anger, there were a few swear words, and some started looking to blame the umpires for the clatter of wickets. We needed to sit down and say 'Look, we're batting like prats, get your heads down, every run counts'. We ought to have been told that by Hansie or Bob Woolmer before the innings started, but no one managed to focus our batters on the next stage of the game – batting England out of the game. Instead, we were dismissed for 208, a shocking effort in the circumstances. We had given England a great chance now, and I was furious.

They needed 242 to win, and Hansie spoke to us before we went out. He said our batting had been appalling, and that we needed two quick wickets to be back in the game that night. We had to bowl tight, squeeze the batsmen and hope that they'd be as careless as us. Butcher and Atherton started positively, but they didn't get off to the flier that finished us off at the Oval in '94. When Pollock had Butcher caught behind, I felt we were entering a decisive phase of the Test. We had to get Atherton that night. What followed was the best duel I've ever had with a batsman over a prolonged period. I've had some great scraps with the Waugh brothers over a short amount of time, but this one with Atherton was 40 minutes of absolute commitment and great determination from Atherton. Plus a huge slice of luck when he got reprieved by the umpire.

Just before I started my second spell, I felt in my bones that the game would be decided by the next few overs. I needed to get the adrenalin flowing right from the off. I followed the philosophy of Alan Jones, knowing that I had to take responsibility, not leaving it to the others. But the rest of the boys needed to be fired up. I shouted over to Mark Boucher, our wicket-keeper that the boys looked a little flat, so he needed to keep us all pumped up. I said, 'I don't want you to shut up for the rest of this day. I want to hear you gee me up after every ball, get in the batsmen's ears'. It felt right from the first over of that new spell, even though Nasser Hussain let the ball go. I told Hansie Cronje that the sparks were going to fly. They certainly did.

For my next over, to Atherton, I went round the wicket after one ball. The first delivery from the new angle got him – or so I thought. It was a short one, Atherton gloved it to the keeper, and I ran past him in triumph to the boys behind the stumps. But Atherton stayed put. I didn't attach any significance to that, perhaps he was just disappointed. We both knew he'd gloved it. But then I saw the frozen look on the faces of the guys in the slips. 'This can't be true' I thought. I looked at umpire Steve Dunne in disbelief, saw Hansie Cronje smiling sarcastically at Atherton. I thought 'I'll kill him', I was absolutely seething. I said to Atherton 'You better be f****** ready for what's coming, because there'll be nothing in your half'. He didn't say anything, he knew there'd be some short, fast stuff coming up.

Walking back to my mark, I slowed myself down deliberately, telling myself not to get carried away. 'Don't let him get away now, you've got him', I told myself. The crowd was really pumped up now, they sensed something special was happening, my team-mates were roaring out encouragement, and Atherton looked very isolated. Next ball, he inside edged me for four, when he could easily have played on. I gave him a long look, and called him a 'f****** cheat' – in English, not in Afrikaans. Atherton said after the match that he couldn't understand a word I was saying to him out in the middle, because it was all in Afrikaans, but I wouldn't be so stupid to do that, I wanted him to understand what I was saying to him. It was important around that time to keep calm, to get the ball in the right spot. I was sure I'd get Atherton if I kept taking deep breaths. I didn't feel tired at all, because I'd never experienced such an adrenalin rush, with the crowd pulling me to the crease in my run-up. I knew I'd get tired at some stage, so I just had to make each ball count. Atherton was getting the big staring treatment from me, but he wasn't to be distracted. He was again lucky when he spliced a short one from me into the fine leg area, and that annoyed me, because I had thought about putting a fielder back for just that mistimed shot. It was all going Atherton's way, despite my speed, hostility and the baying of the crowd. Somehow, I managed to block out the crowd, except when I was at the top of my run-up, breathing in deeply, trying to stay calm. I was in such a zone that it was a case of him or me.

Atherton's partner, Nasser Hussain was irrelevant to me during that period. But then I faced up to him after Atherton had taken almost every ball so far from me. Off the first delivery to Hussain, I thought I had him caught behind, but then instinctively I realised I was wrong. I smiled at Hussain, he smiled back and I told him 'It's bit hot out here'. I was loving the battle, the competitive struggle, but I needed a wicket to keep my adrenalin surging. The next ball was nicked by Hussain for a regulation catch to the keeper, Mark Boucher, and I ran down the wicket, shouting 'Catch!' But it rushed onto Boucher, and he fumbled it. On the TV replay, I later saw Jacques Kallis running towards me from second slip in triumph and Darryl Cullinan getting out of Boucher's way at first slip. If Jacques had stayed where he was, he'd have pouched the rebound, but he was certain that the keeper would take the nick and was too keen to get to me. I stood there, dumbstruck, and shouted 'No!' as loud as I could. Eventually, I turned round, walked slowly back to my mark, telling myself, 'Relax – you're furious, but don't give him a free ball to hit now'. Boucher was shattered, I've never seen such disappointment on a player's face. At the end of the over, I took my place at fine leg, with the crowd going berserk all around me. I suddenly realised how awful poor Mark must be feeling, so I ran up to him, patted him on the backside and said 'You've got to stay with us now – hang in there, don't lose your focus', but he went into his shell after that, and didn't give us the vocal support we needed. Understandable really, it was a bad miss and he knew it. A wicket then and we might have surged on against new batting. Atherton couldn't bat at both ends.

Hussain and Atherton survived till the close. That night, I thought we'd lost it, although Hansie thought we could still do it next day, if I was fresh enough. But I was feeling very low after watching every ball on the video in Bob Woolmer's room. I said, 'Why is it always me? I don't know if I can come up with a spell like that one tomorrow', and I admit I was feeling sorry for myself. Hansie told me 'You're the only guy who can do it for us', and although I said I'd heard that from him often enough, he told me that it comes with the territory of being rated as the world's number one bowler. I was depressed, my ankle was sore and I simply didn't know how I was going to get fired up for the next morning. But I eventually realised that my responsibility was with my players, who expected me to come roaring in again. I wouldn't let them down, and somehow my first ball at eleven o'clock next morning would be as fast and straight as possible.

Next morning, I had another cortisone injection in my ankle, and kept telling myself in the warm-ups that I had to be as fired up as the night before. They still needed another 137 to win, with nine wickets left, and a quick wicket would expose one end. But Hussain was tight, and Atherton was just Atherton. Eventually, I got Hussain but then Alec Stewart came in and really laced into us. They raced home to win by eight wickets, which was a distortion, but the fact is that we had thrown away the Test. I sat in the dressing-room for ages, thinking about how we had failed to win at Old Trafford, and it still bugged me. Atherton came to see me, saying he wanted to share a beer with me, and we chatted amicably enough for a while. He knew he'd gloved it, and we had a laugh about the fallibility of umpires. He said 'What would you have done?' and I said I wouldn't have walked either. I had no problems with Athers. I admired the guts he showed and the way he brazened it out. He was out there, batting for his country, and perfectly entitled to stand his ground if the decision went his way. Throughout our duel, he never said a word, just stared back at me, even when I shouted at him 'Come on! I've got you in my pocket!' He knew that if we'd got through him that Sunday night, England might have easily lost, because some of the later batsmen wouldn't have relished the pressure as much as Athers. In the end, Athers and I had a good laugh together, especially when I asked him for the offending glove as a prize for my benefit the next year. He even signed it – wonder what price it will fetch. I won't be bidding for it!

At the end of the Test, I went home to Birmingham for a few days' rest, hoping that my ankle would recover in time for the deciding Test at Leeds the following week. The tendon injury was coming and going, it was just below the lateral side of the left ankle. I knew that eventually I would need surgery, but hoped that I'd get through at Leeds. A few days before the Headingley Test, I had even more important things on my mind. I faced a ban from the match itself. It was all very innocent on my part, stemming from a complete misunderstanding. Merv Kitchen had been quoted in the *Daily Telegraph* by one of their writers, Simon Hughes, to the effect that he'd had a bad game at Trent Bridge, and he was wondering if he was up to it at Test level anymore. I assumed that Merv had gone on the record and that his words were taken from a press conference. When you've grabbed a precious few days off with your family, and you're worried about your sore ankle and depressed about the defeat at Trent Bridge, you tend not to read too many papers, so I didn't know that Merv Kitchen's remarks were made to Simon Hughes in the car park at Nottingham before he drove home. I'd seen Merv's reaction at the medals ceremony, when he grabbed his medal and scuttled away, looking very downcast. He knew he'd had a horrible Test, but that can happen to anyone, and I felt sorry for Merv. I've had great respect for him as an umpire since I'd first played county cricket in 1987. He'd been a fine umpire, strict but fair, who had put me in my place a couple of times, and quite right too. So that was the background to my live interview on BBC Radio at Chelmsford on the Sunday before the Leeds Test. I was asked for my reaction to Merv's comments in the paper, and I responded honestly, believing that he had willingly gone public. I said it was common knowledge that Merv had had a shocker at Trent Bridge, that I was sorry to hear he was thinking of standing down from international cricket, but it's all about pressure at the highest level, and how to deal with it. It might have sounded insensitive, but I was speaking on behalf of all international cricketers, who have suffered from umpiring errors. Merv had fronted up publicly, so what was wrong with me agreeing with him? I soon realised I might be in trouble when Gerald de Kock, of SABC Radio, sitting alongside me during the interview, said to me straight afterwards, 'Who's going to pay your fine?' Then one of our reporters came to me, saying 'Allan, I've just written down what you said on the radio, told my editor and he said I'd better check it out with you'. I read what he'd written down and told him that was the gist of it. What was wrong with commenting on what Merv himself had said publicly? Next day, Simon Hughes came to me and said 'I think I've got you in trouble'. So my build-up to the Leeds Test was going to be hampered by uncertainty about my part in the game. I was summoned to see the match referee on the day before the Leeds Test was due to start.

I was given a very fair hearing by Judge Ebrahim, a

Zimbabwean lawyer. He allowed me to explain the background to my comments, and my misunderstanding of Merv Kitchen's remarks. Then, after listening patiently, Judge Ebrahim said, 'I'm going to make an example of you', and I thought, 'Oh, no – I'm going to cop a suspension'. But then he said, 'Allan, you're a very nice guy, we all know that. You've apologised profusely, this is your first offence, so I'm only going to fine you'. He warned me about doing any interviews on the subject and I came out of that meeting, relieved, with a big smile on my face.

So now I had to get my head around the Leeds Test. One big push needed from us all now. We had a long team meeting in our hotel the night before, and a lot was said about being ready for England to come at us very hard. They'd been aggressive at Trent Bridge and it worked, so they'd be up for the same here. There had been a few niggles building up between the sides during the series, so we should expect a lot of tension over the next few days and we mustn't back down. I looked across at big Brian McMillan, who was brought back for his first Test of the series and he was very quiet, not even having a beer. Despite his apparent confidence and bristling aggression, 'Big Mac' was never the most positive of players. He seemed to worry a lot about his performances and he only bowled well when he was getting runs. A mood player, Big Mac. We needed his big-match experience and competitiveness at Leeds, and I hoped he was in the right frame of mind for the challenge ahead. I really couldn't be sure, though. Next morning, there was hardly a word spoken on the coach on its way to Headingley. Everyone was lost in their own thoughts. The tension was obvious when we got into our dressing-room at the ground. Bob Woolmer was very annoyed at the cramped quarters and threw his clothes angrily on the floor. He shouted 'Come on! Get out there now for fielding practice!' but after a good session, he was more relaxed. Hansie had a quiet word with us, and then I repeated what I'd said the night before at the team meeting: 'If we lose the toss on a flat wicket, we must still expect to bowl them out for 220'. We did lose the toss, they decided to bat first and standing in the tunnel just before we went out onto the pitch, it was just like going out to play in a big rugby match. Tension crackled through the air, as we huddled together, leaving England's two openers to feel isolated. We all shouted, 'Come on, let's stick it up them!' loud enough so that the openers could hear us. Game on!

We did very well to bowl them out for 230, and without Butcher's century, they would have been in a real mess. I didn't bowl all that well, but the rest of the guys chipped in, especially Makhaya Ntini. That night, at our team meeting, we agreed that we must look to bat just once, get past 400, and then squeeze England. I looked around the guys and wondered yet again who really fancied it at this stage of a hard series. Were some of the batters going to leave it to someone else? We soon found out. Getting bowled out for 252 wasn't good enough, even if some of the umpiring decisions went against us. A Pakistani called Javed Akhtar was standing in this Test, alongside Peter Willey. He had come to Leeds out of season, with hardly any match practice. He'd stood in a rain-affected second XI match at Uxbridge the week before, and that was it. That was wrong. He ought to have stood in at least one county match, to get the feel of it all out in the middle. There was also a bit of history between South Africa and Javed Akhtar, dating back to the Test series the year before. Pat Symcox and

Brian McMillan had given him a lot of abuse for some poor decisions, and they were rightly disciplined for severe dissent. Our boys clearly didn't think too much of him, and Javed Akhtar wouldn't have been human if he hadn't stored those incidents away in his memory. I'm not saying he was biased, but some of his decisions at Leeds were very influential. There were even media rumours going round that his hearing wasn't very good! In our first innings, he gave me out lbw, after nicking Angus Fraser onto my pad. It was a very loud nick, and I was amazed to be given out. I turned round, walked off the field, determined not to show any dissent, because I knew I was walking a tightrope after my comments about Merv Kitchen. I was booed by the fans on the Western Terrace as I walked out to bat and cheered when I left, after offering my bat to them, giving a heavy hint that I'd hit the ball.

Mike Atherton was the next to suffer from Javed Akhtar's raised finger. On the Sunday morning, when we needed quick wickets, he nicked me onto his pads, but that didn't stop me from going up with the lbw shout. After Atherton's lucky escape at Trent Bridge, I had no qualms about appealing for anything, but I must admit I was surprised to get this one. It was a clear sound, definite wood. The bad umpiring decisions were beginning to multiply amid unbelievable tension. Mark Ramprakash had been done in the first innings, when TV replays had clearly shown that the ball had bounced just before being caught by Mark Boucher. Ramps was very unhappy about that, but after being disciplined at Lord's for bad-mouthing Darryl Hair, he had to swallow his medicine. But that didn't stop him handing out some choice verbals when he was in the field, and he got anywhere near our batsmen. And we weren't slow at handing it out, either. Things were coming to the boil, with no one prepared to give ground.

On the Saturday night, after Nasser Hussain had played a fantastic innings, I felt that I'd finally hit the wall. I sat in the bath, feeling very flat. We were in danger of throwing away yet another Test through careless batting, and I felt I had nothing left to give. I told our assistant coach, Corrie van Zyl 'I've gone, finished, there's nothing left' and Corrie's answer was brutal. 'I hate to say this to you, but tomorrow you've got to get out there and do it one more time'. I went to bed very early, and woke up feeling better, but still subdued. We got an immediate boost when Shaun Pollock got the nightwatchman, Ian Salisbury out in the first over. That boosted me. I'd heard the Yorkshire blokes abusing me behind my back when I was fielding down at fine leg, and told myself I'd quieten them down. I decided to go round the wicket to Nasser Hussain, and the first ball went through at chest height. That felt better. I shouted 'Yeah! Come on!' and the whole team got behind me. I got Hick and Flintoff out in the same over, with slower deliveries. I was particularly pleased with the Hick dismissal. I told Hansie to make extra cover hang back a bit, because he wouldn't expect the slower ball so early in his innings. I was sure he was determined to play his shots and would be looking to drive. The slower ball worked a treat and as he played it uppishly, I jumped in the air with delight. I knew that Gary Kirsten was about to catch it. In the celebrations, I offered a quiet word of thanks to Franklyn Stephenson for teaching me how to bowl that slower one when he played for Free State.

Shaun Pollock and I breezed through England that morning. They lost their last eight wickets for just 36 and I was proud that we'd answered Hansie's call before the start of play. 'This is the biggest session you'll play in your career' he told us, and we knew we had to strike back hard that morning. As we came off the field, I was given the honour of leading off the team, not just because I'd taken five wickets, but because it was obviously my last Test in England. My family and many of my friends were there to see it, and the reception given to me by the England supporters was marvellous. I waved to them all, and felt very gratified that I'd managed to keep going for that one final push. Now we had a great chance to win. Just 216 needed, with the sun out, drying the pitch, so that it would be playing better than at any stage in the game. If we could manage to get to lunch without losing any wickets, we would be in with a great chance.

Poor Gerry Liebenberg didn't make it, though. Just to cap a miserable series, he was given out lbw by Javed Akhtar when he knocked the cover off the ball. We heard a big nick when we were outside watching the game, and it looked even worse on the TV replay. The nick was loud, the deviation clear, so why was he out? Gerry is a devout Christian, but that didn't stop him from cursing and swearing when he got back to the dressing-room and his helmet and bat also bounced off the wall. Soon, we were in deep trouble at 27 for five. Some bad shots were played, and Hansie Cronje was so sure he hadn't nicked his one that he walked away with a smile on his face, a subtle form of dissent. But everyone was appealing for anything throughout this match, because we had lost confidence in the umpires, particularly Javed Akhtar. On the first morning, our guys were convinced that Butcher had gloved me down the legside to the keeper, but he survived. That set the tone for the rest of the match, it was a case of every man for himself. And things were getting very heated between a few players. Brian McMillan and Dominic Cork had taken a real dislike to each other and they squared up as they were walking off the field at the tea interval. We all thought Cork was just a big showpony, who didn't like the verbals when directed at him. He was all talk, and nowhere near as good a bowler as he thought. We still hadn't forgotten the send-off he'd given Jonty Rhodes in the previous Test at Trent Bridge, so we were all waiting for Cork. When Big Mac told Cork that he talked more than he could think, Cork responded with 'Yeah, big nose – let's see how you go after tea'. That made it even more disappointing after tea, when Cork suckered Big Mac out. He'd been blocking solidly, while Jonty played superbly and they'd got us back in the game with a magnificent partnership of over a hundred. Cork came on, made a big show of putting a man out for the mis-hook, and after ducking a couple of them Mac fell for the bait, hook line and sinker. I couldn't believe a man of his experience getting conned out by a blusterer like Cork. In their second innings, Cork had been hit on the elbow by Ntini, and he pranced around as if his arm had dropped off. He couldn't stop bellyaching and shouted, 'We'll see, Goughy, what they're like when they have to bat on this!' It was laughable, and I walked past him, telling him he was just a big baby. He then told me to shut up. Lots of witty repartee out in the middle, so nice to see both sets of players getting on so well!

After Jonty Rhodes got out, playing too soon, I came out to join Shaun Pollock. It didn't look good for us, but Shaun started to play some fine strokes, and we began to believe we still had a chance. Alec Stewart passed me and said 'I hope you're enjoying your last Test in England, mate' and I shouted 'I am, and it's not over yet, pal!' and then Cork pitched in. He hit me on the breastplate with a short ball and said 'Oh, look at the big fellow now!' I screamed down the pitch 'F**** off!' and when I got to the other end, I told him,'You're the big f****** pretender, let's see how you go!' Cork may fancy himself as a big cricketer, but I find it difficult to have much respect for him, unlike an Ian Botham or a Dennis Lillee. At least they put in the top performances year after year. Cork just likes to get under your skin, rather than bowl you out.

With so much tension out in the middle, it was easy to lose sight of the overall goal. Our best chance of victory suddenly appeared to be in claiming the extra half-hour, especially as Shaun was seeing the ball like a football and playing beautifully. Cork had shot his bolt, Darren Gough looked tired and Angus Fraser was having trouble with his back. From what I could gather out there in the middle, Ian Salisbury was due on next with his leg-spin and I was sure we could get after him. I knew vaguely about the possibility of claiming the extra half-hour, and when Peter Willey asked me if we wanted to stay on, I looked to our players' balcony and saw nothing to tell me what to do. So I said, 'We'll go off'. Finally Paul Adams ran on with a message from Hansie. We were to stay out there. The umpires asked Alec Stewart what he wanted to do, and he said immediately, 'We're going off'. When we got back to the dressing-room, we found a furious captain. Adams had got to the middle too late. The rules state that it only needs one captain to claim the extra half-hour, and that it should be taken if in the opinion of the umpires, a result is possible that night. According to the rules as they were then, the batsmen out in the middle represent their captain, so we should have had a message before the last ball was delivered. Then we would have been allowed to stay out. The target was 33 in eight overs – the bowlers tired, the light excellent, the pitch playing well, and the leg-spinner was due on next over, having not bowled in the innings so far. He could easily go for a lot very quickly against Shaun. Staying out was our best chance of winning, so we should have worked out our tactics earlier than the last ball.

The pendulum had swung against us on that final morning. The bowlers were refreshed, the humid conditions favoured their swing bowlers and the crowd was willing England to victory. I still thought we had a good chance, especially with Shaun looking so composed. The fielders were in our faces, the crowd cheering every ball – it was unbelievably tense. After the first over, I told Shaun 'Look, we've got to block Gus and try to score off Goughy, because he'll be attacking and we might get some loose stuff off him. Don't try to block Goughy, have a go at anything loose'. We then had a good over from Goughy – including four leg byes, we picked up eight runs. At the end of the over, I said to Shaun, 'Look at them now, their heads are down, we can do this!' The chirrup had disappeared, some of them were kicking the ground in frustration and the zip was ebbing away. Then I got out to Fraser. I thought I had just nicked the back of my pad, rather than the ball. Peter Willey gave me out, caught behind, and I wasn't sure either way. I kicked the ground in disgust, but that was because I'd got out, not at the umpire's decision. It wasn't until I got back to the dressing-room that I realised my reaction might be construed as dissent. I was so angry at myself. I felt I'd been playing well, supporting Shaun and now I was out.

Now it was all down to Makhaya Ntini. He had faced one ball in a match on tour before this Test, and only four in the first innings, but he was very confident. As he passed me, he said, 'Don't worry, partner – I'll do it for you'. He blocked a couple of deliveries, but then lost out to a marginal lbw decision to Darren Gough. Javed Akhtar the umpire again. On the replay, it was going slightly down the legside, but number elevens usually cop them. In the end, our number wasn't on it, and we had lost. We sat in stunned silence, and eventually I snapped out of it, and went outside to shake the English players' hands. There was nothing more to give, nothing else to be said. Mark Butcher came to me with a champagne glass in his hand and I said, 'I bet that tastes nice'. He looked straight at me and said, 'It sure does'. That moment hurt. I should have been the one offering him a victory glass. Eventually we all snapped out of our depression. I stood up and said 'Look, we've got to be strong now. Pick ourselves up and get over this tonight. We must get ourselves right for the one-day series that's coming up'. Hansie picked up the point and said decisively 'Right, get the beers out – let's have a fines meeting'. So we had a few laughs, fining players for daft things and eventually we were in a better frame of mind, as we filed onto our coach. I'm proud to say that we had enough good grace to sign a lot of autographs on our way to the coach, even though the taunts of 'Two – one! Two – one!' were rather unnecessary. I can think of one or two national teams who wouldn't have taken this crushing disappointment as diplomatically as we did.

Before we left Headingley, I had a simple question to

ask Mark Boucher, our young wicket-keeper. Had he gone to apologise to Mark Butcher? Earlier in the game, Boucher had copped a lot of stick from the England boys for catching Ramprakash on the bounce. Butcher and Ramprakash were particularly hard on him when he came to the crease, calling him a cheat and other unmentionables. Boucher then responded in a silly fashion, getting dragged into it and handing out similiar retaliation. It all got a bit out of hand with Butcher in particular getting some fearful stick from Boucher. It was totally out of order, no matter what provocation the young lad was under. In the team coach I said to Boucher 'You are a South African, representing a new country. The old ways have gone for good. Go and find Butcher and apologise'. He did, and there were no hard feelings, but that underlined what a relentless, hard contest it had been. England really climbed into us, and the aggro was worse than any match I've ever known against Australia, the disciples of hard cricket. No wonder Peter Willey said to me during that Leeds Test, 'I'd rather face you on a green wicket than be standing here, with so much going on'.

Neither side helped the umpires at all in that Leeds Test, and I suppose we got what we deserved. There was so much appealing that there were bound to be some bad decisions. I'm not suggesting that there was any bias, but I do believe we copped more bad decisions than England. Yet the umpiring was a red herring. We had to look at ourselves as a unit, honestly and courageously. In our heart of hearts, we knew we hadn't done all that we could over the last two Tests. Gary Kirsten was honest enough to admit the batting failures during the Leeds Test. He came up to me when he was out in the second innings on Sunday and apologised on behalf of the batters. He told me 'I'm sorry, Al, after the efforts of you and Shaun this morning that was unacceptable. It's been a poor effort from us this series, we've let you down'. We had panicked under pressure in the last two Tests, and lost the series, even though we felt we were the better side over the five Tests. That was no consolation at all, in fact it made it even worse. Being named Man-of-the-Series for my 33 wickets meant little to me, because we had lost the series. I could only imagine how our defeat would be going down in South Africa. We tend to strut around a lot when we're on top and we're bad losers. I'm sure many of our supporters back home were expecting to coast through the series after going 1–0 up at Lord's, and there would be a backlash when we got home. The inquests would rage for some time. The inescapable fact is that we bottled it when we needed consistency and determination by the bucketful. No amount of complaints about umpires would alter that. We could only hope that the disappointment of that England tour might mark the period when we moved onto a greater level of performance.

CHAPTER SEVENTEEN

Who'd be an Umpire?

At the end of our tour to England in 1998, the South African players were paid for winning the series, even though we lost it 2–1. This was the decision of Ali Bacher, the managing director of the United Cricket Board of South Africa. He felt that we had been hard done by through umpiring errors in the last couple of Tests, and that if we had enjoyed the rub of the green, we would have won at least one of those Tests – especially the last one at Leeds. I'm sure that Dr Bacher's decision went down well with all of the players – after all, who would ever turn down a bonus? – and certainly it backed up the general feeling of our outraged supporters in South Africa, but we mustn't lose sight of the fact that we lost the series through our own defects, rather than getting stuffed by the umpires. At the end of the Leeds Test, Hansie Cronje was asked to comment on the umpiring and I admired the diplomatic way he faced the minefield. He could have easily sounded off about the dubious lbw decisions in the Leeds Test, at some key errors at Trent Bridge and Headingley that went against us, but he said all the right things, and wouldn't be drawn into rash comments. Hansie didn't lose sight of the fact that we didn't play well enough, and umpiring defects weren't as crucial as that. I was proud of Hansie's dignified response, because I can think of a few other international captains who would have waded in with some hostile observations. Nevertheless, some nagging worries remain about the standard of umpiring and what can be done to help them improve.

The first thing to say is that I don't believe the standard of umpiring has deteriorated during my career. It has got more difficult to do the job, but that's not the umpires' fault. We players have to look closely at ourselves, and take some of the blame. We all know that the more times you appeal, the greater chance you have of getting lucky. So every team is at it more now than a few years ago, taking the attitude that you get nothing if you don't ask. The game is more intensely played now, because the financial rewards are greater, the media profile higher, and nobody makes it easy for the opposition on the field. Hardly anybody 'walks' these days, to help the umpire, unless they've scored a bucketful and it was obvious it was out. It's dog-eat-dog out in the middle. The players have seen they can get away with it if they're lucky, and they're happy to let the umpire take all the aggro if the decision is wrong. The 1998 series between England and South Africa was a very tense, hard battle all through the summer, with both sides trying to outdo each other in appeals, and pressurising the umpires. There were bound to be some errors as we kept asking the questions at the top of our voices, then looking amazed when the decisions didn't go our way. We put too much pressure on the umpires, and we shouldn't have complained when wrong decisions started to stack up, because we had sown the seeds of doubt in the umpires' minds. I sympathised with Mark

Ramprakash eventually at Lord's, when he was given out by Darryl Hair, caught behind off my bowling, because on closer inspection he didn't hit it. But Ramps didn't help himself when he muttered some uncomplimentary views to Darryl Hair as he passed him, on his way back to the pavilion. Ramps must have known that these decisions are part of the modern game, now that we're all out to gain an advantage, and he shouldn't complain when it doesn't go his way. We'll all take a wrong decision that's in our favour, so why should we be so shocked when we get a bad one?

It was significant that at Trent Bridge, Hansie Cronje had some harsh advice for us before we went out to field in the second innings. He said, 'Guys, these umpires are under tremendous pressure. If it's close enough, I want to hear appeals, and I expect you to SCREAM the appeals'. I admit it all started to get out of hand in those last two Tests, but I was surprised that one of the umpires who escaped much of the flak was Steve Dunne. He gave the massively important decision to reprieve Mike Atherton off my bowling when he was out, and that could easily have cost us the match. Yet Merv Kitchen took much of the criticism for Trent Bridge. Also, at Leeds, it wasn't Javed Akhtar's fault that he was rusty, having stood in just one rain-affected second eleven match the week before. The ICC officials who decided that each Test should involve one umpire from abroad should take some responsibility. Why not rotate the series with two from abroad, rather than a different one each time? When did they get the chance to acclimatise? Headingley is a notoriously difficult ground for an umpire, because the ball moves around such a lot, and you have to be on the ball throughout, so why throw Javed Akhtar in at the deep end?

I'm all for using all the technology that's available to make the umpires' job easier. If it's there, then use it, even if it means slowing the game down. With all the slow-motion cameras available these days, it doesn't take all that long to get the relevant replay – say, 35–45 seconds. The crowd seem to like the suspense involved, waiting for the red or the green light, and the players know that, all things being equal, the right decision will have been reached. There are stacks of experienced television technicians on the ground during a Test match, and all they have to do is use the video playbacks and give the third umpire greater choice to help him make his decision when it's been referred to him by the two umpires out in the middle. At the moment, such referrals are only made in the case of contentious line decisions – stumpings or run-outs, or if the ball had actually crossed the boundary rope – but I'd like to see the use of technology widened. In South Africa, in our last domestic season, our administrators widened it to bat/pad catches, lbw decisions where the ball has nicked the bat first, and a caught behind when the ball has touched the gloves, the shoulder, the shirt, or anywhere else on the batsman's body. Now South Africa wants that to be extended to international cricket and will press for its introduction at the next ICC meeting in London. This has to be the way forward. Why restrict the use of such sophisticated technology to just line decisions? If the scope had been widened for the last series in England, so many controversial decisions would have been overturned, and perhaps the umpires would have been able to relax more, and give it their best shot, instead of being pressurised by the players into making poor decisions. Mike Atherton would have been out at Trent Bridge, Mark Ramprakash reprieved at Lord's,

Andrew Flintoff given not out from that bat/pad appeal at Leeds, Mark Ramprakash spared from the one that bounced in front of Mark Boucher in the same Test, and Atherton, myself and Gerry Liebenberg escaping lbw decisions when we clearly hit it. So many errors, so many of them avoidable. I read an article in which Darryl Hair deplored the amount of appealing, that was taking the enjoyment out of the umpires' jobs and I honestly sympathise. So let's try to cut down the amount of mistrust and use modern technology to help them.

I can see the day when cameras would be available to help the umpire in lbw appeals. Professor Tim Noakes, at the University of Cape Town, is convinced that a high-speed camera, linked to a computer, placed in line with both sets of stumps, would then give the precise destination of the ball in relation to the stumps, when it hit the pad. It would also help in terms of faint nicks off the bat. There's even talk of a sensor placed in the ball to judge its direction. It's an interesting idea. So is Ali Bacher's suggestion that we should adopt an idea from tennis and introduce an electronic eye to judge no balls. That way the umpire's gaze can be steady on the business area at the other end, rather than having to look at the bowler's feet, then bring his head up quickly to look at the destination of the ball. The umpire should be free to concentrate all the time on the batsman on strike, and a bleep would tell him, the batsman and the scorers that there'd been a no-ball. All this may sound revolutionary, but I believe a lot of it is common sense, an awareness that we live in a technological age, and that we should use every available piece of equipment to make the umpires' job easier, and reduce the level of sharp practice by the players. The amount of television coverage these days of the big games only serves to magnify all the errors, and reduce the authority of the umpires when they are seen to make mistakes. The sophisticated cameras highlight the cock-ups, so why not enlist them to make the umpires' job easier? I don't believe for a moment that umpires are worse than they were a decade ago. The difference is that they're bang in the firing line, because other elements in the game – especially the players – are making their job that much harder. I like Hansie Cronje's suggestion that red and yellow cards should be introduced to punish persistent offenders. He believes that a batsman who hangs around at the crease, when he clearly has nicked the ball and is looking to bluff the umpire ought to be given a yellow card warning, then a two-match ban if he offends again in that series. Bowlers who appeal excessively should be treated the same way. Not suspended bans, designed as a rap over the knuckles, but a proper ban. Hansie says the players have to be forced to become more honest, and he hopes to sell it to the other international captains when they have their annual meeting in London after the World Cup. I think it's a very sound principle, and it would force all of the players to look at their own failings before banging on about dodgy umpires.

One recent technological innovation that I want to see reduced is the giant screen replay at the matches. I believe using it is very counter-productive, giving players an extra grievance, driving a bigger wedge between them and the umpires, inflaming passions on the field and getting the spectators on the back of the umpire when he's made a mistake. Too often in the recent series against England, a batsman lingered when he'd been given out, turning around to look at the giant screen before he walked into the dressing-room, shaking his head, showing what he thought of the decision. That to me is blatant dissent and Alec Stewart was obviously guilty of that in the second innings at Lord's, when he was given out. The bowlers pause at the end of their run-up, waiting for the replay of the previous ball, and if they're not happy with the not-out decision, they make it very clear. So do the fielders. It gets to the umpires. I've seen them on their walkie-talkies at the end of the over, checking with the third umpire if they've made a ricket. When they get the bad news, that affects their judgements, and there's the risk of a 'make-up' decision, where the unlucky bowler wins a subsequent decision he may not have deserved from that single delivery. I believe the replays on the giant screen should only be used for a great piece of cricket that will entertain the crowd, not anger them: a stump cartwheeling out of the ground, a wonderful piece of fielding, a spectacular boundary. There are enough of them in a days' play without having to focus on a possible umpiring error. The umpires are much more uptight, now that their difficult decisions are magnified up on the giant screen, and the spectators start to jeer at them. Who would want to be an umpire with all that going on?

Among the players, there is an obvious readiness to call for the television replay when they think they might get a favourable decision. At Trent Bridge, Nasser Hussain dived forward at backward point, to take what he thought might have been a catch to dismiss Hansie Cronje. There was some doubt whether the ball had carried, and Hussain, still lying on the ground, signalled the square with his hands – the usual request from the umpire for a television replay. Hussain was out of order doing that, because that is the umpire's job. If he wasn't sure – and making the signal surely indicated that – he should have said simply that, and left it to the umpires. If you're not sure, then it's not-out, according to the laws of cricket. I didn't like seeing a player cross the divide between honest doubt and suggesting that the television replay should determine the matter. That incident showed how much the reliance on the television replay is creeping into the minds of the players. If there's any doubt, then try it on. We're all as guilty as any other group of players. At the Cape Town Test of 1996, Hansie Cronje was wrong to call for the television replay to determine whether England's Graham Thorpe had been run out. It didn't matter that to the naked eye, Thorpe was out by two yards. I was right behind the stumps when Andrew Hudson's throw came in and I was amazed that umpire Dave Orchard gave it in. I said 'Orchie, you must be joking', and then Hansie stopped the game, because he could tell from the crowd's reaction that the television replay proved Thorpe was lucky. Hansie stood there, with his hands in his pockets, arguing the toss with the umpires, saying that they should call for the television replay. He said 'The technology is there, so why don't we use it?' and eventually they did. Thorpe was given out, and he was rightly very cross at Hansie interfering. Hansie was wrong. The umpires are the sole judges of what is in or out in the game, and he shouldn't have interfered. He was fined half his match fee, and that was justified, because the umpires had buckled under the pressure. It was a classic case of using modern technology to force an umpire to change his decision. Hansie would have been furious if the boot had been on the other foot.

The fact that Dave Orchard was standing in only his

second Test was relevant. Too many umpires who lack experience are standing in Tests. An experienced umpire would not have allowed himself to be dragooned into calling for the television replay that day. Word gets around on the international circuit which umpires can be pressurised, and which ones stand firm. You don't always get those with enough experience, though. Each Test-playing country nominates umpires to the ICC panel, but not every one of them is sufficiently qualified for such a high-pressure task. Zimbabwe's Russell Tiffin's initial game as an umpire in first-class cricket just happened to be a Test match. When he joined the ICC panel, so that he would officiate around the world in international games, he had stood in just one Test. I'm not saying Russell isn't up to the job, but the quota system, whereby each country is represented on the umpires' panel, can sometimes lead to distrust from the players and an erosion of respect. The general view is that English umpires are the best, because they do the job more often than anyone else, but I'm not so sure. All those years of standing in Tests didn't alter Dickie Bird's attitude to lbw appeals. He was a famous 'not-outer' and despite his popular public image he was not a favourite among bowlers. I do believe an Englishman, David Shepherd, is the best umpire in the world. He's been more consistent than anyone down the years – strong, fair, he gets most tricky decisions right. Shep also has a lovely way about him, he doesn't get ratty with the players, but they know they can't take liberties. He's human, likeable with a quiet authority. Yet other countries have good umpires. Australia's Darryl Hair used to be known as a trigger-happy official, willing to keep the bowlers appealing, but he's more consistent now. Steve Bucknor, from the West Indies, used to be excellent, and he still maintains a high standard. Clive Lloyd, who has seen a lot of umpires around the world, says he'd be happy to have two Englishmen standing in all Tests. Certainly England has the greatest representation on the international panel – four to the other countries' two – but that doesn't mean they are collectively the best. Merv Kitchen's performance at Trent Bridge didn't do much for the image of the English umpire, and Merv himself was honest enough to admit he'd had a bad match.

The main point about umpiring at the highest level these days is not where the umpire comes from, but whether the players realise they can't get away with much when that guy is out there, in charge. We have to take some responsibility for the decline in confidence in the umpires. The players are just ekeing away at the umpires' competence, and the ICC must embrace new technology and a red/yellow cards system to haul the players back into line. Otherwise, not enough umpires will have the ambition to graduate into Test cricket, because they'll think it's just not worth the hassle. Then international cricket will be in trouble. Perhaps some good after all will come out of that dramatic Test series in England, when South Africa thought the umpiring went against us. At least we are more willing to try experiments, using the available technology, rather than just rely on the umpires to get it right. Don't forget we were the first country to use the third umpire in run-out decisions, back in 1992. Perhaps this is one area where South Africa will prove to be pioneers, improving the way the game is conducted at the highest level. Certainly the top umpires need help, and it won't come from the players spontaneously. Sadly, international sport doesn't work like that anymore.

CHAPTER EIGHTEEN

What Makes a Fast Bowler?

The short answer to that question is a lot of determination, a high pain threshold, sympathetic coaching and luck. I've been so lucky in my career to have inherited my mother's suppleness. It means that I can glide through my run-up, into my action at the crease without too much strain on my body. So, as I progress through my thirties, I'm not showing many signs of wear and tear, apart from my suspect ankle. A fast bowler is particularly vulnerable to the wearing down process; it catches up on you quicker than in other cricketing disciplines, so that one season you're still pinning the batsmen onto the back foot, and the next they're pulling and hooking you at will. The trick is knowing when to go before it gets too embarrassing. Hopefully, I'll know quicker than anyone else.

I started thinking about the elements that make up a fast bowler in 1991, when I was filmed by a sports scientist called Nigel Stockhill. Nigel is now a fitness coach with England Under-19s, but at the time he was based with the National Cricket Association's Human Resources Unit at Lilleshall. His project in 1991 was to determine precisely what makes a fast bowler. He filmed people like Waqar Younis, Courtney Walsh, Wasim Akram and myself, trying to find out what happens to our bodies at the moment we deliver the ball, and how we can make slight adjustments to prolong our careers. Basically, he was looking for the prototype that makes a modern fast bowler, the common denominators. He filmed me in a net at Edgbaston, under Bob Woolmer's supervision, and he asked me to wear shorts, so that he could highlight what my knee and its associated muscles did at the moments of pressure in delivery. I was scared stiff when I saw the evidence afterwards. I couldn't believe how much my left knee hyper-extended at the crease. The knee basically went backwards and then popped forward again. It looked as if my whole left leg was going to snap in half. I asked Warwickshire's physio, Stuart Nottingham about it and he told me not to worry, that I was lucky. He said I was hyper-mobile, almost double-jointed, so that my knee can bend inwards, going back about 180 degrees, and then pop out again. Stuart said the amount of elasticity in my tissue enabled me to take the strain on the front leg. The lack of pressure on my body at the crease allowed me to be explosive, to glide through my action. That was very reassuring!

After studying me at close quarters and looking at the video close-ups, Nigel Stockhill's conclusion was that I had a safe action – one that wasn't going to let me down and it would prove robust over the years. It's true that my action has basically stayed the same since my teens, give or take a few adjustments. Nigel thought my action was part of a new breed, moving away from the orthodox, classical sideways-on action that was usually offered as the ideal for the fast bowler. But research down the years has shown that fast bowlers who are more front-on tend to last longer, and don't suffer as many injuries as those who look over their left shoulder before delivering the ball after dragging their hips through an exaggerated side-on movement. Someone like Dominic Cork, who has the classical action, has suffered a lot more injuries than Courtney Walsh, Curtley Ambrose and Malcolm Marshall, who are more chest-on. That method reduces the strain on the back hips and knees. Nigel's opinion was that I had a midway action – halfway between the two extremes – but it didn't put my body under great stress, so it was highly satisfactory, because I still generated pace. I don't have a great deal of hip rotation, I tend to get my right side through as quickly as possible, which helps my explosiveness.

I've worked hard in three areas of my bowling action – in the jump, the use of my left arm and the hips. After watching Devon Malcolm in the late eighties, I learned how to leap higher, cocking the wrist, ready to line up the target. Then it was a case of using my left arm as a telescope, dragging my left side up, gathering in the power, getting the stumps in the sights. The left arm had to be dragged quickly past the left thigh to allow the right arm to go through quickly, delivering the ball. Then the hips must whip through the actual delivery of the ball, which is where the pace comes from. Wasim Akram was brilliant at whipping through his leading arm so quickly. I used to love watching him, especially his quick feet at the crease. That meant he was snapping his body through quickly. Stuart Nottingham reckons that fast bowling is made up of various components – twenty per cent run-up, the same amount for hand/wrist action, thirty per cent trunk rotation and the same for the shoulder. The key is to co-ordinate all that at the same time. So timing is essential and that's my problem when I lose rhythm. The ball comes out at the wrong time and I spray it down legside. When I'm going well, I can feel my right arm hitting my left arm as I zip through my action. That means my left arm has been high, and I'm pulling through onto it well with my left arm on its follow-through. It's also crucial to have a still head, to face the target when running in and then delivering the ball. There are also times when my right arm is doing too much during my run-up, and that throws me off-balance just as much as if my head is lolling from side to side. It's all a matter of fine-tuning, knowing that if one of the key components is misfiring, the whole machinery will cough and splutter. Batsmen never have these problems, do they?

So to the big question that's been put to me thousands of times over the years. Why can't England breed fast bowlers? We're not talking about guys who last a season, bowling fast, take a few wickets in several Tests, then fade away. We mean fast bowlers who rock up consistently, season after season, ending up with more than two hundred Test wickets. Most other countries seem to have them, but not England. The last was Devon Malcolm, who I thought was treated badly down the years, never knowing if he was playing his last Test. Devon's physique showed how much time he'd spent working on his body and he had a history of not breaking down, willing to bowl long spells at speed. Yet he was raised in the culture of fast bowling, in Jamaica, where fast bowlers are cherished and encouraged. Devon never seemed to be trusted by the English hierarchy, who didn't appear to understand the mentality of the fast bowler, his need to be supported and tolerated when things weren't going well. Apart from Devon, there's been Darren Gough in my time, yet Goughy is a guy for the fast delivery, rather than the fast spell. I rate Goughy very highly, and

I was delighted to see he kept fit during the Ashes series, but I wouldn't classify him as a genuine fast bowler. So we have to go as far back as Bob Willis to find a consistently fast bowler for England, who performed at the highest level, year in year out.

One thing that Bob Willis and Devon Malcolm had in common was that they weren't overbowled by their counties. Devon was the grateful recipient of Derbyshire's rota system, where their captain Kim Barnett made sure his seam bowlers had enough rest, while Bob's commitment to Warwickshire was inevitably reduced because of the demands put on him by England. And that is the major factor in England's failure to breed top fast bowlers who'll last the course. There is too much cricket being played in England by jaded professionals. The biggest mistake in English cricket is that the national side isn't the number one priority. It is in South Africa, and Australia, where we are contracted to our boards of control, not our provincial sides. The top England players must be told by the English Cricket Board officials when they can play for their counties, rather than just hoping that the county will look favourably on the request to rest the player concerned. At the moment, the chairman of Worcestershire County Cricket Club has more to say about Graeme Hick's welfare than the England coach, David Lloyd, and the same applies to Darren Gough, Alec Stewart and all the other elite England players. I saw at first hand what a strain Test cricket can be on England players when talking to Mike Atherton, when we played at Lord's in the Diana, Princess of Wales Memorial Match. It was halfway through the 1998 season, and Athers was brain-dead. He admitted that after a Test, he's so exhausted that he needs a week off to recharge his mental batteries, but there's no chance of that because he has to play for Lancashire. Would county members prefer their county won a trophy than England had a Test series victory? I think they probably would. England cricket supporters can be very parochial, especially if none of their county players are in the Test team. It's the same in football. I know a lot of Aston Villa fans in Birmingham who are far more bothered about their team winning every week than how the England side are doing.

Bob Willis would not have been able to sustain his hostility and consistency for England if he'd roared in for Warwickshire, match after match, bowling at his fastest. It simply can't be done, given the fixture congestion in England. In South Africa, the top players rarely play for their provincial sides, which is sad but a fact of life. That's because everybody recognises that the interests of the national side must always come first. I remember asking Peter Pollock, our chairman of selectors, if I could play for Free State after a drawn Test against Pakistan. He simply said, 'No, you're not playing, you'll work in the nets at Durban, ready for the next Test. That's the end of the story'. No room for debate. To be fair, Peter Pollock had been a fine Test bowler, and he knew what sort of physical and mental challenges are involved, so he had my welfare at heart. Yet there was no question of thinking about Free State's interests, they just weren't of any relevance.

English professional cricket needs two divisions, giving an extra competitive edge, and only eight championship games a season should be played, to make every match an event. Too many players just go through the motions in the last few weeks of the season. If they faced the danger of relegation, or the prospect of promotion, then they'd soon compete harder. The NatWest Trophy should be reduced to 50 overs a side, standardising the competition with others worldwide, and the Sunday League should be played over 40 overs. Nothing else. There is simply too much cricket being played, and as a result much of it is meaningless. So you get promising young fast bowlers like Alex Tudor getting too much work out in the middle, when he ought to be learning about his trade, polishing up the rough edges, hardening up his body. There's no point in having the genuine article like Tudor, then over-bowling him at a time when his body is still in a transitional stage. That way, he'll keep breaking down, because he's playing at the wrong stage in his evolution into a consistent fast bowler, who can shrug off the injuries. I was very lucky that I didn't play Test cricket until I was 25, because we were still banned. So I learned about dealing with pain, looking after my body, taking preventative action, developing stamina, keeping flexible – all the things that go towards establishing a fast bowler. If I'd had to do all the travelling and playing on the international stage when I was younger, I might not have lasted the course. At the age of 25, I had some sort of idea of what was needed to maintain standards and fitness.

Perhaps English cricket should have regular seminars involving fast bowlers, to examine their particular problems. It's true that some of the young fast bowlers in England don't help themselves. A lot of them appear to break down rather too often, and then wait for someone to help them. I do sense a lack of responsibility and drive, but that may just stem from fatigue and disillusionment with the system. Certainly, not enough of them pay sufficient attention to their bodies when they're eighteen or so, and then when they strive for extra pace without doing the necessary hard physical training, they break down. Then they opt for the easier life, by settling for line and length, rather than trying to blast the batsmen out. Fast bowling is not easy, and you can't make it unless you put the time in, as well as having the natural ability to bowl fast. I think the England side's fitness trainer, Dean Riddle has some progressive ideas and he should be given greater scope to introduce his methods into the county set-up. I believe he should be given the authority to impose a detailed fitness programme on every designated fast bowler on the county staffs. Each county should have their own fitness trainer, as well as a physio, and that specialist should oversee Dean Riddle's regime. Tell the young fast bowlers they are the future, the ones who could win Test matches for England. That's what we do in South Africa. Guys like Roger Telemachus and Makhaya Ntini are told that they must fill the gaps left by Allan Donald and Shaun Pollock eventually, that they must be ready to grasp the opportunity. They're told to watch how the senior fast bowlers train and then work in the nets, how they prepare mentally for the big games. It's made clear to them that they are the future, but hard work is the basis for further promotion. Maybe the willingness to work hard is more central to the South African philosophy than it is in England, but there's a pot of gold at the end of the rainbow for the next young Englishman who becomes a great fast bowler. It's glamorous, it wins Test matches, it gets you fast-tracked into the national team in a short space of time. Fast bowlers are what every Test captain wants, because often they are the main difference between the sides. The incentives are all there for an ambitious young English fast bowler, but does he have the drive and does his country's cricket structure have the vision to create a climate where fast bowlers can thrive? It's no coincidence that they haven't done so in the last twenty years. The situation is holding back the England national side.

CHAPTER NINETEEN

A Dramatic Series

The visit by the West Indies to South Africa at the end of 1998 turned out to be the most dramatic few months we have experienced since returning to international cricket in 1991. Now I know that sounds a hell of a statement when you consider the pace of events during that period, but there was such a lot happening, on and off the field, during that West Indies tour. It began with the genuine threat that it would not take place at all, due to a dispute between West Indies' players and their Board, and it ended with South Africa becoming only the seventh side in Test history to complete a clean sweep of 5–0. We consolidated our position as the second-best team in Test cricket, and with our comprehensive 6–1 thrashing of them in the one-day internationals, South Africa went top of the one-day rankings, ideal preparation for the World Cup.

In the course of that tour, I lost respect for Brian Lara as he made little apparent effort to rally his demoralised players, and for other reasons. On top of all that, South African cricket faced a crisis over the best way to get more non-whites into our national side. With politicians exerting pressure on our administrators to fast-track non-white players into the top bracket, cricket was in danger of becoming a political football, with political correctness swamping commonsense that dictates you play your best eleven, irrespective of colour. The situation became so tense that our captain, Hansie Cronje, openly rebelled against the political dictates, threatening to resign unless he got his own way. The stand-off was averted after hurried, secret talks brought Hansie back into the fold, but the problem hasn't gone away. There is a gap that's getting wider between political aspirations to accelerate the rate of change and cricket's reluctance to accept tokenism in picking the national side. It's a problem unique to South Africa, and I don't know how it can be satisfactorily resolved.

South Africa's failure in England was still fresh in our minds as we prepared for the West Indies tour. Even though Ali Bacher had guaranteed that we would be paid a bonus, as if we had won the series in England, we weren't consoled. It was nice of Dr Bacher to organise that, but the hidden agenda behind this was a sense of frustration at umpiring errors in the last two Tests – and that was only part of the true story. We had let ourselves down, and no amount of bleating over umpiring would obscure that. When we got home, the level of disappointment from our supporters was hard to take. I played golf with one guy, who said he was in tears when we lost at Leeds and he was inconsolable for days afterwards. Now he had some idea how we felt! So there was enormous determination to take it out on the West Indies. That's if we got on the park. We were shattered to hear about their dispute with their Board, a situation that was finally resolved at the last moment. I have no desire to get into the rights and wrongs of the issue, other than to repeat what Courtney Walsh told me – that the row had been rumbling along for some time and was inevitable. I have great respect for Courtney, but I do feel it was the wrong time to get involved in such brinkmanship. Ali Bacher had to fly to a hotel near Heathrow Airport in London to try to broker a compromise, and even our President, Nelson Mandela sent a message, requesting the tour to go ahead. All cricket fans in South Africa were desperate for the tour to proceed. Guys like Lara and Walsh were heroes in the townships, and Lara in particular had done some impressive work for the under-privileged on his previous trips to our country. Whatever the pros and cons of the dispute, I thought it was unfair on leaders of the calibre of Ali Bacher and Nelson Mandela to be dragged into it. I do not know what steps Lara had taken to resolve the player/Board dispute in advance of the tour, but it was perhaps unfortunate that the captain was still involved in the matter on the eve of the tour.

The West Indies players looked weary and demoralised when they finally arrived in South Africa, and they never recovered. Lara lacked the dynamism and professionalism to pull them around, and the younger players in particular looked out of their depth, desperate for strong leadership. Lara spent a lot of time in the company of his friend and vice-captain, Carl Hooper, a man who has had many run-ins with his Board. Even during fielding practice, they stuck together instead of working hard with the other players. There was no team spirit there, and it was very significant that at the end of the third Test, one of their younger players left the field in tears. Rawl Lewis, their leg-spinner, was distraught at the manner of the defeat in Durban that gave us a winning 3–0 lead in the series, and we felt genuinely sorry for him as he cried. Later on, after he had composed himself, Lewis told one of our players he was very depressed at the lack of communication from his captain, who appeared not to rate some of his team, and made little attempt to conceal that fact. Brian Lara had only turned up at some of the official functions, and seemed to enjoy spending time on the golf course instead of rallying the squad and making it more difficult for us. We weren't complaining, because we were also playing superbly, but Lara's distance from the bulk of his players made our job easier.

I've known Brian since 1992, and I was saddened at the change in him over the years. Even though he had been preferred to me as Warwickshire's overseas professional for the 1996 season, I had nothing personal against Brian, and we got on fine. But I was deeply saddened at the way he went about his job in South Africa. I don't know whether his drive had been sapped by all the money he has made since he became a superstar and got what he wanted – the West Indies captaincy – but his attitude was in total contrast to that of another man who has had to come to terms with even more adulation and financial incentives. Sachin Tendulkar is in a different class to Lara as a professional cricketer. He is a model cricketer, and despite the intolerable pressures he faces back home in India, remains a really nice guy. Sachin is also the best batsman in the world, pulling away from Brian Lara every year. I'd love to sit down with Brian over a beer, to tell him what his younger players think about him, to find out if he's bothered about the risk of squandering his amazing batting talent. It could all fade away for Brian over the next few years, unless he re-discovers some hunger and humility. I have respected hugely his talent, but I think he was incredibly lucky to keep the West Indies captaincy after his performance in

South Africa. The superb batting and improved leadership skills he later showed against Australia seemed to suggest the penny had dropped at last, which is good for both the West Indies and Brian.

I found it very hard to have a conversation with Lara on that tour. He gave the impression that he felt superior to me. It dawned on me that perhaps I had never really known him in the past. I tried discussing the disappointing season with Warwickshire, when his captaincy was criticised, but all he would say was that he didn't have a good enough side, particularly in the bowling department. He wasn't man enough to admit he hadn't put in enough for the side – something most of the Warwickshire boys felt – and he looked for excuses. That disappointed me, because I know how some of the younger Warwickshire bowlers felt demoralised at the lack of faith shown in them by their captain. At the end of the one-day series in South Africa, with the whole tour over, I asked Brian for a pair of his batting gloves for an auction item for my benefit year, which was due to start back in Birmingham a couple of months later. Brian was in our dressing-room and just shook his head, without answering me. I was hurt and asked him again. He said 'No' very sharply. I said he needed to learn to speak to people with some courtesy and told him to 'F*** off out of our dressing-room'. Then he back-tracked, saying he hadn't meant to sound like that, and later he returned, to throw me a pair of his gloves, without a word. Perhaps Brian was just disappointed at his tour, his failures as batsman and captain; perhaps he was angry at the way I had got after him. I had targeted Brian right from the start, and managed to get under his skin. In the Test series, I got him five times in the eight innings I bowled at him, and throughout he was too loose for a player of his class, too keen on dominating rather than toughing it out. In the last Test, at Centurion Park, he got after me, creaming me for boundary after boundary. He hit me for six boundaries in twelve balls, and my tail was really up. I'm told it was the most exciting period of play in the entire Test series, but I wasn't aware of that. I wanted Lara's scalp. So I started to give him the verbals, telling him he had no discipline as a batsman and captain and set a bad example. That's typical of the sort of tough talking you get out in the middle, but Brian complained about it to me. I said, 'This is a tough game, tell someone who cares'. We had a drinks interval and I went up to him and shook hands, saying, 'Don't worry, it stays out here – we'll still have a beer together afterwards'. Then I got him caught at gully, fending off a lifter and I was absolutely delighted. At the end of the Test, after we had hammered them again, I went up to Lara, gave him a hug, and wished him well for the coming series against Australia. But he obviously hadn't forgotten how I'd rattled him because a fortnight later, we had that nonsense from him over the batting gloves. I realise now that Brian wasn't taking me very seriously, that perhaps I was joking after giving him a lot of verbals during the series. Perhaps I over-reacted by telling him he needed to be more courteous to people. But that's his problem. The game of cricket will always be bigger than one individual, no matter how talented.

With all the West Indies' troubles clear for all to see on this tour, one fact was slightly obscured. South Africa played superbly to beat them 5–0. They still had some top players in their squad, even though they never settled. When fit, Courtney Walsh and Curtly Ambrose were still awesome fast bowlers, and we had to bat very well against them time and again. Our batters had been put through the mincer at a camp in Bloemfontein before the series started and their resilience was obvious throughout the series. Eddie Barlow had been drafted into the camp, with Bob Woolmer's blessing, and he was terrific at boosting the guys' confidence, homing in on the psychological skills needed. The team that batted better was going to win the series and he told us to stop thinking about umpiring mistakes. Eddie was there for the first two Tests, standing behind the nets, watching each batsman closely, emphasising the importance of playing tightly and with discipline. The players enjoyed having him around and they took the regular Barlow rollickings in the right spirit. I am certain that if we had batted as well in England as we did against the West Indies, we would have won that series. We got out of trouble regularly against the West Indies and that demoralised them in the end. In the first Test, we could have folded, chasing 164 on a slow, low pitch at the Wanderers, with Ambrose and Walsh looking dangerous, but a positive approach brought us victory by four wickets. After that, the West Indies rarely threatened.

We showed our batting depth in the second Test, at Port Elizabeth, by recovering to 245 after being 142 for seven. I hit my highest Test score, 34, and added 66 with Pat Symcox for the tenth wicket and that frustrated them. My reward for that was to be hit on the head in the second innings by Ambrose. It wasn't that short initially, but Ambrose's great height did for me, and the ball hit me square on the head. A dose of my own medicine! I went down like a sack of potatoes, and when I took off my helmet and the ice pack was brought out, I had a large lump on my head. The crowd were right behind me as Ambrose bowled me two bouncers in a row as soon as I recovered. I don't blame him, I'd have done the same, but it got my adrenalin going. After I swished a few, I was bowled by Walsh and ran off the pitch, really angry. I was really pumped up at the start of their innings and I bowled very quickly. I got Lara out, mishooking to mid-wicket and with the traditional band playing lustily inside St George's Park, the atmosphere was electric. We ran out winners by 178 runs, and yet I was disappointed in the newspaper coverage next day. It was all about Donald getting his revenge, and the demoralised West Indies team, but little about another great effort from our blokes. That continued to be the theme throughout. In the third Test, Shaun Pollock bowled brilliantly, Jonty Rhodes made a typical 87 and we strolled home by nine wickets. The next Test, in Cape Town, was dominated by Jacques Kallis, who scored 198 for once out, and took seven wickets, and the final Test showed the importance of batting all the way down the order. We were 98 for five, having been put in to bat, with Walsh bowling superbly, but Kallis helped pull us round and then our wicket-keeper, Mark Boucher, scored his maiden hundred, coming in at number eight. We all supported him and that put the game beyond the West Indies. They just faded away, to lose by 351 runs. It was a great team effort and that was recognised by the adjudicator for the Man of the Match award, Dennis Lindsay, when he gave it to the whole side, rather than an individual. So many of our players advanced their reputations throughout the series. Jacques Kallis looked the best all-rounder in the world – batting maturely, bowling quickly, and taking some wonderful catches at first slip. Shaun Pollock took 29 wickets in the series and looked a stunning fast bowler, with pace, bounce and late swing. His batting continues to develop, and soon he will be scoring Test centuries. Mark Boucher is second only to Ian Healy as a wicket-keeper/batsman at Test level, while Herschelle Gibbs impressed as an opener as the series progressed. He's not as flashy as he used to be, having tightened up his game, and his brilliant fielding only added to our high standard. With Gibbs and Rhodes on either side of the wicket, I felt we had the best two fielders in international cricket.

As for myself, I was just delighted to have had the all-clear on my damaged ankle a week before the start of the first Test. After a strenuous programme of restoring fitness to my ankles and calves, I started slowly in the series, as I usually do after a long lay-off. I was pummelled a bit early on in the first Test, but found my rhythm in a one-day game at the Wanderers, and after that I kicked in again. At times against the West Indies, I bowled as fast as I've ever done, and I was very happy with 23 wickets in the series, especially as I bowled just 21 overs in the last two Tests, due to a hamstring injury.

By the time the one-day series started against the West Indies, attention was sharply focused on just who was playing for South Africa, and what was the colour of the individual's skin. Pressure was mounting on our selectors to pick at least one non-white player for the national side, an issue that had been rumbling along for at least a year. There had been understandable criticism that the Development Programme had not been throwing up enough international-class players in the years since we had returned to official international cricket, and that view was shared by the architect of the Programme, Ali Bacher. During the 1998 home Test series against Pakistan, Dr Bacher had voiced his dismay at the presence of an all-white eleven representing South Africa. He felt it was high time that a country with an overwhelming non-white population ought to be better represented on the international field, and Dr Bacher warned that something would have to be done to redress the balance. The dilemma was eased for a time when South Africa took three non-white players on the England tour – the Cape Coloureds Paul Adams and Roger Telemachus, and Makhaya Ntini, the first black African to represent our country at cricket. All were there on merit. Telemachus was in the squad for the experience – sadly he was injured in the first week of the tour and had to return home – Adams is the only wrist-spinner in South African cricket while Ntini I rate highly. At the age of twenty, when he first played Test cricket, he was a more complete fast bowler than I was at that age, and he impressed when he played in the Test series against England.

So it seemed that the pace of racial integration into South Africa's Test eleven was satisfactory enough after the England tour. But then a few matters came to a head and brought the racial issue firmly into the public domain. At the start of our domestic season, Adams was out of form and getting little bowling for Western Province; the same applied to Ntini – and then a rape charge laid against him in December obviously altered his focus. Herschelle Gibbs, a Cape Coloured, who had played for South Africa in Tests in 1996/97, was also out of form at a time when an opener's spot in the West Indies series was there for the taking. And Telemachus was still recovering from the shoulder operation that ruined his tour to England. Victor Mpitsang, a nineteen-year-old fast bowler who had been spotted at a Development clinic in Kimberley by Corrie van Zyl, was in his maiden first-class season. Raw, but highly promising, Victor had opened the bowling for South Africa in the Under-19 World Cup, and at the end of his debut season in first-class cricket, he came with us to New Zealand on the senior tour – but at the time when the clamour began to fast-track Development players, Victor just wasn't ready for the big time. That is a fact, not a racial observation. Since returning to international cricket in 1991, South Africa's players have been selected on cricket merit alone, but now that was becoming a controversial stance to take. Politics and sport were starting to become closely linked again, and many felt that it was wrong for an all-white team to represent a country which numbered just five million whites in a population of 38 million.

Throughout the nineties, as South Africa regained respectability in world opinion, the African National Congress were fantastic supporters of our national side and Dr Bacher's Development Programme. We all felt we were in the same boat, rowing in unison, and the white players were heartened by the growing awareness in non-white communities that we were acceptable role models. Change was coming – for the good – and the only issue was the rate of that change. I never had any doubts that in a few years, the South African cricket team would predominantly comprise non-whites, and we all knew it was Dr Bacher's dream. We respected that, and had no problems with that ideal, as long as the eleven was picked solely on merit, without tokenism. The non-whites who had played international cricket for us had all been easily assimilated into our dressing-room, enjoying the banter, respecting the team ethos. No problem. But the external pressures have increased in the past year, led by the ANC. Many of the leading ANC officials believe that, five years after the first democratic general election, and nine years after apartheid was officially dismantled, the old system still exists in cricket. Players are still being coached, selected and discovered along racial lines according to the ANC, and that it is so much more difficult to come through to the top if you are poor and black. Of course, we all sympathise with that point of view and it would be stupid to suggest that South Africa is close to solving this particular sporting problem. But the ANC is clearly running out of sympathy with the established order. Steve Tshwete, the Sports Minister, went on the record after our first Test against the West Indies in November 1998, saying that a 'lilywhite' team representing South Africa was no longer acceptable to him. He said that he would find it very difficult to support South Africa in both the cricket and rugby World Cups in 1999 if both sets of selectors continued to select just white players. This was serious, especially as Mr Tshwete had been greatly admired in the cricket community by all colours for his genuine support throughout this last decade.

For the second Test, in Port Elizabeth, the Cape Coloured opener, Herschelle Gibbs replaced Adam Bacher, but that was not a reaction to Mr Tshwete's threat. Bacher had failed twice and his technical flaws had been exposed by Walsh and Ambrose. Gibbs was now a fine player at the age of 25 after a faltering start to his international career and his wonderful fielding was also a plus. He stayed in the side for the rest of the series, making useful scores and looking the part. He was not a token selection, and there was every reason to believe he would be part of the national side for a few years to come. But the political stakes were getting higher in election year. The ANC needed to retain its popularity in the wake of President Mandela's retirement, and in a sports-mad country like South Africa, it was inevitable that the politicians would seize on this sort of issue. Steve Tshwete warned that, if necessary, he would legislate when he believed there was genuine discrimination on grounds of colour and race. He said it was up to the respective national selectors in the various sports to ensure that legislation wasn't necessary. Affirmative action in sport was now a hot issue in South Africa. Clearly, the ANC felt rapid changes were needed, even down to picking players on the colour of skin rather than cricketing skills. It began to look like apartheid in reverse – a sad contrast to the ANC's previous unstinting and generous support of Ali Bacher's progressive ideas.

Throughout the West Indies tour, Dr Bacher was under enormous pressure from the Government to speed up the transitional process. It must have been desperately difficult for a man of Dr Bacher's liberal background, who had also captained his country and would not have taken kindly to being told who he should be picking for the final eleven. At the end of the Test series, he called the squad to a meeting in Johannesburg. We were due to start the one-day series in four days' time and Dr Bacher spelled out to us the reality of the current situation. He told us how much flak he was getting from the politicians about the need for quotas, and that experiments might be needed to keep them at bay. The suggestion was that South Africa might soon be picking an eleven on a different basis to simple merit. Hansie Cronje, our captain, exploded at that. He said a South African cap has to be earned on merit alone, and that he would have no part in anything else. Throughout that two-hour meeting, Hansie made it quite clear how annoyed he was at the political interference. He said any experimenting with quotas should be done at provincial level, that the international set-up must not be devalued for the sake of keeping the ANC happy. Paul Adams and Herschelle Gibbs were both in the meeting and they fully supported Hansie, who made it clear he was thinking of resignation. Dr Bacher couldn't persuade Hansie to think about quotas at international level, and when I flew back home to Bloemfontein with Hansie later that day, he was still dogmatic about that point. Yet I was surprised how cool he was after his outburst in the meeting and I got the feeling that he knew what he was doing; I wondered if Hansie was trying to force the hands of the politicians. That night, I rang him at home, telling him that the ANC would come down really hard on him and our administrators if this developed into a public spat. I told Hansie he could screw things up for the whole country, even though I agreed with his sentiments. He was so calm and collected about it all that I felt he had a fall-back procedure mapped out, and just wanted to wake up our administrators to the amount of anger he and his players felt at such interference. Over the next few days, Hansie had a lot of phone calls from important cricket officials, and after he and Dr Bacher met for a three-hour meeting in Johannesburg, the matter was hushed up and Hansie had been talked out of resignation. I don't know how far he would have pushed the issue, but I've known Hansie for almost all my life and I knew how determined he was over the principle of non-interference.

The matter won't go away, though. Dr Bacher is genuinely trying to do his best for all concerned, but he's had to make public statements to keep the politicians happy. Dr Bacher has said that all-white national teams are no longer acceptable. A policy document drawn up by the United Cricket Board had originally stated that 'The national team must be a team of colour, wherever possible', but in February Dr Bacher said the words 'wherever possible' had been dropped. Meanwhile Hansie Cronje and our coach Bob Woolmer kept their heads down on the New Zealand tour, after that latest policy reversal. It needed all of Hansie's diplomatic skills to avoid getting publicly pinned on the issue, although Bob Woolmer was more forthright, saying he'd never taken any notice of politicians and had no plans to do so now. Non-white players would only be selected if they improved South Africa's chances of winning a match. It was reassuring to hear support from one of the non-whites who had been dropped after the first of the one-day internationals in New Zealand. Herschelle Gibbs said, 'Nothing in life comes free and the same should apply when it comes to representing your country. You must be picked on merit'. I know that's the view of every South African who has represented his country in my time, irrespective of their colour, and I'm certain that was the sole criterion when the squad for the World Cup was picked. The politicians simply don't understand the atmosphere of a sports dressing-room, the fact that any player who has been picked for reasons other than merit would be embarrassed to be there, just as a token gesture. South Africa is in a unique position because of its history of denying basic human rights to the majority of the population, but I believe the only problem now is the pace of change in sporting considerations. Hansie Cronje was right to stand up at that meeting on behalf of all South African cricketers, and I hope Ali Bacher can hold the line for what is fundamentally right. I wonder what sort of pressure would have been exerted if 1999 hadn't been an election year in South Africa, and if Nelson Mandela was still leading our country, bringing his massive moral authority to bear on the issue?

I think we'll get there, with patience, understanding and some diplomatic silences from influential politicians and cricket administrators. The changes planned for our domestic cricket for the 1999/2000 season will definitely speed up the process. All eleven provincial sides will have to play at least one non-white player in an eleven, and each squad of seventeen must contain at least three who are non-white. There will also be a pool of those who aren't contracted to a province, and other provinces will be able to dip into that pool, with an eye towards picking non-whites as a priority. That will help the many talented Cape Coloureds who can't get into the Western Province side; they can play first-class cricket elsewhere, getting crucial experience. The chief executives of the eleven provincial sides have agreed that they will ensure that they fast-track as many non-white players as possible, and that the obsession with winning trophies will not count against these selections. Critics of the pace of change tend to forget that at youth level, a lot of non-white players are coming through encouragingly. Representative youth teams are already 50–50 in racial mixes and that is the shape of things to come in South Africa. The provinces are the areas that need an infusion of non-white players, so we can judge their temperaments under pressure, against experienced opponents who have played at the highest level. You just can't throw a player in at the deep end who hasn't a clue about the particular demands. The pool of talent of non-whites must be deeper, and I expect to see encouraging progress in the next year. Equality of opportunity was rightly one of the main planks of the Anti-Apartheid Movement's argument, and that is all we want in South African cricket. Give the disadvantaged players every chance to make the grade, then let's see who can grab the chance. If you prove yourself, then you go up the ladder, and so on until you get handed your South African cap. You can't forgo the chance of playing your best eleven in any form of international sport, just to keep the politicians happy. I hope things will settle down after the general election, and dedicated administrators like Ali Bacher will be left alone to try fulfilling his life's dream. Give him time, and South Africa's Test side will reflect the make-up of the 'Rainbow Nation' and most whites I know won't complain about that – provided they are in the team on merit, and merit alone.

CHAPTER TWENTY

Just One Run!

The English summer of 1999 will stay in my memory for all the wrong reasons. It brought home to me that no matter how long you play professional sport, you'll never be able to assume anything. Sport's knack of hitting you hard when you could be entitled to think the odds are in your favour was never demonstrated more clearly to me than during a three-month period in 1999. My morale was greatly tested over those weeks, when I contributed to a heartbreaking, narrow loss in the World Cup semi-final, then saw my season with Warwickshire in ruins through injury, ending up with my international and county career in doubt. All this in my benefit year at Edgbaston, at a time when I really wanted to be out there on the park, to show my gratitude to the Warwickshire supporters and the club for such marvellous support down the years. Yet I was breaking down with my ankle problem. I didn't even take a wicket in the championship season and I was very embarrassed that it should happen at a time when so many people were supporting my benefit season. I felt as if I was taking money under false pretences and I vowed to repay all that loyalty before I finished my career at Warwickshire. But would I get the chance to come back to Edgbaston? That was another worrying consideration as that nightmare season ended. Was my time up? Would that vulnerable ankle curtail my career? So many things left me depressed and I kept brooding about my bad luck. I couldn't get the World Cup semi-final out of my mind, and that awful moment when I was run out, when we needed just one more run to beat Australia. I still can't believe what went wrong.

South Africa had come into the World Cup as favourites, and that was justified by our strong showing in one-day matches over the preceding year. Bob Woolmer and Hansie Cronje worked very positively with us in our training camp before we left for England and the spirit was excellent. They impressed on us that although nothing should ever be taken for granted, we deserved to be the tournament favourites because of our consistency. We had to accept the responsibility of being favourites, and see it as a compliment and an extra incentive. I certainly think we played confidently enough in the World Cup – apart from that final, shattering ball in the semi-final at Edgbaston – and in terms of preparation, morale and cricket skills we were ready to grab the prize that we felt we should have taken in the previous World Cup, when one bad game against the West Indies saw us eliminated at a time when we were playing fantastically well. This time, we were desperate to make amends.

As for me, it was a bit of a race against time to get fit for the tournament, starting in the middle of May. There was always the chronic injury to my left ankle at the back of my mind, with the threat that it could flare up again at any stage, but I had also picked up a nasty stomach muscle injury in New Zealand, just a few weeks before we were due in England. I missed one Test and two one-dayers in

New Zealand, and there was inevitable speculation that I might not be ready for the opening matches of the World Cup. But medical specialists in South Africa reassured me, and I was fired up for what I knew would be my last World Cup. I came through the warm-up games well enough, and then it was time for us to come to the party – at Hove, against India.

The atmosphere that day was fantastic – with around 5,000 Indian fans making a tremendous noise – and I thought we played really well to chase 253 and win by four wickets with a couple of overs to spare. I felt I bowled well – going for just three an over and working up good pace – while Jacques Kallis showed what a world-class all-rounder he had become by playing maturely for his 96. But the story of the day was our experiment with a radio system out in the field, which allowed us to be wired up to Bob Woolmer in the dressing-room.

Now Bob has always been at the forefront of experimenting with technology in sport, having studied sports coaching in the USA, and he was frustrated with the limited amount of time that cricket coaches, in particular, could spend with their players off the field during breaks. His argument was, why should coaching stop once the players were out there on the field? So much happens during a cricket match, especially in a one-dayer, that Bob felt this new system of communication was worth trying out. So Hansie Cronje, as captain, and myself, as leading bowler and an avid supporter of Bob's ideas, wore the earpieces through which the coach could communicate in an instant – but the experiment only lasted half-an-hour, until we were spotted by a television cameraman. The match referee, Talat Ali told us during the first drinks interval that it wasn't on, so we had to dispense with the electronic aids. It was no big deal, but I thought there was a bit of an over-reaction to what I felt was a genuine attempt to speed up the game. Instead of having the twelfth man on and off the field, relaying suggestions or instructions, what was wrong with having a direct input to the dressing-room? It's just a facility – Bob wasn't treating Hansie as captain like a robot, merely offering a different perspective, like different angles for the fielders or another area for the bowler to consider. For me, it was good to have advice while out on the field from a coach I respected so much, and who knew my game inside out. I suppose we should have cleared it beforehand with the ICC, who felt such an experiment couldn't be sanctioned in a World Cup match, but I'm certain that Bob Woolmer will push for it again in the near future. It works okay in American football, where specialist coaches sit in the stand, giving detailed instructions, so why not in cricket? In a few years' time, we'll wonder what all the fuss was about.

At least we were off the mark in the tournament. We could have slipped up at Hove, against a dangerous Indian side, and the way we steamrollered Sri Lanka in the next match was even more impressive. The 1996 holders were, in my book, slight favourites to retain the trophy, because of their brilliant batsmen, a genius in the off-spinner Muttiah Muralitharan and their mental toughness – and when we were 122 for eight, they must have fancied their chances. But Lance Klusener played an amazing innings to reach 52 off 45 balls, including 22 in the final over, and he took three cheap wickets as they folded against the target of 200. We were really fired up over a couple of umpiring decisions that didn't go our way when we batted, and we turned it to our advantage very positively. With England next up at the Oval, we were beginning to build up momentum very nicely. We knew the importance of the first three matches, the necessity of winning plus boosting our net run rate, and so far it was going according to plan.

We looked like champions in beating England by a massive margin, in one-day terms, of 122 runs. We had made only 225 for seven on a good pitch after being put in, and although some of our batters had played some loose shots, we were awesome in the field, bowling them out for 103 to win with nine overs to spare. I came on second change – after being first change the previous game, because the new white ball just didn't suit me – and I found my control and rhythm straight away. My analysis of four for 17 off eight overs was a great boost to my confidence, and we were all on a high, having come through three tough games with a hundred per cent record. Support for us was growing, as more and more South Africans came over for the later stages of the tournament, and although we remained cautious and low-key, we were quietly confident. Our fielding couldn't be bettered by any other side – and Jonty Rhodes' fantastic catch at backward point to get Robert Croft at the Oval summed up the standard – and with so many of us experienced in English conditions, there seemed no reason why we couldn't at least get to the semi-finals. Then, who knows? Could this be our year after the disappointments of '92 and '96?

The next match, in Amsterdam, was a clinical win by seven wickets over Kenya. Some felt that Hansie Cronje and Bob Woolmer should have rested a few key players, with some tough matches to come, but Hansie wanted to maintain our level of intensity. I don't blame him for that.

That intensity is ingrained in the South African mentality – 'you *will* win' – and although that sometimes rebounds on us, making us tense up, we do have a massive competitive instinct. This goes through homework at school, training hard at sport and giving absolutely everything on the field of play. Only Australia shade us in that respect, as they were to prove in two momentous matches in this 1999 World Cup.

Four straight wins then, and we were now firm favourites to lift the trophy. We weren't complacent, though – we'd had enough setbacks in the two previous World Cups to take anything for granted – and our next match, against Zimbabwe was a real wake-up call. What a time for Zimbabwe to beat us in any form of cricket for the first time – by 48 runs. We were definitely motivated for this one, in front of a packed crowd at Chelmsford. Victory would have given us an easier passage through to the semi-finals, allowing us perhaps to rest one or two players for the next game against Pakistan. There is always an extra incentive when we play our neighbours, Zimbabwe, because they believe we patronise them for their lack of experience and depth of players. Whether that's true or not, no South African wants to lose to Zimbabwe, and I can't put my finger on why we bowled badly and batted stupidly. At 40 for six, chasing 234, we were deep in trouble, and although Lance Klusener again batted superbly for another unbeaten half-century, my dismissal saw us go down by 48 runs with sixteen balls to spare. That was very annoying, because it meant we now had to regain our momentum against Pakistan, then New Zealand to be in contention for a semi-final place.

We had to dig deep against Pakistan to beat them by

three wickets in a great match at Trent Bridge. Needing 221 to win, in poor light, we were 58 for five at one stage, but Klusener did it again. With Shoaib Akhtar bowling very rapidly, supported by Wasim Akram's great experience, you would have fancied Pakistan to nail down the win. But Klusener smashed 46 off 41 balls, keeping his nerve so impressively, and we stormed home with an over to spare. As long as Klusener was there in the closing overs, we felt that any total was achievable and with batsmen like Mark Boucher, Shaun Pollock and Steve Elworthy there as support in the lower order, we felt confident. Our next match – at Edgbaston against New Zealand – proved to be a surprisingly routine outing, as we played very professionally to ease in by 74 runs. So now we were one game away from the semi-final of the World Cup – again. Could we at last go one better than '92? Apart from that blip against Zimbabwe, we felt we had played well so far, although our batsmen could have made a few more runs. But all the other sides had struggled in the top order, with no pinch-hitting heroics against the white ball, swinging and seaming around in typical English conditions at the start of a damp summer. South Africa's lower order – marshalled by Klusener – kept getting us out of trouble, and our experience of English conditions made us a handy outfit when we bowled. And our fielding remained outstanding.

Our opponents in the next game were the Australians. We felt we'd never have a better chance of beating them, and in the process eliminating them from the tournament. Because of the complicated scoring system, we were virtually assured of a place in the semis, provided we didn't get hammered in this match at Leeds. On the other hand Australia, after a few faltering performances in the

tournament, simply had to beat us to stay alive. We were
without the injured Jacques Kallis, who had a strain in his
abdomen, but we batted really well to make 271 for seven,
with Herschelle Gibbs making a brilliant hundred. Poor
'Hersch'. He was to prove the fall-guy before the end of
the match. We had them 48 for three, with just one key
wicket left before we could be confident of victory. That
wicket was Steve Waugh's. One of the greatest competitors
I have ever played with or against, he was the difference
that day between victory and defeat. If he had got out for
less than a hundred, we would have won and Australia
were out. He should have gone for 56, when he clipped
Klusener to Gibbs at mid-wicket. Gibbs, who had fielded
brilliantly all tournament, dropped the comfortable catch.
It was the way he dropped it that demoralised us, though.
Hersch is a confident cricketer, a bit of a showman, and
when he takes a catch, he likes to throw the ball over his
shoulder almost as soon as he has the ball in his hands.
This is what he did with this offering from Waugh – except
that he took his eye off the ball before he had it under
control, and he spilled it. We were all running towards him
in celebration, and we stopped dead in our tracks as the
ball hit the turf. I thought, 'Oh, no, not Waugh' and sure
enough, he grabbed the lifeline. He went on to play one
of the greatest one-day knocks I've seen. He was merciless,
aggressive, running superbly between the wickets and his
120 not out brought them victory by five wickets with two
balls to spare. It was no consolation to us that it had been
a fantastic match, and that Waugh had played remarkably
to make the authentic captain's innings. We had thrown
away victory – literally – and no one was in any doubt
that the Australians would be stronger psychologically,

now that they had looked down the barrel of elimination and survived. We had played enough tight games against those guys in recent years to know how tough they were, how they were used to winning in tense situations – something we still had to master, especially against Australia. They'd done us again. How significant would that be for the rest of this World Cup?

Our dressing-room was very quiet that night at Headingley. We were still in the World Cup, we had got to the semi-final due to our satisfactory net run rate, but the chance to eliminate Australia had gone that day. At least we'd have another go at them in four days' time. As luck would have it, Australia versus South Africa was to be the second semi-final, on my home ground of Edgbaston. Would that be a lucky omen for me and my team? We would know the other finalist before our game, because Pakistan were up against New Zealand the day before, at Old Trafford. What a time to get revenge against Australia! We had beaten them many times before in one-day matches, but rarely when the chips were down, when it really mattered. A World Cup semi-final really mattered – not least to Herschelle Gibbs. Understandably, he was very down after Leeds, and the papers went to town on an alleged remark from Steve Waugh when he spilled that catch. It was reported that Waugh said to him, 'Congratulations, Hersch – you've just dropped the World Cup', and although some of our fielders confirmed that, Hersch said he hadn't heard it. He was too busy cursing himself for his over-confidence, but it's the sort of thing that Waugh would have the bottle to say to him. One of these days I'll ask Steve Waugh about that.

Hansie Cronje and Bob Woolmer did their best to gee

up Hersch in between Leeds and Edgbaston, telling him he mustn't brood about it. 'Go out and put it to bed,' Hansie told him, and I must admit that Hersch and the rest of us practised very hard and effectively in the build-up to Edgbaston. We had one day off, when we played golf, and after that we were very focused, watching videos of the Australians, planning how we could maximise our strengths to negate them. We felt that it was good to have the chance so soon to hit back at the Aussies, that Steve Waugh couldn't do it again. Our time was now.

On the morning of the match, our team bus was very quiet as we headed towards the ground. Headphones on, no one spoke, we were all in our private thoughts, fully aware of what faced us. Our warm-ups on the outfield were tense, yet committed, lacking our usual high spirits – but if you can't get edgy before a match of this nature, when could you? We knew the Aussies would be feeling exactly the same. We felt hugely encouraged by the over-whelming support for us on the ground. Everywhere you looked, there were green jerseys, with hardly a peep from the Aussie fans. It was a special Edgbaston atmosphere – a packed house, a glorious June morning, with the adrenalin pumping overtime. This is what you play international sport for. I felt it was going to be our day.

It went very well for us early on, after we had stuck them in on a slow pitch which helped the seamers and didn't do much for strokemakers. It wasn't a particularly good pitch for such a big occasion, with a few deliveries stopping on the batsmen, so it was hard to judge how good their score of 213 was. They had recovered from 68 for four through half-centuries from Michael Bevan and, inevitably, Steve Waugh, but Shaun Pollock and I hit back at the death, taking nine wickets between us. As I walked off the field, at the end of their innings, I thought, 'We can't complain at needing 214.'

We started very well. Gibbs and Gary Kirsten put on 48 for the first wicket, seeing off the dangerous Glenn McGrath. Soon it was 53 for three, as a truly great bowler took the game by the scruff of the neck. Shane Warne came on, well aware that he had to do something special – and quickly. He did. Three wickets to Warne in the space of eight balls. The one that got Gibbs in his first over really started the alarm bells ringing, as Hersch's off-stump was hit by a ball that pitched outside leg-stump. It wasn't a great idea to try working that delivery through legside, but it turned a mile, and this great bowler for the big occasion was off and running. He was lucky to get Hansie Cronje – given out, caught at slip when the ball hit his boot, not bat – but Warne was superb in that first spell. Darryl Cullinan's run out stemmed from the pressure and soon we were 61 for four.

I couldn't stand the tension in our dressing-room any-more, and I escaped to a room occupied only by the fourth umpire, Roy Palmer. I stayed there for the next 33 overs, praying that I wouldn't have to walk out there and bat. Surely the Aussies weren't going to do us again? But Warne had to come off after bowling eight overs, and they had to mix their part-time bowlers up. Jacques Kallis and Jonty Rhodes calmed our nerves by adding 84, and it looked as if we were getting there as we entered the last ten overs with seventy needed and six wickets left. We might not even need Klusener! But then Jonty got himself out for 43 and when Warne returned for his last two overs, we needed 61 from 48 balls. Just see off Warne, and we're home! His last over went for fifteen – including a majestic six over long-on from Shaun Pollock. But Jacques tried to play him through extra cover with an inside-out drive and he was caught for 53. Pollock and Mark Boucher then went soon after, and at 196 for eight, I was beginning to realise I might be needed.

Lance Klusener was playing remarkably, though. The Aussies took a chance in keeping the deep mid-wicket area open, and Lance plundered that part of the ground. He smashed 23 off his first twelve balls, and yet he never looked in any trouble. There was no sense of panic, he just picked his spot calmly. I was dreading having to bat. What if it came down to me, with Lance helpless at the other end? How would I remember where all the fielders were? What if I got one on my legs, I tried to guide it down to the fine leg boundary, and I just hit it straight to a fielder? How do I get Klusener on strike when all the gaps are plugged? No one was talking to me at that stage in the dressing-room because the hope was that I wouldn't be needed. Everyone else was too busy cheering on big Lance, as he smashed the bowling around. Steve Elworthy was out there with him – a vastly experienced cricketer, a highly competent batsman, the ideal person for this sort of situation. All Steve needed to do was support Lance, and I wouldn't be needed.

But Elworthy was run out, going for a second run that didn't need to be attempted. We were up with the required rate, Warne was bowled out, and a few more blows from Klusener would see us through. This isn't meant to be a criticism of Steve, because I soon showed what pressure can do to an experienced cricketer – but I reckon we would have won it if Steve had stayed in, rather than go for that second run when it was bound to be tight. All this is being wise after the event, though, because my pulse was racing as I picked up my bat and gloves and went out to join Lance Klusener. I can't remember anything the boys said to me as I left the dressing-room. I suppose there wasn't much to offer, really. We all knew what I had to do – give it to Klusener and run when I was told.

Lance was unbelievably calm when I joined him out in the middle. On the way out, the din from the crowd was remarkable. No packed ground in England generates more atmosphere than Edgbaston, yet it seemed to calm Lance, rather than intimidate him. I was close to panic, with fifteen needed, but he just said, 'Don't worry about it, we'll be fine' as if it was a benefit match! Over the next few minutes, he showed an amazing big-match temperament, and I'm still in awe at his calmness as I think about the bedlam out in the middle, and the stakes that we were playing for.

The penultimate over was bowled by Glenn McGrath, a guy perfectly capable of dismissing Klusener, never mind me. His fifth ball was clubbed by Klusener for six over long-on, but through the hands of Paul Reiffel, as he back-pedalled towards the rope. It was a desperately close thing, but you wouldn't know from the look of Lance. You could see the heads of the Aussies drop as Reiffel threw the ball back, and when Lance took a single off McGrath's final over to get the strike, they looked down. Klusener now looked in complete control. All I had to do was just stay there, and hope I didn't have to face another ball. There was nothing really to say as Lance and I met between overs, we just had to look at the lack of confidence in the Aussies to tell it was going our way. I just wished my partner good luck and went back to the non-striker's end, waiting for

Damian Fleming to start the final over. Nine to win, one wicket to fall, six balls left.

The first ball was smashed through the offside cordon to the extra cover boundary, beating the sweeper out there by three yards to his left. I don't think I'd ever seen a ball hit harder. Until the next delivery. This one travelled at a rate of knots to the right of Mark Waugh at long-off, and it raced over the ropes. What an amazing shot – what nerve! I threw up my arms in delight at that second boundary, convinced we had won it now, and the crowd's excitement was deafening. I looked around the Aussie fielders, at Shane Warne with his hands disconsolately on his hips, at Steve Waugh clapping his hands, trying to shout something positive – and I thought 'We've got them!' One more run needed, four balls left.

Waugh then showed his experience and tactical shrewdness, although I didn't think so at the time. Fleming had been bowling reverse swing and to the left-handed Klusener; that was ideal for the batsman, because he was just hitting through the line to deliveries that were starting on middle and moving away to the off. So Waugh told Fleming to go around the wicket and try to tuck up the left-hander. Amid all the hubbub from the crowd, I thought it was just a delaying tactic to see if they could prey on our nerves, but I had complete faith in my batting partner. One more ball from Fleming should do it, I thought. Wonder if he'll smash another offside four to end it in spectacular fashion? The third ball did cramp Lance for room, and he jabbed it out to Darren Lehmann at mid-on. He made a great diving save to his left, and as I raced down the pitch, I was sent back by Lance. As I turned, I realised I'd be struggling if Lehmann hit the stumps direct with his favoured left-hand throw. The ball just missed the stumps. I'd have been out by a couple of feet if it had hit. Sprawled on the floor, my heart pounding, I thought, 'Thank God, we've got away with it. We'll be okay now.'

I walked down the pitch to have a word with Lance, but amid all the noise, it was a waste of time. He was wild-eyed, but calm. He still looked in control of himself as I told him, 'Pick your spot, and hit it out of the park.' Three balls to go, one run needed to win. Fleming bowled a yorker. Lance dug it out with the bottom of his bat and it bounced past the bowler. I was in the crease until the moment when the ball passed Fleming and only then did I start to run. I looked up at Lance, saw him rushing to my end and so I started to run as well. My legs felt like jelly, as if I wasn't making any headway at all down the other end. I heard the Aussies shouting 'Keeper! Keeper!' as I tried to get my legs moving properly. It was a dreamlike sequence, almost in slow motion. I ended up dropping my bat, and was run out by ten yards at least. The Aussies fell into each others' arms and my world just fell apart. The match ended in a tie – with both sides all out for 213 – but they went through to the Final on net run rate. We knew that would be the case if the scores were level, so we had no one else to blame but ourselves. Or more particularly – me.

I couldn't bring myself to watch that final over on video until a few days later. I then pieced together the elements of that final ball. Was I right to stay in my ground until the ball had passed the bowler? I think so. After all, that narrow escape from Lehmann's throw off the previous ball had shown how risky it would have been to charge down the pitch too early. Yet I should have run instantly the ball beat Fleming because although Mark Waugh was very close at mid-off, he would still need time to get down to the ball, pick it up and get it back to Fleming. Surely Lance would have been home at the bowler's end in that space of time? But I was too slow in getting out of the blocks and Fleming had the time to gather Waugh's throw, under-arm it down to the wicket-keeper's end, leaving me stranded. It looked terrible – amateurish, panicky, the sort of thing you see on the village green every Sunday. Not in a World Cup semi-final, featuring a guy who has played for his country for more than a decade. Nothing you do in your career can prepare you for a moment like that. I had let down my batting partner, my team and my country.

Along with most of the boys, I was in tears in our dressing-room. I just felt worse as the night wore on, as Jonty Rhodes came to console me, followed by Hansie Cronje. Both told me it was bad luck, but I knew that wasn't the case. I had blown it. I was still in a state of shock when Lance came over and apologised. 'For what?' I asked. He said, 'It was my fault, I should have left it, there were two balls to go after that one. We still had time.' We spent the rest of the night trying to take the blame while absolving the other, but it served no purpose, I suppose. I couldn't be consoled by anyone. In the end, Hansie called us together for a group huddle. He thanked us all for our efforts, that it just wasn't meant to be. The more I apologised, the more I was told it wasn't my fault, but the boys were just being kind. Then Bob Woolmer stood up to thank us all for supporting him down the years. That's when it dawned on me that Bob had coached us for the last time. He had decided to finish after the World Cup, and that was now for South Africa. Bob broke down, and we all started to cry again. It was horrible, just horrible.

We sat in the dressing-room for at least two hours, stunned, emotional and inconsolable. Many of our supporters waited for us outside to cheer us, and that made it even worse. One wasn't quite so understanding. He shouted, 'Why didn't you f*****g run, Donald!' and he was quickly led away by a security official. I wouldn't have been able to answer that question myself. I went home to Harborne that night – just ten minutes' drive – and it was like entering a different world. It did my heart good to see the smiling faces of my two children, to give me some perspective on what had happened. They still loved their daddy, no matter what happened in the final over of a cricket match. Next day, I went to the team hotel, to say goodbye to the boys, and pick up my kit. I looked at the newspapers, and the pictures of the despairing South African supporters at the ground brought it all back to me again. Forget my anguish – what about all those folk who had paid so much to come over and see me throw it away with one moment of panic? You could put it down to human error, but an experienced international froze at the crucial time. And that was me.

Over the next few weeks, I was heartened by many kind messages from South African supporters. There were just a couple of abusive messages, and I couldn't have complained if there had been hundreds of them. Friends at Warwickshire and my family were marvellous to me for the rest of that English summer, but I couldn't get the events of that Fleming over out of my mind. I watched the tape over and over again, and just felt annoyed at myself. In my last World Cup, I had contributed to the biggest disappointment of my career. Bob Cottam, our bowling coach at Edgbaston said to me one day, 'Al – you look terrible. You need some time off.' It's true that I was emotionally drained, and very tired. I wasn't sleeping very well, my mind still pored over that daft moment. Warwickshire were very understanding, and gave me a fortnight off. It took me at least four months to get that match out of my system. Having worn out that video tape, I never want to watch that run out ever again.

My nightmare summer in England didn't improve all that much after that semi-final. When I returned after licking my wounds, my ankle problem flared up again. I broke down five times over the next ten weeks, and I got through a few one-day matches for Warwickshire, but with no great comfort nor success. I didn't take a single wicket in the championship, and by the end of the season, I knew that some influential people at Edgbaston were wondering if I was finished. Could they take a chance on me and offer me another contract, when there was no guarantee that I'd last a full season? I could fully understand those views, but no one could have been more depressed or worried than me. I had to fly out to South Africa during the championship match at Durham, after I broke down again – and I was a very worried man when I went to see the specialist Dr Fief Ferreira. I realised that an operation was the favoured option, but that would probably put me out of the forthcoming Test series against England, due to start in two months' time. A satisfactory recuperation from such an operation would normally take around four months, and there was no guarantee that it would rescue my career. I told Dr Ferreira and the South African cricket team's physiotherapist Craig Smith that I preferred taking a chance on a scan and injection, rather than an operation. They agreed to give it a go. They found some inflammation in the ankle, but not an excessive amount of damage. An injection at last hit the spot. It was agony, but we felt it would do the trick. Two days later, in the middle of September, I flew back to Birmingham, under strict instructions to stay off my feet for as long as possible. My career was still alive, but I knew I had been lucky. The upcoming series against England meant so much to me as I advanced on my target of three hundred Test wickets. I needed another 35, and couldn't contemplate falling short.

I also owed it to Warwickshire to prove the doubters wrong. Everyone was so generous to me during my benefit, and yet I couldn't repay so many kindnesses. First I was away until the middle of June on World Cup duty, then my depression took me out of it for a fortnight, and finally my ankle gave way. And all the while, the collection buckets were going around Edgbaston, various functions were being handsomely supported. My good friend Ernie Els attended a marvellous golf day at the Buckinghamshire Club, just before he played in the Open, while my book launch dinner was graced by Jack Charlton, Ernie Els, Gareth Edwards, Francois Pienaar, Michael Lynagh, Rory Bremner and all the South African cricket team. So much goodwill from so many people left me rather embarrassed at my lack of success on the field in 1999. I owed it to many to get back into the thick of things and start taking wickets again. It was time to stop feeling sorry for myself.

CHAPTER TWENTY-ONE

Looking Down the Barrel

I returned to South Africa in September 1999 to face what proved to be the most demanding period mentally of my career. As usual with a sportsman, the psychological doubts grow as the body starts to send out warning signals – and there were enough of them, as I tried to recover from the ankle problem that seemed to be ever-present. I had managed to stave off another operation on that left ankle, because that would have meant missing out on a Test series I really fancied – at home against England – but my state of mind wasn't very positive as that series approached. I was in a mess with my bowling, and at times wondered if I'd ever be the same bowler again. Over the next six months, there were to be many low periods, a lot of self-doubt and I needed the great support I received from many important areas. The quest for my 300 Test wickets soon appeared irrelevant to me, as I was more concerned at a decline that I hoped was only temporary. That I took another 32 Test wickets during this difficult time proves that you don't always get personal success when you're at your peak, firing on all cylinders. It wasn't until the Bangalore Test in March that I felt I was bowling as well as I'd done in the World Cup, nine months earlier, but at least I could honestly say that I'd come out of the dark tunnel in a stronger mental state. And my tally of 297 Test wickets was yet another incentive to keep going as I neared the ripe old age for a fast bowler of 34!

Before the England series, we played two Tests in October and November against Zimbabwe. It was a very close call for me, because I'd been off my feet just a few weeks earlier, resting my dodgy ankle while hoping that the psychological scars from that World Cup semi-final would disappear. I was picked for the first Test – in my home city of Bloemfontein – but throughout practice, I kept hoping that my rustiness would disappear once the adrenalin of the match kicked in. The ankle was still at the back of my mind, and I was tentative, with no rhythm. The ball kept spearing down legside, my wrist wasn't in the correct upright position, and there was no fire or genuine pace there. Shaun Pollock and Jacques Kallis comfortably outbowled me and I just told myself I had to keep running in, hoping I'd get back in sync. I needed miles on the clock, but I kept thinking, 'How on earth am I going to get picked against England, when I'm bowling this rubbish?' We wanted revenge after the '98 series defeat, we needed to bounce back after the World Cup, I wanted to get to my 300 target – but the meter was ticking as we went into November and I was struggling.

In the build-up to the first Test against England in Johannesburg, all the media hype concerned Donald versus Atherton, and the revival of our duels down the years. All I knew was that Athers was in far better nick than me, from what I'd seen of him so far on the tour. He remained the English wicket we all prized most. Well, judging by my awful preparation for that first Test, I'd have been happy with Alan Mullally's wicket, never mind Athers'! On the eve of the Test, after a hard session in the nets, I went out into the middle with the other fast bowlers, to try to simulate a match situation. I was dreadful – the wrist was floppy, the ball was slipping down legside, there was no zip there. After another session in the nets, I felt better, but there was no consistent rhythm. I told myself I just had to bowl through it in the Test, hoping that it would come good. Hardly an optimistic base from which to operate at the start of such an important series.

Because I was nervous and short of confidence, the ideal scenario for me was to bowl first on a favourable wicket, hoping to regain some form. That's exactly what happened. We were lucky to get the chance, though. Hansie Cronje won what proved to be a crucial toss, and by the third over, we had four batters out for just two runs, including their experienced trio of Michael Atherton, Nasser Hussain and Alec Stewart, all for nought. A dream start, but we shouldn't have started in bad light. The pitch was damp, because the groundsman wanted to make sure that cracks wouldn't develop, but it was also dark. A nightmare for the batting side, and the light wasn't good enough for batting early on. We would have been disappointed if we'd had to bat in those conditions, but England needed to tough it out early on, and they didn't. That's the mark of a top side. We had the responsibility of getting the ball in the right place, especially as it was swinging around so much, so there was a bit of pressure on us as well. That's why I was so thrilled to take three wickets in my first two overs, including the key one of Atherton in the first over. That was one of the most satisfying wickets of my Test career, because it was planned. Hansie Cronje told me at our team meeting that I'd bowl him in the first over, and that's why I pointed to Hansie in jubilation when I did just that. We had worked out that Atherton, who is such a good leaver of the ball early on, has a tendency to get slightly off-side of the ball in his keenness to cover his off-stump. Because I seemed to be bowling a lot of inswingers due to my wrist action being faulty, I thought I had a chance of sneaking in the in-ducker. That's what happened, and he left quite a gap, and I knocked his off-pole out. A dream start. I ended up with six for 53 and we bowled them out for 122. A huge relief for me.

It's true that England were unlucky with the toss and conditions early on, but I don't think it was a wicket to be bowled out on for 122. They had their chance after tea on the first day, but in the thirty overs available to them, they took just one wicket. They didn't make us play often enough, and wasted their advantage with the new ball. Hansie said that anything above 350 was a bonus, so to get to 403 for nine was tremendous. Herschelle Gibbs and Darryl Cullinan gave a masterly example of how to leave the ball when it's rising too steeply, and England just didn't bowl with enough accuracy and control. That was the key to this Test, not our great start on the first morning. If they'd bowled us out for 200, they were back in the game, especially on a pitch where the odd ball kept low and even the old ball swung around and moved off the seam. We would have had to bat last, but in the end they did that, because we beat them by an innings on the fourth morning.

I was really pleased by my five for 74 in the second innings, especially a spell of four for 11 inside fifteen balls, when I worked up good pace. My rhythm was good, the ball came out well and smacked into Mark Boucher's gloves. But then I lost it again on the fourth morning. It was mystifying how my rhythm came and went, and although I had taken eleven wickets in this Test, I wasn't fooled. I knew I was still a long way off the standards I had set myself, aware that I'd bowl a lot better in future and take just a handful of wickets. I went back to play a four-day match for Free State, in between the first and second Tests, and still I couldn't recapture my consistency. My confidence was still low, but the new South African coach, Graham Ford was very good around this time. He just said, 'Forget about all the technical worries, just go out there and bowl. Enjoy it.' I tried to, but I can't say I was enjoying it all that much. It was nice to go one-up in the series straight away, though.

We might have won the next Test, at Port Elizabeth, if Nasser Hussain hadn't batted so brilliantly to see out the final day. We batted too slowly on the fourth evening, as we tried to set up a total that would tempt England but not allow them to win. In the end, it was 302 in 79 overs, and when we had them 5 for two – including Atherton's wicket – we had a genuine chance. But Hussain dug in, the wicket was dead, and the fact that we had taken too long when we batted, meant we couldn't take a second new ball. So the match petered out, with us needing another four wickets, and England miles away from the victory target. I was very impressed with Hussain. In the past, he has given you a chance because of his desire to play his shots, and the fact that he plays with an open face defensively, but he tightened up his game and I liked his 'over my dead body' attitude at Port Elizabeth. The captaincy has helped make him a better player, and by the end of the Test series, his was a key wicket to take.

The crucial factor in the draw was the pitch. It was a disgrace for Test cricket, because it gave the bowlers little hope. The year before, the West Indies Test had ended inside three days, and I'm sure the sponsors and the United Cricket Board were worried that this Test wouldn't go the distance, especially after the one at Johannesburg lasted only until lunch on the fourth day. When we got to look at the wicket on the first morning, all the grass had disappeared, and it rolled out flat and dead. On the final afternoon, as we tried desperately for a breakthrough, I leaned towards the stump microphone and said into it, 'Let's have a big hand for the groundsman.' It was sheer frustration from me, because I thought the prospect of South Africa winning the series over England was more important than seeing the match last five days. You'd expect that from a player, though, wouldn't you?

There was one big plus for South Africa from the Port Elizabeth Test. Nantie Hayward made his debut and immediately impressed as a fast bowler of Test class. He was too loose on our tour of England in '98, but he spent a lot of time in the gym, getting his upper body and legs stronger. His control had also greatly improved. No longer did he spray it around and on this flat pitch, he definitely looked South Africa's premier fast bowler of the future. Already he's quicker than me by a long way. He needs to look closely at the way he's going to develop as a fast bowler, but he has all the natural aggression and common-sense to be the genuine article for years to come. He won't be the next Allan Donald, he'll be the first Nantie Hayward and he should take a stack of wickets for South Africa.

Going into the third Test, in Durban, I was still down on myself. My form was around seventy per cent, still erratic in spells, still unsure that the ball was going to go exactly where I wanted it. I wasn't a great deal better in Durban, although the extenuating circumstances were the draining heat and humidity as well as a pitch that was dreadfully slow after days and days of heavy rain. The groundstaff did fantastically well to get the pitch ready for the start, because some parts of the playing area were still muddy the day before – so I suppose we can't complain too much. The circumstances behind the turgid pitch were totally different to Port Elizabeth. Yet nothing went sideways at Durban, the bounce was uniform and the wicket would probably have lasted for another three days. It was ideal for the batsman prepared to graft – in this Test, that was Nasser Hussain and Gary Kirsten. They both showed great character and physical resilience, but the pitch was loaded in favour of the batsmen. That's why we were so annoyed at being bowled out cheaply in our first innings, and made to follow on. Getting bowled out for 156 was very poor, even though Andy Caddick bowled brilliantly to take seven wickets. I'd always thought Caddick would be a threat in this series, with his extra bounce, and willingness to bowl lots of overs. He should have played more Tests for England, whether or not he's had an attitude problem. That's up to the management and captain to sort out. He bowled a beautiful line at Durban, and yet we didn't concentrate enough in that first innings. Too many cavalier shots on a pitch that didn't encourage the strokemaker.

We made amends for it in the second innings, chiefly through Gary Kirsten's monumental 275 and Mark Boucher's brilliant hundred, but I wonder if Hussain made an error in enforcing the follow-on. There was a case for giving his bowlers a day's rest, so that we would have to bat out the final day and a bit against bowlers who had some respite from the heat. But Caddick, Darren Gough and Chris Silverwood were on their knees on that final afternoon, with England having been on the field for the last three days. Yet we could have lost it. When Mark Boucher came in as nightwatchman, we were just 34 ahead, with six wickets left and a whole day stretching ahead. But Boucher's a great man to have around in these situations, and he took the pressure off Gary Kirsten, who had struggled all series and was playing for his place. Boucher never looked like getting out until he got his hundred, and the mature way he batted underlined how lucky we are to have someone of his quality coming in at number eight or nine in a Test match. As for Gary, that was a real pressure innings from him. A very quiet and popular team-man, Gary just gets on with his batting, playing within his limitations, doing the simple things effectively. A broken finger at the start of the season had set him back and he had lacked confidence until this innings at Durban. He knew he had to bat and bat to save the Test, and that sort of pressure brought out the best in him. It was just a shame that he couldn't get one more run to set a new record for the highest individual Test score for South Africa, but he was left tied on 275 with his team-mate, Darryl Cullinan, who was sat in the dressing-room, watching Gary close in on him. Darryl was as disappointed as everyone else when Mark Butcher surprised even himself by squeezing one through onto the leg-stump, to bowl Gary. Darryl wanted Gary to beat his record, and he made that quite clear to everyone. That's a measure of the popularity of Gary Kirsten. He'd played for the team, helping to save the Test, and created history at the same time.

So we went to Cape Town, still one-up in the series, boosted psychologically by frustrating England at Durban. We came out of that one the stronger of the two sides. They must have been physically shattered, having to spend three whole days in the field, in very difficult conditions, while we had the satisfaction of denying them a victory that they must have felt was theirs when they bowled us out so cheaply in the first innings. There would only be two clear days for both sides to recover before taking the field at Cape Town, but we would surely be fresher than Caddick and company. The 1998 series was still fresh in our minds, when we were one-up with two to play, yet still lost the series. Surely this wouldn't happen again?

For the first time in the series, we picked the best-balanced eleven and it showed, as we hammered England by an innings. Hansie Cronje had been under pressure as captain to pick an eleven that was deemed to be more representative of the new South Africa, so non-white players would be encouraged. That had led to confusion. Paul Adams was picked ahead of the seamer David Terbrugge for Johannesburg, where a spinner was totally superfluous. Then at Port Elizabeth, when we could have done with Adams' wrist-spin on such a flat wicket, he was twelfth man. At Durban, Jonty Rhodes was controversially dropped in favour of Nantie Hayward. We were all very surprised about that, because Jonty gives us so much in the field, and he was set to play on his home ground. He had made two fifties in the previous Test, and looked to be playing his way back to form. I don't believe Hansie wanted to drop Jonty, but the six selectors appeared to be torn between all sorts of considerations, so Jonty was dropped to accommodate an extra bowler, including Paul

Adams. Now in Cape Town, both Jonty and Paul played, and we looked a better unit as a result. But it was proving a difficult series for Hansie. He wasn't batting very well, scoring few runs, and it looked as if he wasn't getting the team he wanted for the Tests.

The toss was going to be crucial at Cape Town. England wouldn't have fancied bowling on day one after their exertions in Durban, and they were glad to bat first on a flat pitch. To bowl them out for 258 was a great effort, especially after Atherton and Butcher had started off with a first-wicket stand of 115. I got them both, and it was very satisfying after bowling a very poor opening spell. At lunchtime, we had a chat, and we agreed that we needed to bowl one of two lengths – either full, inviting the drive off the front foot, or short, tempting the batters to have a go with the cut, pull or hook. We'd stick a man out and hope they took the bait. It worked perfectly after lunch. Atherton had been taking on the short ball all morning, and this time he dragged one around to Gary Kirsten at deep backward square leg. Butcher's dismissal was even more pleasing. After lunch, I had bowled four maidens in a row at him, and then I suggested to Hansie that I should try a short one outside off-stump, to see if he'd go for the cut. Hansie said, 'Go over the wicket to him, make it bounce high and see if he takes you on.' It worked beautifully. The ball went straight down Kirsten's throat at third man. In that second spell of the day, after lunch, I took two for 2 in seven overs and it was the only time in the series that everything felt right for me. I just couldn't understand why the switch kept flicking on and off, but at least I was still taking wickets. I ended up with four on that first day at Cape Town. Andy Caddick, the nightwatchman, got out to me, driving loosely, and I wondered if his fatigue from Durban contributed to that dismissal. I was much happier, though, about the third wicket. Alec Stewart had played really well to get to 40, attacking the bowlers, enjoying the challenge, climbing into the short ball in particular. I've always relished my duels with Stewie, a batsman I rate very highly, who can look after himself when the verbals start flying around. I started to test him with a few observations when he just missed a hook shot off the first ball of my new spell. I stared down the pitch to him and said, 'Don't cock it up for your team', and when he mistimed another pull shot, he walked down the pitch and smiled at me. I said, 'Is it really necessary to be that compulsive?' and he replied, with a smile, 'No.' I told him, 'I've got a feeling you're going to cock it up'. He hooked me to deep backward square leg and as he left the crease, I shouted, 'Told you so!' That may sound childish, but you do get wound up in a tense Test match, and Stewie is well able to look after himself. We had a laugh about it afterwards.

I ended up with five wickets in that innings, which was personally very satisfying and great for the team, because it gave us the chance to bat England out of the game. The conditions got better for batting – very hot after the breeze on the first day – and England ran out of steam. I think the big effort in Durban took a lot out of them. Jacques Kallis and Darryl Cullinan both got fine hundreds and we passed 400, with two days left to bowl them out. We did it by tea-time on the fourth day, to win by an innings. They didn't bat with a great deal of spirit, and with Andrew Flintoff missing with a broken bone in his foot, plus a long tail, they were swept away once Atherton went for 36. The wickets were shared around, and although I only got one

– Caddick obligingly carving a short one to cover point – it was a great feeling to walk off my favourite Test ground, having clinched the series in style. The crowds had been marvellous all four days, with both sets of supporters really getting behind their sides. My family were on the ground, and as I walked off the ground at the end, waving in their direction, I wondered if this was to be the last time I played Test cricket at Newlands. I knew I was about to make some significant decisions. I couldn't put them off any longer.

I'd been grappling with the problem of keeping both South Africa and Warwickshire happy for some years now, and here it had come to a head in January 2000. I had been offered a one-year contract by Warwickshire, but that was dependent on my being available for the whole of the 2000 season. They had missed out on my services for the bulk of the 1999 season, through World Cup duties, then my ankle injury, and they were in no mood to compromise further. I understood that. I would always appreciate Warwickshire's support and faith in me, and I still owed them after being awarded a benefit in 1999. Yet South Africa had a huge claim on my loyalty also. Dr Ali Bacher, on behalf of the United Cricket Board of South Africa employed me, not Free State – and Dr Bacher wanted me to pledge myself to my country's cricket tours all the time. Australia were due in South Africa in April for three one-day matches, then we would return to Australia in August for a return one-day tournament. This one in Melbourne would be a ground-breaking series, to be played indoors. The hype would be massive, the box-office potential huge and both Dr Bacher and his Australian equivalents would be very keen to have me there in August, rather than playing for Warwickshire for England. What was I to do? Whatever I decided, I'd be disappointing either South Africa or Warwickshire. Bob Woolmer, who had decided to return to coach at Warwickshire, was in South Africa at the time, doing media work during the Test series, and told me that the county wanted a decision by the end of January, because they needed to secure a replacement if I was to let them down. The added complication was that if I dipped out of my international commitments with South Africa, I might not be picked again. The next home Test – in November against New Zealand – would see me past my 34th birthday, and perhaps the selectors would judge me to be past it. And here I was, stranded on 290 Test wickets. Of course, reaching that landmark was less important than playing in a successful South African side, while trying to keep my two employers reasonably happy – but it would be frustrating to miss out on such a personal landmark.

I announced my decision during the last Test, at Centurion Park. I told a packed press conference that I had asked the South African Board for a sabbatical. They would release me from my contract, so that I could play a full season for Warwickshire. I'd miss out on those one-day series against Australia and take my chances later in the year, when I returned from England. I would again be available for the two Test series against New Zealand, then Sri Lanka, plus all the one-dayers. I made it clear that I didn't expect to walk back into international cricket. I was hopeful, of course, but willing to be judged on merit when the next domestic season started in South Africa. I felt I needed some quality time with my family for the next six months or so, and that I would get that in England, with Warwickshire. Recharging my batteries by getting away for a time from the international treadmill would hopefully prolong my career with the national side, but I realised that my form and fitness would be the only criteria for my possible comeback. In return for releasing me from my contract, the Board had asked me to go to India, a month after this England Test series. That was a tough one. We'd only be playing two Tests, and I wouldn't be needed for the one-dayers. I'd be in India for just seventeen days maximum. Yet I felt very tired at the end of that series against England. Physically jaded, mentally gone. Could I rouse myself for that trip, or should I just opt out and get myself ready for a long summer with Warwickshire? I asked Dr Bacher for a few days to think about it. He said there was no pressure on me, but I felt there was. I needed to go back to Bloemfontein and talk it over with Tina.

As it turned out, I got back home earlier than I thought from Centurion Park. I didn't play in the Test because of an attack of gout. Unbelievable – and people say I'm a good athlete! I can see the funny side of it now, but not on the first morning of the Test, when I thought there was a recurrence of the foot problem that caused me grief in England on the '94 tour. I was in agony, walking into the ground at Centurion Park, and when I mentioned it to Hansie, he laughed and said, 'Don't worry, it's probably only gout!' Our doctor took one look at me and agreed. He took X-rays on the affected bone and to my relief, they were fine. It really was gout and it would clear up in a couple of days. I have suffered from it now and then – it's an hereditary thing, and my mother has it now and then – but what an anti-climax, with everyone wondering about the next stage in my career, and whether or not I'd ever get that 300th Test wicket! In hindsight, I would not have got anywhere near those ten wickets I needed at Centurion Park, because it rained for three days and we wouldn't have got on the park.

So I was back home in Bloemfontein for that eventful final day in the Centurion Park Test, won by England in a run chase. They did well to get those runs, but I can't help feeling that if Paul Adams hadn't dislocated and fractured his finger in the field before he'd even bowled one ball, they might have lost. Adams has really improved as a spinner, with greater control and discipline and at no stage in the series did England get to grips with him. Nantie Hayward bowled excellently at the death, when it got really tense and I thought it was a great finish. Hansie's declaration would not have been offered if the series had been all-square, or we were just one up, but it made for a great final day. The game of cricket received a boost, and although our guys gave everything, they lost what was, in effect, a one-day game. The record books will say we won the Test series 2–1, but I think we were better than that. When I saw the England tour party in the previous September, I said that they were at least one experienced batsman light, and that we ought to beat them. They relied far too much on Stewart, Hussain and Atherton, and their tail began at seven. I knew that Chris Adams would struggle, because he plants his left foot straight down the pitch, opening him up to the ball that leaves him. So he was vulnerable to catches in the slips and behind the stumps. Michael Vaughan looked to have a good temperament, who knew where his off-stump was, but this Test series was always going to be a learning period for him.

Vaughan's one for the future, so he couldn't be expected to make many runs. I couldn't understand why they didn't pick Graeme Hick and Mark Ramprakash. They have experience at Test level, and Hick remains the English batsman most feared by us. I thought their pace attack was the best we'd seen from them in recent years. Caddick was a revelation, Gough still has class, Silverwood is a great trier and Mullally gives them variety and control. Their fielding definitely improved as well. But, overall, I don't think anyone will disagree that we were the better side.

I was looking forward to the one-day series against England after the Centurion Park Test, but to my dismay I wasn't picked. I was angry about this. I love the day/night games in South Africa – the packed grounds, the close finishes, the noise and excitement. It really gets you up for the series. Instead, I was told that South Africa was looking to the future in one-day terms, and that I wouldn't be picked. It seemed strange to me that one of our fast bowlers making his international debut in this one-day series was Henry Williams – at 33, the same age as me! Building for the future? Gary Kirsten, Hansie Cronje and Jonty Rhodes were all still included for the England series, and so they should be – but if the selectors were really aiming for the future, they should also have gone the same way as me. I was the only experienced player to be left out, and my pride was hurt. When injuries mounted up during the triangular series – Zimbabwe were also involved – the call still didn't come for me. I was at home, watching the matches on television, and the selectors knew I was available and would have loved to be drafted in. It was a slap in the face and I felt very frustrated. I couldn't help feeling that I was being penalised for not making myself available for those two

Australian series, in April and August. It was hard being at home during the Triangular series. Every time I spoke to one of the South African players, they said there was a huge hole in the absence of myself and Darryl Cullinan, who had retired from one-day cricket. But Darryl had taken that decision himself, whereas I was being punished for taking a sabbatical for just six months, from April to October.

During the Triangular series, I was still being put under pressure by Dr Bacher to make myself available for the visit of Australia in April. I was at home, watching the South Africa versus England match in East London, when Dr Bacher rang to say, 'Allan, you've got to play in the Australia series.' He'd just got back from the ICC meeting in Singapore, where his Australian counterpart, Malcolm Speed had told him how important it was for me to be in Melbourne for the one-day series indoors. Apparently the hype in Australia has been enormous. It's a new concept, there's a chance for South Africa to get revenge from the last World Cup, and Malcolm Speed thinks this sort of cricket will appeal hugely to the younger generation. It'll be a big marketing exercise and Dr Bacher felt his star players should all be in Melbourne, and available for the first series, in South Africa. But I reminded him about my contract with Warwickshire, and that he had given his blessing to my sabbatical only a few weeks ago. I was also disgruntled about being left out of the Triangular series, but I let that pass. Dr Bacher told me that he'd sort it all out with M J K Smith and Dennis Amiss at Edgbaston and I felt relaxed about that. He has a habit of getting things done, and he has always appeared to have a good relationship with the Warwickshire officials. But Dr Bacher's approach was quickly shot down. Bob Woolmer nearly fell off his chair, said there was no chance of any leeway, and the chairman, Mike Smith said there would be no contract if I stayed in South Africa in April to play against Australia. Fair enough. I wasn't pushing for it, but Dr Bacher felt Mike Smith was being unreasonable. I must admit that there might have been a bit of give-and-take from Warwickshire, because I would only have missed three Benson & Hedges Cup matches, and no championship games. But I realise that Warwickshire are desperately keen to make a good start after last season's disappointments that included relegation in the championship. So Bob Woolmer wants us all focused right from the off at the start of April and I accept I have to be there. It's been the biggest country vs county dilemma I've faced in my career, and I'm glad it was all sorted out before it got nasty. But it was none of my making, I was just stuck in the middle.

During all the toing and froing between Dr Bacher and Warwickshire for my services, I had taken the decision to go on the short tour to India. Dr Bacher had made a personal request to me, and despite my misgivings due to fatigue, I had agreed after a week's reflection. I'm glad I went, because you can't beat the pleasure of being in a winning side in sport, especially when you're up against it, away from home in unfavourable conditions. It's a hard place to tour, but Geoffrey Boycott had told me I should go, because the two Tests were being played on grounds that favoured the quicker bowlers. The ball certainly went through at times in Mumbai and Bangalore, and it also turned for the spinners, so both Tests were full of incident, with the batsmen having to work hard for their runs. So the wickets were shared between our bowlers in the two

Tests. I ended up with seven, which left me on 297, but I had no problems over that. We'd had a long discussion between ourselves about the best way to approach going to India, and we agreed that they'd be vulnerable after a disastrous tour of Australia, with Sachin Tendulkar set to hand back the captaincy again. We needed to hit them hard straight away, to get in their faces and unsettle them. It worked. The first Test, at Mumbai, could have gone either way, but we won by four wickets, with Jacques Kallis playing with great maturity and Mark Boucher playing his shots when we were up against it. Mark decided to sweep the spinners out of the rough and he executed it brilliantly. It was a great win, and I was first on the field to give the boys a big hug of congratulations.

The second Test victory was a justification for aggressive batting. We bowled them out cheaply, after losing the toss, and we were determined just to bat once on a pitch that was going to turn sharply as the game went on. It worked a treat. Kallis, Klusener and Cullinan all batted positively, Nicky Boje chipped in with a nightwatchman's 85, and the Indians never stood a chance, despite a fantastic hundred from Azharuddin, who smashed us all over the place. I got the key wicket of Tendulkar in the second innings, as he chased a wide half volley to be caught at cover, and once he was out, one end was open. We won by an innings, a very satisfying performance, after we had decided to play all our fast bowlers on a spinners' pitch. We fancied that we could overwhelm them with sustained aggression and it paid off. It was important to continue winning Test series, at home and abroad, and this was our fourth series victory in a row.

I'm glad I went to India for team and personal reasons.

By the end of the series, I was bowling better than at any time in the past nine months. The ball was shaping nicely from my hand, I felt in control. No longer was I dreading that huge inswing, which meant that my wrist action was wrong. I could run to the crease with confidence again. To this day, I still don't know why it all went wrong for me, but at least I never gave up trying to put it right. It just seemed to return in India, and I reckon that by the end of that tour, I was only about five per cent off my best. That long lay-off in England didn't help, of course, and I was erratic for a long time afterwards. I'm relaxed about my pursuit of my 300th Test wicket. I've had a look at South Africa's home Test itinerary later this year, and I see that the first Test against New Zealand is on my home ground, Bloemfontein. If I can force my way into the side, it would be marvellous to get those three remaining wickets in front of my friends and family.

I now feel really strong about my game again. I'm really looking forward to the new season with Warwickshire, and I know that Bob Woolmer will be doing all he can to revive our fortunes, and get us back into the top division after we were surprisingly relegated last season. The boys know that we seriously under-achieved last year, and Bob will be coming hard at them. Bob and I spoke a lot in South Africa, and I'm excited by his vision and drive. At this stage of my career, the 2000 season in England is a huge challenge. I owe it to the Warwickshire fans to perform on the field after my embarrassment last season. I don't want to be seen as a beneficiary who took the money and gave little back. I'll never lose my affection for the club or its supporters, even though South Africa will still be claiming my attention again once the English season ends. That's the kind of professional challenge I enjoy, I love the dog-fight out in the middle. I pray it will stay that way for a few more years yet.

Career Statistics

Compiled by WENDY WIMBUSH
(as at 20 March 2000)

Career Milestones

1966   Born in Bloemfontein, 20 October.

1985   First-class debut: Orange Free State v Transvaal

1987   8–37 Orange Free State v Transvaal
Debut for Warwickshire: Edgbaston v Glamorgan
B & H Cup debut v Scotland
Sunday League debut: v Derbyshire
NatWest debut: v Staffordshire
100th first-class wicket: P J Newport (Worcestershire) at Worcester, 6 July

1989   200th first-class wicket: T E Jesty (Lancashire) at Old Trafford, 18 May
Capped for Warwickshire, after returning figures of 7–2–12–5 against Wiltshire at Edgbaston
86 wickets @ 16.25. Top of English bowling averages

1990   300th first-class wicket: R C Ontong (Northern Transvaal) at Bloemfontein, 21 January
400th first-class wicket: M A Robinson (Yorkshire) at Edgbaston, 1 June

1991   83 wickets @ 19.68
International debut: v India (Calcutta, 10 Nov) in a limited-overs international, taking 5–29

1992   One of Five *Wisden* Cricketers of the Year 1992
Played in South Africa's first World Cup match: v Australia at Sydney, 26 February
Test debut v West Indies (Bridgetown, 18 April)
500th first-class wicket: C A Walsh (Gloucestershire) at Bristol, 20 June
74 wickets @ 22.25

1993   600th first-class wicket: P E Robinson (Leicestershire) at Leicester, 23 July
50th Test wicket: M J Slater (Australia) at Adelaide (Third Test), 30 December

1995   700th first-class wicket: A C Parore (New Zealand) at Auckland, 6 March

BB 6–15 v Yorkshire (Edgbaston) – figures for Warwickshire in any Sunday League match

89 wickets @ 16.07. Top of English bowling averages

800th first-class wicket: A Flower (Zimbabwe) at Harare, 15 October. 8–71, his best in Tests.

100th Test wicket: G A Hick (England) at Johannesburg (Second Test), 3 November

1996	100th limited-overs international wicket: 6–23 v Kenya (Nairobi), 3 October
1997	150th Test wicket: I A Healy (Australia) at Centurion Park (Third Test), 21 March

900th first-class wicket: Saqlain Mushtaq (Surrey) at Edgbaston, 3 July

60 wickets @ 15.63. Top of English bowling averages

1998	1000th first-class wicket & 200th Test wicket: S T Jayasuriya (Sri Lanka) at Centurion Park

33 wickets @ 19.78 in series v England (5 Tests)

250th Test wicket: R N Lewis (West Indies) at Durban (Third Test), 28 December

1999	Took 100th first-class catch (M D Bell) in Test Match against New Zealand at Auckland, 1 March

200th limited-overs international wicket: A D R Campbell (Zimbabwe) at Chelmsford, 29 May

Involved in run-out drama in the World Cup semifinal against Australia at Edgbaston, 17 June

Because of injury he played only two championship matches and six limited-overs matches for Warwickshire

2000	Injured groin in second innings of Fourth Test against England (Cape Town) and missed Fifth Test (Centurion) because of gout. He ended the series with 22 wickets @ 19.18

Took seven wickets in two Tests against India, to end on 297 Test wickets, equalling Derek Underwood

First-Class Matches

Season	M	I	NO	HS	Runs	Av	50	Ct
†1985–86	7	9	3	17*	45	7.50	–	1
†1986–87	10	13	8	21	64	12.80	–	2
1987	11	10	3	37*	111	15.85	–	1
†1987–88	9	13	6	25	54	7.71	–	4
1988	7	10	3	29	74	10.57	–	4
†1988–89	8	12	5	21	74	10.57	–	3
1989	19	22	6	40	215	13.43	–	3
†1989–90	9	9	3	12	58	9.66	–	3
1990	16	22	6	25*	148	9.25	–	–
†1990–91	9	9	5	46*	94	23.50	–	7
1991	21	21	9	18	96	8.00	–	10
†1991–92	3	4	2	9*	15	7.50	–	1
‡1991–92 WI	1	2	0	0	0	–	–	–
1992	21	22	10	41	234	19.50	–	14
‡†1992–93	8	9	5	14*	36	9.00	–	3
1993	10	12	4	19	68	8.50	–	8
‡1993–94 SL	4	4	2	4*	5	2.50	–	3
‡†1993–94	6	6	3	15*	27	9.00	–	5
‡1993–94 A	5	6	3	10	22	7.33	–	–
‡1994	8	6	3	27	68	22.66	–	4
‡†1994–95	3	3	0	15	34	11.33	–	–
‡1994–95 NZ	2	2	1	4*	8	8.00	–	1
1995	15	16	5	44	194	17.63	–	7
‡1995–96 Z	1	1	0	33	33	33.00	–	–
‡1995–96	8	9	4	32	95	19.00	–	2
‡1996–97 I	3	5	1	17	34	8.50	–	1
†1996–97	6	9	1	26	80	10.00	–	–
1997	11	13	6	29	140	20.00	–	5
‡1997–98 P	2	3	0	8	10	3.33	–	2
‡1997–98 A	4	5	3	55*	61	30.50	1	1
‡†1997–98	6	8	2	18	55	9.16	–	2
‡1998	7	6	3	7*	29	9.66	–	1
‡†1998–99	7	10	3	33	90	12.85	–	1
‡1998–99 NZ	2	–					–	1
1999	2	4	2	10	14	7.00	–	1
‡1999–00 Zim	1	1	1	17*	17	–	–	1
‡†1999–00	7	7	0	9	27	3.85	–	2
‡1999–00 Ind	3	2	1	7	8	8.00	–	–
TOTALS	282	325	122	55*	2437	12.00	1	104

† denotes in South Africa
‡ denotes including Test matches

Overs	Runs	W	Av	5wI	10wM	BB	S/R
175.2	504	21	24.00	2	–	5–43	50.09
358.3	1116	47	23.74	2	1	8–37	45.76
301.4	1012	39	25.94	2	–	6–74	46.41
263.1	755	25	30.20	–	–	4–39	63.16
180.4	534	26	20.53	1	–	5–57	41.69
260	815	28	29.10	1	–	5–46	55.71
537.1	1398	86	16.25	6	–	7–66	37.47
291.1	784	37	21.18	1	–	5–54	47.21
391	1089	29	37.55	–	–	3–28	80.89
274.5	752	29	25.93	1	–	5–39	56.86
522.3	1634	83	19.68	8	2	6–69	37.77
137.5	402	16	25.12	–	–	4–64	51.68
45	144	6	24.00	–	–	4–77	45.00
576.2	1647	74	22.25	6	–	7–37	46.72
307.1	696	26	26.76	2	1	7–84	70.88
268.1	811	30	27.03	2	1	7–98	53.63
128	310	13	23.84	1	–	5–69	59.07
246.1	780	22	35.45	–	–	4–32	67.13
193.1	552	17	32.47	–	–	4–83	68.17
212.2	775	25	31.00	2	–	5–58	50.96
104.2	269	13	20.69	–	–	4–36	48.15
69.5	223	11	20.27	–	–	4–39	38.09
535.3	1431	89	16.07	6	1	6–56	36.10
50.1	113	11	10.27	1	1	8–71	27.36
308.5	823	34	24.20	2	–	5–44	54.50
91.2	209	17	12.29	–	–	4–37	32.23
241.2	644	31	20.77	2	–	5–36	46.70
387.5	938	60	15.63	3	1	6–55	38.78
67.4	226	7	32.28	–	–	3–108	58.00
142.4	383	17	22.52	1	–	6–59	50.35
199.2	583	35	16.65	2	–	5–54	34.17
302.2	785	39	20.12	5	–	6–56	46.51
175.2	583	25	23.32	2	–	5–99	42.08
53.5	114	5	22.80	–	–	3–54	64.60
50	136	0	–	–	–	–	–
19	35	2	17.50	–	–	2–25	57.00
272.3	693	32	21.65	4	1	6–53	51.09
74	166	9	18.44	–	–	2–23	49.33
8817	24864	1116	22.27	65	9	8–37	47.40

First-Class Matches (continued)

Matches in South Africa

	M	I	NO	HS	Runs	Av	50	Ct
Free State	66	79	35	46*	444	10.09	–	28
Pres XI	2	2	0	12	16	8.00	–	–
SA Def Force	2	2	1	3*	4	4.00	–	–
Unofficial SA	2	2	1	21	28	28.00	–	1
Official SA	34	45	13	33	356	11.12	–	7
TOTALS	106	130	50	46*	848	10.60	–	36

Matches for Warwickshire

	M	I	NO	HS	Runs	Av	50	Ct
Champ	127	145	50	44	1210	12.73	–	52
v OU	1	–	–	–	–	–	–	–
v SL	2	2	2	4*	4	–	–	–
v NZ	1	2	1	25*	26	26.00	–	–
v Eng A	1	2	0	33	49	24.50	–	–
v Aus	1	1	1	5*	5	–	–	1
TOTALS	133	152	54	44	1294	13.20	–	53

Official South African Teams outside South Africa

	M	I	NO	HS	Runs	Av	50	Ct
	43	43	18	55*	295	11.80	1	15
TOTALS	282	325	122	55*	2437	12.00	1	104

Overs	Runs	W	Av	5wI	10wM	BB	S/R
2209.1	6187	232	26.66	8	–	8–37	57.13
34	81	2	40.50	–	–	2–21	102.00
69.3	212	13	16.30	1	1	7–63	32.07
90	224	12	18.66	–	–	4–29	45.00
1214.1	3495	162	21.57	12	2	7–84	44.96
3616.5	10199	421	24.22	21	3	7–84	51.54

Overs	Runs	W	Av	5wI	10wM	BB	S/R
3648	10323	512	20.16	34	5	7–37	42.75
20	44	2	22.00	–	–	2–44	60.00
33.5	95	1	95.00	–	–	1–35	203.00
15	33	0	–	–	–	–	–
24	68	1	68.00	–	–	1–68	144.00
10	67	0	–	–	–	–	–
3750.5	10630	516	20.60	34	5	7–37	43.61

Overs	Runs	W	Av	5wI	10wM	BB	S/R
1449.2	4035	179	22.54	10	1	8–71	48.58
8817	24864	1116	22.27	65	9	8–37	47.40

Test Matches

Season	Opp	M	I	NO	HS	Runs	Av	50	Ct
1991–92	WI	1	2	0	0	0	–	–	–
‡1992–93	Ind	4	5	3	14*	29	14.50	–	–
1993–94	SL	3	3	2	4*	5	5.00	–	2
1993–94	Aus	3	4	3	10	11	11.00	–	–
‡1993–94	Aus	3	5	3	15*	22	11.00	–	2
1994	Eng	3	4	2	27	46	23.00	–	1
‡1994–95	Pak	1	1	0	15	15	15.00	–	–
1994–95	NZ	1	1	1	4*	4	–	–	–
1995–96	Zim	1	1	0	33	33	33.00	–	–
‡1995–96	Eng	5	6	3	32	68	22.66	–	1
1996–97	Ind	2	3	0	17	21	7.00	–	1
‡1996–97	Ind	3	4	1	26	35	11.66	–	–
‡1996–97	Aus	3	5	0	21	45	9.00	–	–
1997–98	Pak	2	3	0	8	10	3.33	–	2
1997–98	Aus	2	3	2	4*	6	6.00	–	–
‡1997–98	Pak	3	4	1	11	12	4.00	–	2
‡1997–98	SL	2	3	0	18	36	12.00	–	–
1998	Eng	5	6	3	7*	29	9.66	–	1
‡1998–99	WI	5	7	2	33	76	15.20	–	1
1998–99	NZ	2	–					–	1
‡1999–00	Zim	1	1	0	2		2.00	–	–
1999–00	Zim	1	1	1	17*	17	–	–	1
‡1999–00	Eng	4	4	0	9	16	4.00	–	1
1999–00	Ind	2	2	1	7	8	8.00	–	–
TOTALS		62	78	28	33	546	10.92	–	16

‡ in South Africa

		M	I	NO	HS	Runs	Av	50	Ct
In South Africa		34	45	13	33	356	11.12	–	7
Overseas		28	33	15	33	190	10.55	–	9
v West Indies		6	9	2	33	76	10.85	–	1
v India		11	14	5	26	93	10.33	–	1
v Sri Lanka		5	6	2	18	41	10.25	–	2
v Australia		11	17	8	21	84	9.33	–	2
v England		17	20	8	32	159	13.25	–	4
v Pakistan		6	8	1	15	37	5.28	–	4
v New Zealand		3	1	1	4*	4	–	–	1
v Zimbabwe		3	3	1	33	52	26.00	–	1
TOTALS		62	78	28	33	546	10.92	–	16

Overs	Runs	W	Av	5wI	10wM	BB	S/R
45	144	6	24.00	–	–	4–77	45.00
175	394	20	19.70	2	1	7–84	52.50
102	232	12	19.33	1	–	5–69	51.00
127.2	373	13	28.69	–	–	4–83	58.76
128	425	12	35.41	–	–	3–66	64.00
89.3	410	12	34.16	1	–	5–74	44.75
32	116	4	29.00	–	–	2–53	48.00
40.4	1322	5	26.40	–	–	4–88	48.80
50.1	113	11	10.27	1	1	8–71	27.36
173.5	497	19	26.15	1	–	5–46	54.89
63.2	141	10	14.10	–	–	4–37	38.00
119.2	319	20	15.95	1	–	5–40	35.80
122	325	11	29.54	1	–	5–36	66.54
67.4	226	7	32.28	–	–	3–108	58.00
86.4	214	12	17.83	1	–	6–59	43.33
80.2	262	16	16.37	1	–	5–79	30.12
88	257	14	18.35	1	–	5–54	37.71
243.2	653	33	19.78	4	–	6–88	44.24
117.2	395	23	17.17	2	–	5–49	30.60
53.5	114	5	22.80	–	–	3–54	64.60
33	83	1	83.00	–	–	1–58	198.00
19	35	2	17.50	–	–	2–25	57.00
145.2	422	22	19.18	3	1	6–53	39.63
58	133	7	19.00	–	–	2–23	49.71
2260.4	6415	297	21.59	20	3	8–71	45.67
1214.1	3495	162	21.57	12	2	7–84	44.96
1046.3	2920	135	21.62	8	1	8–71	46.51
162.2	539	29	18.58	2	–	5–49	33.58
415.4	987	57	17.31	3	1	7–84	43.75
190	489	26	18.80	2	–	5–54	43.84
464	1337	48	27.85	2	–	6–59	58.00
652	1982	86	23.04	9	1	6–53	45.48
180	604	27	22.37	1	–	5–79	40.00
94.3	246	10	24.60	–	–	4–88	56.70
102.1	231	14	16.50	1	1	8–71	43.78
2260.4	6415	297	21.59	20	3	8–71	45.67

Test Matches (continued)

Highest Scores & Best Bowling

v West Indies	33	(Port Elizabeth) 1989–90
	5–49	(Port Elizabeth) 1998–99
	5–49	(Centurion) 1998–99
v India	26	(Durban) 1996–97
	7–84	(Port Elizabeth) 1992–93
v Sri Lanka	18	(Cape Town) 1997–98
	5–54	(Centurion) 1997–98
v Australia	21	(Johannesburg) 1996–97
	6–59	(Melbourne) 1997–98
v England	32	(Durban) 1995–96
	6–53	(Johannesburg) 1999–00
v Pakistan	15	(Johannesburg) 1994–95
	5–79	(Durban) 1997–98
v New Zealand	4*	(Auckland) 1994–95
	4–88	(Auckland) 1994–95
v Zimbabwe	33	(Harare) 1995–96
	8–71	(Harare) 1995–96

Comparative Test Summary

	M	I	NO	HS	Runs	Av	100	50	Ct
C E L Ambrose	88	129	27	53	1297	12.71	–	1	16
C A Walsh	112	153	52	30*	834	8.25	–	–	26
Wasim Akram	92	132	16	257*	2503	21.57	2	6	37
G D McGrath	60	74	23	39	295	5.78	–	–	16
S M Pollock	42	61	12	92	1444	29.46	–	8	24

Ov	Runs	W	Av	5wI	10wM	BB	S/R
3306.2	7865	369	21.31	22	3	8–45	53.76
4117.1	10849	426	25.46	17	2	7–37	57.98
3391.4	8857	383	23.12	22	4	7–119	53.13
2396	6255	281	22.55	17	2	8–38	51.16
1545.5	3558	175	20.33	10	–	7–87	53.00

Limited-Overs Internationals

Season	Opp	M	I	NO	HS	Runs	Av	50	Ct
1991–92	India	3	–					–	–
1991–92	World Cup	9	1	0	3	3	3.00	–	1
1991–92	West Indies	2	2	1	5*	5	5.00	–	–
†1992–93	India	7	–					–	1
†1992–93	Total Series	6	4	3	5*	6	6.00	–	–
1993–94	Sri Lanka	3	1	0	0	0	–	–	1
1993–94	Hero Cup	5	2	2	5*	6	–	–	1
1993–94	B&H World Series	8	3	1	7*	7	3.50	–	1
†1993–94	Australia	2	1	0	0	0		–	–
†1994	England	1	1	1	2*	2	–	–	–
†1994–95	Pakistan	1	–					–	–
1994–95	NZ Centenary	3	2	1	0*	0	–	–	–
1995–96	Zimbabwe	2	1	1	5*	5	–	–	–
†1995–96	England	5	–					–	2
1995–96	World Cup	4	–					–	–
1996–97	Kenya Centenary	4	1	–	0	0	–	–	1
1996–97	Titan Cup	7	1	–	0	0	–	–	–
†1996–97	Standard Series	8	–					–	4
†1996–97	Australia	7	1	0	6	6	6.00	–	–
1997–98	Jinnah Cup	3	1	0	0	0	–	–	–
1997–98	Carlton & United	9	2	0	11	15	7.50	–	2
†1997–98	Standard Series	3	–					–	–
1998	England	3	1	1	6	6	–	–	–
1998	Emirates	2	1	0	12	12	12.00	–	–
1998–99	New Zealand	4	1	1	0*	0	–	–	–
‡1998–99	West Indies	1	–					–	–
1999	World Cup	9	3	1	7	10	5.00	–	2
TOTALS		121	30	13	12	83	4.88	–	16

† denotes in South Africa

348

Overs	Runs	W	Av	4wI	BB	RPO
27.4	120	9	13.33	1	5–29	4.33
78	329	13	25.30	–	3–34	4.21
18	96	2	48.00	–	2–47	5.33
69	233	9	25.88	–	3–27	3.37
60	202	7	28.85	–	3–27	3.36
24	76	5	15.20	–	2–28	3.16
29	131	2	61.50	–	1–15	4.51
74.2	282	12	23.50	1	4–40	3.79
19	106	1	106.00	–	1–60	5.57
10.2	47	2	23.50	–	2–47	4.54
8	25	3	8.33	–	3–25	3.12
26	125	2	62.50	–	2–43	4.80
18	49	2	24.50	–	1–21	2.72
49	248	12	20.66	1	4–41	5.06
34	126	8	15.75	–	3–21	3.70
35	119	14	8.50	1	6–23	3.40
65.4	294	17	17.29	1	4–31	4.47
76.1	319	18	17.72	2	4–37	4.18
63.5	284	9	31.55	–	3–67	4.44
30	148	5	29.60	–	2–46	4.93
73.2	250	17	14.70	2	4–29	3.40
20	61	2	30.50	–	1–12	3.05
25.4	112	7	16.00	–	3–32	4.36
17	81	4	20.25	–	2–40	4.76
32	115	8	14.37	–	3–34	3.59
8	33	0	–	–	–	4.12
82	325	16	20.31	2	4–17	3.96
1073	4336	206	21.04	11	6–23	4.04

Limited-Overs Internationals (continued)

	M	I	NO	HS	Runs	Av	50	Ct
In South Africa	40	6	3	6	12	4.00	–	7
Overseas	81	24	10	12	71	5.07	–	9
v India	24	3	2	5*	6	6.00	–	4
v Australia	28	8	1	11	24	3.42	–	4
v New Zealand	13	3	2	4	4	4.00	–	1
v West Indies	9	3	2	5*	5	5.00	–	–
v Pakistan	12	4	2	5*	6	3.00	–	2
v Sri Lanka	10	5	1	12	18	4.50	–	1
v Zimbabwe	8	2	1	7	12	12.00	–	2
v England	13	2	2	6*	8	–	–	2
v United Arab Emirates	1	–					–	–
v Holland	1	–					–	–
v Kenya	2	–					–	–
TOTALS	121	30	13	12	83	4.88	–	16

Highest Scores & Best Bowling

In South Africa	6	v Australia (Durban) 5.4.97
	4–37	v Zimbabwe (Centurion) 25.1.97
Overseas	12	v Sri Lanka (Trent Bridge) 14.8.98
	6–23	v Kenya (Nairobi) 3.10.96
v India	5*	(Chandigarh) 22.11.93
	5–29	(Calcutta) 10.11.91
v Australia	11	(Sydney) 4.12.97
	4–29	(Perth) 18.1.98
v New Zealand	4	(Adelaide) 6.12.97
	4–43	(Brisbane) 9.1.99
v West Indies	5*	(Kingston) 7.4.92
	3–27	(Port Elizabeth) 11.2.93

Overs	Runs	W	Av	4wI	BB	RPO
373	1511	61	24.77	3	4–37	4.05
700	2825	145	19.48	8	6–23	4.03
222.1	898	42	21.38	1	5–29	4.04
248.4	1053	43	24.48	4	4–29	4.23
118.2	424	23	18.43	1	4–43	3.58
77.4	286	10	28.60	–	3–27	3.68
103.2	440	15	29.33	–	3–25	4.25
81.3	309	17	18.17	–	3–42	3.79
67.2	242	14	17.28	2	4–37	3.59
121	577	29	19.89	2	4–17	4.76
10	21	3	7.00	–	3–21	2.10
6	21	2	10.50	–	2–21	3.50
17	65	8	8.12	1	6–23	3.82
1073	4336	206	21.04	11	6–23	4.04

v Pakistan	HS	5*	(Verwoerdburg) 21.2.93
	BB	3–25	(Johannesburg) 12.1.95
v Sri Lanka	HS	12	(Trent Bridge) 14.8.98
	BB	3–42	(Wellington) 2.3.92
v Zimbabwe	HS	7	(Chelmsford) 29.5.99
	BB	4–37	(Centurion) 25.1.97
v England	HS	6*	(Old Trafford) 23.5.98
	BB	4–17	(Oval) 22.5.99
v Kenya	HS	–	
	BB	6–23	(Nairobi) 3.10.96

Limited-Overs Internationals

Four Wickets in an Innings

1.	5–29	India	Calcutta	10.11.1991
2.	4–40	Australia	Sydney	23.1.1994
3.	4–41	England	Durban	17.1.1996
4.	6–23	Kenya	Nairobi	3.10.1996
5.	4–31	Australia	Faridabad	25.10.1996
6.	4–37	Zimbabwe	Centurion	25.1.1997
7.	4–46	Zimbabwe	Johannesburg	31.1.1997
8.	4–43	New Zealand	Brisbane	9.1.1998
9.	4–29	Australia	Perth	18.1.1998
10.	4–17	England	Oval	22.5.1999
11.	4–32	Australia	Edgbaston	17.6.1999

Domestic Limited-Overs

Four Wickets in an Innings

1.	4–28	Scotland	Perth	9.5.1987	B&H
2.	5–24	Staffordshire	Burton-on-Trent	24.6.1987	NW
3.	4–32	Middlesex	Edgbaston	28.5.1989	Sun
4.	5–12	Wiltshire	Edgbaston	29.6.1989	NW
5.	4–26	Northamptonshire	Northampton	2.8.1989	NW
6.	4–55	Somerset	Edgbaston	2.5.1991	B&H
7.	4–16	Yorkshire	Edgbaston	26.6.1991	NW
8.	5–28	Staffordshire	Edgbaston	24.6.1992	NW
9.	4–23	Surrey	Oval	19.7.1992	Sun
10.	4–69	Kent	Edgbaston	7.7.1993	NW
11.	5–41	Derbyshire	Derby	1.8.1994	NW
12.	6–15	Yorkshire	Edgbaston	25.6.1995	Sun
13.	5–25	Lancashire	Edgbaston	2.5.1997	B&H
14.	4–32	Yorkshire	Edgbaston	18.5.1997	Sun
15.	4–54	Somerset	Edgbaston	9.7.1997	NW
16.	5–37	Sussex	Edgbaston	14.8.1997	NW
17.	5–10	Essex	Chelmsford	31.8.1997	Sun
18.	4–24	Gloucestershire	Edgbaston	14.9.1997	Sun

Four Wickets in an Innings

1.	4–18	Orange Free State	Western Province	Cape Town	22.3.1989	B&H
2.	5–25	Orange Free State	Northern Transvaal Country Districts	Pietersbury	23.11.1991	NS
3.	4–32	Orange Free State	Western Province	Bloemfontein	9.12.1991	B&H
4.	4–8	Orange Free State	Natal Country Districts	Empageni	3.10.1992	Total
5.	4–21	Orange Free State	Natal	Durban	11.3.1994	B&H
6.	4–33	Free State	Border	East London	20.12.1996	Stand

Sunday League

Season	M	I	NO	HS	Runs	Av	50	Ct
1987	5	4	2	13*	23	11.50	–	2
1988	4	3	2	18*	25	25.00	–	1
1989	11	7	2	17*	63	12.60	–	2
1991	8	1	0	7	7	7.00	–	3
1992	9	2	1	1*	1	1.00	–	1
1993	9	2	0	1	1	0.50	–	1
1995	11	3	3	5*	14	–	–	2
1997	14	2	2	5*	5	–	–	4
1999	4	–					–	–
TOTALS	75	24	12	18*	139	11.58	–	16

Highest Score 18* v Middlesex (Lord's) 24.7.1988
Best Bowling 6–15 v Yorkshire (Edgbaston) 25.6.1995

Benson & Hedges Cup

Season	M	I	NO	HS	Runs	Av	50	Ct
1987	3	1	0	0	0	–	–	1
1989	4	3	3	23*	30	–	–	–
1990	1	–					–	–
1991	5	3	2	6*	8	8.00	–	1
1992	3	1	0	10	10	10.00	–	–
1993	1	1	0	9	9	9.00	–	1
1995	3	2	0	2	2	1.00	–	–
1997	6	4	3	17*	28	28.00	–	1
1999	1	–						
TOTALS	27	15	8	23*	87	12.42	–	4

Highest Score 23* v Leicestershire (Leicester) 2.5.1989
Best Bowling 5–25 v Lancashire (Edgbaston) 2.5.1997

Overs	Runs	W	Av	4wI	BB	RPO
40	163	10	16.30	–	2–34	4.07
28	133	2	66.50	–	1–30	4.75
87	342	14	24.42	1	4–32	3.93
58	264	8	33.00	–	2–7	4.55
51	185	9	20.55	1	4–23	3.62
83.4	340	10	34.00	–	3–41	4.06
84.4	311	19	16.36	1	6–15	3.67
85.5	336	30	11.20	3	5–10	3.91
25	132	6	22.00	–	3–45	5.28
543.1	2206	108	20.42	6	6–15	4.06

Overs	Runs	W	Av	4wI	BB	RPO
23.2	91	7	13.00	1	4–28	3.90
42.5	158	2	79.00	–	1–28	3.68
11	42	1	42.00	–	1–42	3.81
49	266	11	24.18	1	4–55	5.42
33	102	4	25.50	–	2–33	3.09
10	47	2	23.50	–	2–47	4.70
31	131	3	43.66	–	2–39	4.22
47.5	159	8	19.87	1	5–25	3.32
8.4	40	1	40.00	–	1–40	4.61
256.4	1036	39	26.56	3	5–25	4.03

NatWest Trophy

Season	M	I	NO	HS	Runs	Av	50	Ct
1987	3	–	–	–	–	–	–	1
1989	5	1	0	0	0	–	–	–
1991	4	2	1	2*	3	3.00	–	–
1992	4	2	2	14*	23	–	–	–
1993	3	2	1	2*	2	2.00	–	–
1995	5	–	–	–	–	–	–	2
1997	5	3	2	3*	4	4.00	–	1
1999	1	1	0	7	7	7.00	–	–
TOTALS	30	11	6	14*	39	7.80	–	4

Highest Score 14* v Northamptonshire (Edgbaston) 12.8.1992
Best Bowling 5–12 v Wiltshire (Edgbaston) 29.6.1989

Domestic Limited-Overs Summary

Comp	M	I	NO	HS	Runs	Av	50	Ct
Sundays	75	24	12	18*	139	11.58	–	16
B&H	27	15	8	23*	87	12.42	–	4
NatWest	30	10	6	14*	32	8.00	–	4
TOTALS	132	50	26	23*	265	11.04	–	24

Overs	Runs	W	Av	4wI	BB	RPO
29.2	88	10	8.80	1	5–24	3.00
47.4	137	14	9.78	2	5–12	2.87
42	132	6	22.00	1	4–16	3.14
45.5	108	11	9.81	1	5–28	2.35
30	120	6	20.00	1	4–69	4.00
57.5	215	11	19.54	1	5–41	3.71
52.1	223	15	14.86	2	5–37	4.27
10	53	2	26.50	–	2–53	5.30
314.5	1076	75	14.34	9	5–12	3.41

Overs	Runs	W	Av	4wI	BB	RPO
543.1	2206	108	20.42	6	6–15	4.06
256.4	1036	39	26.56	3	5–25	4.03
314.5	1076	75	14.34	9	5.12	3.41
1114.4	4318	222	19.45	18	6–15	3.87

First-Class Records
Five-Wicket Innings

1.	5–46	Orange Free State	Eastern Province	Bloemfontein	1985–96
2.	†5–43	Orange Free State	Northern Transvaal	Bloemfontein	1985–86
3.	†7–63	SA Defence Force	Griqualand West	Kimberley	1986–87
4.	8–37	Orange Free State	Transvaal	Johannesburg	1986–87
5.	†6–74	Warwickshire	Essex	Chelmsford	1987
6.	5–42	Warwickshire	Leicestershire	Edgbaston	1987
7.	5–57	Warwickshire	Yorkshire	Headingley	1988
8.	†5–46	Orange Free State	Border	Bloemfontein	1988–89
9.	†5–18	Warwickshire	Surrey	Edgbaston	1989
10.	7–66	Warwickshire	Middlesex	Edgbaston	1989
11.	5–103	Warwickshire	Essex	Ilford	1989
12.	5–67	Warwickshire	Gloucestershire	Edgbaston	1989
13.	5–57	Warwickshire	Kent	Canterbury	1989
14.	5–40	Warwickshire	Somerset	Taunton	1989
15.	5–54	Orange Free State	Eastern Province	Bloemfontein	1989–90
16.	†5–39	Orange Free State	Transvaal	Bloemfontein	1990–91
17.	5–42	Warwickshire	Yorkshire	Headingley	1991
18.	†5–54	Warwickshire	Yorkshire	Headingley	1991
19.	5–38	Warwickshire	Glamorgan	Swansea	1991
20.	5–36	Warwickshire	Glamorgan	Swansea	1991
21.	†5–33	Warwickshire	Gloucestershire	Edgbaston	1991
22.	†5–48	Warwickshire	Sussex	Coventry	1991
23.	†6–69	Warwickshire	Northamptonshire	Edgbaston	1991
24.	6–84	Warwickshire	Somerset	Taunton	1991
25.	†5–69	Warwickshire	Worcestershire	Edgbaston	1992
26.	5–82	Warwickshire	Sussex	Hove	1992
27.	5–44	Warwickshire	Gloucestershire	Bristol	1992
28.	†6–49	Warwickshire	Surrey	Guildford	1992
29.	7–37	Warwickshire	Durham	Edgbaston	1992
30.	†5–36	Warwickshire	Middlesex	Lord's	1992
31.	5–55	SOUTH AFRICA	INDIA (T3)	PORT ELIZABETH	1992–93
32.	†8–84	SOUTH AFRICA	INDIA (T3)	PORT ELIZABETH	1992–93
33.	‡7–98	Warwickshire	Yorkshire	Edgbaston	1993
34.	6–57	Warwickshire	Leicestershire	Leicester	1993
35.	5–69	SOUTH AFRICA	SRI LANKA (T1)	MORATUWA	1993–94
36.	5–58	South Africans	Hampshire	Southampton	1994
37.	5–74	SOUTH AFRICA	ENGLAND (T1)	LORD'S	1994
38.	6–56	Warwickshire	Middlesex	Edgbaston	1995
39.	6–64	Warwickshire	Surrey	Edgbaston	1995
40.	5–21	Warwickshire	Yorkshire	Edgbaston	1995
41.	†6–95	Warwickshire	Northamptonshire	Edgbaston	1995
42.	5–37	Warwickshire	Gloucestershire	Edgbaston	1995
43.	†5–65	Warwickshire	Derbyshire	Edgbaston	1995
44.	†8–71	SOUTH AFRICA	ZIMBABWE	HARARE	1995–96
45.	5–44	Free State	Eastern Province	Port Elizabeth	1995–96
46.	5–46	SOUTH AFRICA	ENGLAND (t5)	CAPE TOWN	1995–96
47.	5–40	SOUTH AFRICA	INDIA (T1)	DURBAN	1996–97
48.	†5–36	SOUTH AFRICA	AUSTRALIA (T3)	CENTURION	1996–97
49.	†6–55	Warwickshire	Surrey	Edgbaston	1997

50.	†5–98	Warwickshire	Nottinghamshire	Trent Bridge	1997
51.	5–50	Warwickshire	Essex	Chelmsford	1997
52.	†5–59	SOUTH AFRICA	AUSTRALIA (T1)	MELBOURNE	1997–98
53.	5–79	SOUTH AFRICA	PAKISTAN (T2)	DURBAN	1997–98
54.	†5–54	SOUTH AFRICA	SRI LANKA (T2)	CENTURION	1997–98
55.	†6–56	South Africans	Worcestershire	Worcester	1998
56.	5–32	SOUTH AFRICA	ENGLAND (T2)	LORD'S	1998
57.	†6–88	SOUTH AFRICA	ENGLAND (T3)	OLD TRAFFORD	1998
58.	5–109	SOUTH AFRICA	ENGLAND (T4)	TRENT BRIDGE	1998
59.	†5–71	SOUTH AFRICA	ENGLAND (T5)	HEADINGLEY	1998
60.	†5–49	SOUTH AFRICA	WEST INDIES (T2)	PORT ELIZABETH	1998–99
61.	5–49	SOUTH AFRICA	WEST INDIES (T5)	CENTURION	1998–99
62.	5–47	Free State	Western Province	Bloemfontein	1999–00
63.	6–53	SOUTH AFRICA	ENGLAND	JOHANNESBURG	1999–00
64.	†5–74	SOUTH AFRICA	ENGLAND	JOHANNESBURG	1999–00
65.	5–47	SOUTH AFRICA	ENGLAND	CAPE TOWN	1999–00

† Denotes second innings

Note: The only English county against whom Donald has not taken five wickets in an innings is Lancashire. He has taken five wickets in an innings at Edgbaston on 16 occasions. Numbers 17–20 were in successive innings and numbers 56–59 in successive Test Matches.

Ten Wickets in a Match

1.	11–154	SA Defence Force	Griqualand West	Kimberley	1986–87
2.	10–96	Warwickshire	Yorkshire	Headingley	1991
3.	10–74	Warwickshire	Glamorgan	Swansea	1991
4.	12–139	SOUTH AFRICA	INDIA (T3)	PORT ELIZABETH	1992–93
5.	10–129	Warwickshire	Yorkshire	Edgbaston	1993
6.	10–136	Warwickshire	Northamptonshire	Edgbaston	1993
7.	11–113	SOUTH AFRICA	ZIMBABWE	HARARE	1995–96
8.	10–119	Warwickshire	Surrey	Edgbaston	1997
9.	11–127	SOUTH AFRICA	ENGLAND	JOHANNESBURG	1999–00

Pair

1988	Warwickshire	Somerset	Bath
1991–92	SOUTH AFRICA	WEST INDIES	BRIDGETOWN (Test debut)

Highest Scores & Best Bowling

In South Africa

President XI	12	v Australian XI (Pretoria) 1985–86
	2–21	v Australian XI (Pretoria) 1985–86
SA Defence Force	3*	v Griqualand West (Kimberley) 1986–87
	7–53	v Griqualand West (Kimberley) 1986–87
Unofficial South Africa	21	v Australian XI (Port Elizabeth) 1986–87
	4–29	v England XI (Johannesburg) 1989–90
Free State	46*	v Western Province (Cape Town) 1990–91
	8–37	v Transvaal (Johannesburg) 1986–87
Official South Africa	33	v WEST INDIES (PORT ELIZABETH) 1998–99
	7–74	v INDIA (PORT ELIZABETH) 1992–93

For Warwickshire

Championship	44	v Essex (Ilford) 1995
	7–37	v Durham (Edgbaston) 1992
v Oxford University	dnb	
	2–44	(Oxford) 1987

v Sri Lankans	4*	(Edgbaston) 1990
	1–35	(Edgbaston) 1990
v New Zealanders	25*	(Edgbaston) 1990
	–	
v England A	33	(Edgbaston) 1995
	1–68	(Edgbaston) 1995
v Australians	5*	(Edgbaston) 1993
	–	

Official South African Teams outside South Africa

55* v Tasmania (Devenport) 1997–98
8–71 v ZIMBABWE (HARARE) 1995–96

Benson & Hedges Series and Standard Bank League & Cup (Day/Night matches)

	M	I	NO	HS	Runs	Av	100	50	Ct
1985–86 Imp	2	2	1	4	5	5.00	–	–	1
1986–87 Imp	5	3	1	3*	6	3.00	–	–	–
1987–88 OFS	6	5	3	6	11	5.50	–	–	–
1988–89 OFS	9	2	2	19*	20	–	–	–	1
1989–90 OFS	7	3	1	3	3	1.50	–	–	–
1990–91 OFS	7	–					–	–	1
1991–92 OFS	6	1	1	2*	2	–	–	–	–
1992–93 OFS	7	1	1	0*	0	–	–	–	2
1993–94 OFS	4	1	0	2	2	2.00	–	–	–
1994–95 OFS	5	2	0	15	15	7.50	–	–	–
1995–96 FS	5	1	0	0	0	–	–	–	4
1996–97 FS	2	–					–	–	–
1998–99 FS	5	1	0	3	3	3.00	–	–	1
1999–00	3	–							
TOTALS	73	22	10	19*	67	5.58	–	–	10

Nissan Shield & Total Power Series

	M	I	NO	HS	Runs	Av	100	50	Ct
1986–87 OFS/GW	3						–	–	–
1987–88 OFS	6	4	4	1*	2	–	–	–	1
1988–89 OFS	4	1	1	9*	9	–	–	–	–
1989–90 OFS	4	1	1	2	2	2.00	–	–	–
1990–91 OFS	5	–					–	–	1
1991–92 OFS	6	1	1	2*	2	–	–	–	–
1992–93 OFS	6	1	1	6*	6	–	–	–	1
TOTALS	34	9	8	9*	21	21.00	–	–	3

The Benson & Hedges series is a day-night series, played now over 45 overs. In 1985–86 and 1986–87 Donald played for a composite team called the Impalas, but from 1987–88 Orange Free State were able to enter their own team. In 1996–97 the sponsorship changed to Standard Bank and the competition took two forms: the Standard Bank League, played on a round-robin basis and the Standard Bank Cup, which was contested by the top League teams. In 1999–2000 the format changed again, consisting of the Standard Bank Cup, played on a League basis.

Overs	Runs	W	Av	4wI	BB	RPO
17	73	2	36.50	–	1–15	4.29
39	204	3	68.00	–	2–20	5.23
48	188	5	37.60	–	3–21	3.91
66.3	224	15	14.93	1	4–18	3.36
58	186	8	23.25	–	3–35	3.20
44.2	190	2	95.00	–	2–44	4.28
49	148	11	13.45	1	4–32	3.02
57.2	182	8	22.75	–	2–10	3.17
35.1	87	6	14.50	1	4–21	2.47
36.4	155	9	17.22	–	3–35	4.22
35	120	9	13.33	–	3–20	3.42
17	93	5	18.60	1	4–33	5.47
37	141	3	47.00	–	2–35	3.81
24	115	2	57.50	–	1–36	4.79
564	2106	88	23.93	4	4–18	3.73

Overs	Runs	W	Av	4wI	BB	RPO
21	91	1	91.00	–	1–39	4.33
58	213	8	26.62	–	3–26	3.67
33	141	5	28.20	–	2–45	4.27
42	160	1	160.00	–	1–35	3.80
49.3	133	7	19.00	–	3–18	2.68
57.3	180	9	20.00	1	5–25	3.13
56.4	182	9	20.22	1	4–8	3.21
317.4	1100	40	27.50	2	5–25	3.46

The Nissan Shield was played on the same lines as the English Benson & Hedges Cup in 1986–87 and 1987–88. In the first year Orange Free State and Griqualand West formed a composite team. The competition continued over the next few seasons, with various alterations, including the use of 15 players (6 substitutions) in 1990–91. The spnsorship changed to Total Power in 1992–93, but this was the last year of the competition.

In 1996–97 Orange Free State became Free State.

Index

Adams, Chris 330
Adams, Jimmy 110,
    195–6
Adams, Paul 9, 190–1,
    235–6, 256, 289, 293,
    324–5, 330
Adelaide 105, 137, 139–41,
    222–3
African National Congress
    (ANC) 2–3, 131, 190,
    290, 291, 292–3
Ahmedebad 205
Aldridge, Brian 102
Ambrose, Curtly 104, 110,
    117, 195, 273, 286–7
Amiss, Dennis 45–6, 167,
    182, 183, 332
Amsterdam 301
ankle injury 238, 248, 297–8,
    314–15
apartheid 17–20, 43
army service 19–20, 50
Asif Din 66, 181–19
Atherton, Mike 275–6, 317
    Dirt in the Pocket Affair
        154
    England captain 191–2
    Test matches 155, 156–7,
        160, 188–9, 229, 236,
        237, 243–8, 252,
        318–19, 325, 326
athletics 13
Auckland 103
Australia
    attitude to cricket 99
    one-day indoor series, 2000
        332
    rebel tours 21–5, 32–8
    1992 World Cup 101–2
    1999 World Cup 303–5
    see also TEST SERIES
Azharuddin, Mohammad 126,
    207, 209, 334

Bacher, Adam 208, 232,
    291
Bacher, Dr Ali 136, 187, 190,
    202–3
    approach to AD on behalf
        of Warwickshire 38
    Cricket Development
        Programme 71, 78, 124,
        289
    disciplinary actions 129,
        232–3
    English rebel tour 71

Bacher, Dr Ali – *contd.*
  managing director of United
    Cricket Board 78, 183,
    261, 327, 329, 332–3
  political pressure for non-
    white representation
    292–4
  and South African coach
    appointment 160–1
  and South Africa's return to
    international cricket 78
  support for AD 145, 183
  tour of England 1994 149
  tour of India 1991 91, 93
  on use of technology 265
  West Indies 1998 tour 281,
    282
Baker, Arthur 14–15
Bangalore 333
Barbados 109–10
Barlow, Eddie 99–100, 132,
    161, 286
BBC Radio interview 249
Benaud, Richie 223
Benson and Hedges Cup
    England 215
    South Africa 131
Best, Carlisle 109
Bevan, Michael 212, 306
Biokinetics 198
Bird, Dickie 47–8, 269
Birmingham *see* Edgbaston;
    Warwickshire
Bishop, Ian 114, 195
'bleep' test 199–200
Blewett, Greg 211
Bloemfontein 7–8, 18–19, 70,
    317, 330
  childhood/youth in 8–16
Boje, Nicky 334

Boon, David 101, 138
Border, Allan 45, 137, 138,
    141–2
Botha, Naas 13
Botham, Ian 219
Boucher, Mark 9, 244, 246,
    259, 287, 288, 303, 308,
    319–20, 322–3, 334
bowling
  action 16–17, 272, 273–4,
    317, 335
  fast bowlers 271–9
  goal of 300 Test wickets
    316, 335
  reverse swing 176–8
  rhythm in 58, 59–60,
    174–5, 319–20
  run-up 59–60, 174–6
  slower ball 98–9
  South Africa Test wickets'
    record 221
  200th Test wicket 225
Boycott, Geoffrey 333
Bremner, Rory 315
Brisbane 104–5, 141–2
Broad, Chris 26, 27
Brown, David 38–9, 47
Brown, Dougie 170, 173,
    178, 200, 216
Brown, Roger 127–8
Bucknor, Steve 105, 126, 194,
    269–70
Burge, Peter 154, 157
burnout 145–6, 183
Butcher, Mark 230, 243, 251,
    254, 258, 259, 323, 325
Byas, David 173

Caddick, Andy 322, 323,
    325–6, 327, 331

Calcutta 92–3
cameras, use in decision-
    making 125–7, 264–5
Canberra 105
Canterbury 171, 171–2, 215
Cape Town 70, 115, 124,
    143–4, 191, 192, 207–8,
    268, 287, 324–7
Carr, John 57
Centurion Park 187, 213–14,
    218, 225, 329–30
Charlton, Jack 315
Chelmsford 302
childhood/youth 8–16
Christchurch 104
Clarke, Sylvester 52–3
Colombo 133, 134
Commonwealth Games 203
Cook, Jimmy 27, 93, 96,
    126–7
Cork, Dominic 238, 255,
    256, 273
Cottam, Bob 53–4, 58, 63,
    72, 73, 74, 76, 313–14
County Championship win
    1995 169–72
Crawley, John 189
Croft, Robert 236, 238, 301
Cronje, Ewie 15, 36, 39, 50
Cronje, Frans 15, 22
Cronje, Hansie 11, 23–4,
    134, 160
  boyhood friendship with
    AD 15–16
  car accident/change of
    lifestyle 127–8
  fitness 199, 201
  Free State cricket 98, 99,
    132
  maiden Test hundred 127

political pressures 281,
    292–4
South Africa captain 161,
    189–90, 194–5, 209,
    222–3, 236, 238–9, 243,
    246–7, 251, 254, 256,
    298, 301, 305–6, 312,
    318–19, 324, 325
Test matches 138, 139,
    158, 230–1, 241,
    242
umpires/umpiring 261–2,
    263, 266, 268
1992 World Cup 102–3,
    105
1999 World Cup 307
Crowe, Martin 48–9
Cullinan, Darryl 10, 111,
    134–5, 230, 307, 323,
    332
  Test matches 155, 159,
    220–1, 227, 242, 319,
    326, 334
Cummins, Anderson 109–10
Curran, Kevin 176
Currie Cup 22, 23, 25–31,
    50–2, 99
  Free State win 131–2
Curtis, Tim 64

Daily Telegraph 248
Dakin, Geoff 93, 106
Davis, Steve 223
de Klerk, F.W. 3, 102–3, 106,
    107
de Kock, Gerald 249
de Villiers, Fanie 137, 138,
    139, 157, 195
DeFreitas, Phil 150, 157
discipline 9–10, 20

Donald, - (grandfather) 14, 17
Donald, Andrew (brother) 8–9
Donald, Des (uncle) 14, 67
Donald, Francina (mother) 8–9, 16
Donald, Stuart (father) 8, 12, 13, 14, 35–6
Donald, Tina (wife) 2, 7, 8, 42, 88, 120, 210, 229, 329
Dravid, Rahul 208–10
Dunne, Steve 244, 263
Durban 27–8, 124–5, 145, 189–90, 206–7, 208–9, 282, 321–3
Dutch Reformed Church 18

East, Robbie 27, 29
Ebrahim, Judge 249–50
Edgbaston 234
    Test match 229–30
    1999 World Cup 303, 306–11
    see also Warwickshire
Edwards, Gareth 315
Eksteen, Clive 134
electronic aids to communication 299–300
Elliott, Matt 213
Els, Ernie 315
Elworthy, Steve 242, 303, 308
England
    fast bowlers 274–5, 277–9
    organisation of cricket 275–7
    rebel tour of South Africa 69–71
    1992 World Cup 105, 107–9
    1999 World Cup 301
    see also TEST SERIES

Faisalabad 194, 217–18
Fearnley, Duncan 74, 75
Ferreira, Anton 30
Ferreira, Dr Fief 314–15
fielding drills 198
fitness training 197–202
Fleming, Damian 310–12
Flintoff, Andrew 240, 253, 326
foot injury 147–50, 162–3
Ford, Graham 320
Fotheringham, Henry 27
Fowler, Graeme 72
Fraser, Angus 235, 238, 239, 242, 257
Free State
    1985/86 season 25
    1987/88 season 50–3
    1989/90 season 67–9
    1990/91 season 77
    1991/92 season 98–9
    1992/93 season 131–3
    1999 320
    debut against Australian rebels 22–4
    first-class debut 26–7
Free State Schools 22

Gallian, Jason 192
Gatting, Mike 69, 70
Gibbs, Herschelle 288, 289, 291–2, 319
    opposition to tokenism 293, 294

1999 World Cup 304, 305–6, 307
Gifford, Norman 46–7
Giles, Ashley 170, 171, 236, 238
Gillespie, Jason 212
Gooch, Graham 150, 160
Gough, Darren 150, 157, 177, 229, 238, 257, 258, 274–5, 323, 331
gout 329
Gower, David 58
Greatbatch, Mark 103
Grey College, Bloemfontein 10–12, 14
Gwalior 94
gym work 200–1

Hadlee, Richard 48, 58
Hair, Darryl 140, 232, 263, 265, 269
Harare 186
Harmony Oval, Virginia 32–4
Hayden, Matthew 218–19
Haynes, Desmond 65
Hayward, Nantie 321, 324, 330
Headingley, Leeds 148–9, 155, 234, 250–260, 303–5
Healy, Ian 142, 212–13
Henry, Omar 97–8, 125, 132
Hick, Graeme 64, 87, 98–9, 240–1, 253, 331
Hirwani, Sultan 193–4
Hogg, Rodney 24–5, 33–4, 37
Hohns, Trevor 23
Holder, Vanburn 25–6
Holland 194

Hollioake, Adam 170, 219
Hollioake, Ben 240
Hookes, David 205
Hooper, Carl 282
Hove 299
Hudson, Andrew 92, 142, 190
Hughes, Kim 21, 32, 36, 38
Hughes, Merv 142, 143
Hughes, Simon, cricketer 66
Hughes, Simon, journalist 248, 249
Humpage, Geoff 44, 64, 117
Hussain, Nasser 200, 233, 245–7, 253, 267–8, 318, 320, 322

Ijaz Ahmed 205
Illingworth, Raymond 161, 187, 189, 191–2
India
  cricket crowds 92, 93–4
  welcome for South African tourists 90–1
  1992 World Cup 105
  1999 World Cup 299
  see also TEST SERIES
Indian subcontinent, benefits of touring 205–6
injuries
  ankle 238, 248, 297–8, 314–15
  foot 147–50, 162–3
  stomach muscle 298–9
International Cricket Conference (ICC) 217, 233, 263, 264
  South Africa's reinstatement 78, 80
  umpires' panel 269

Inzamam-ul-Haq 104, 164

James, Steve 230
Javed Akhtar 251–2, 254,
    258, 263
Jayasuriya, Sanath 225
Johannesburg 26–7, 142–3,
    163, 188–9, 211–12,
    234, 317–23
Jones, Alan 178–80, 244

Kallicharran, Alvin 51, 64
Kallis, Jacques 235, 246, 287,
    299, 304, 307, 308, 326,
    334
Kapil Dev 127, 130
Karachi 185, 194–5
Kasprowicz, Mike 221
Kenya 205, 301
Kimberley 31–2, 190
King, Collis 28
Kirsten, Gary 132, 138, 158,
    227–8, 253, 259, 307,
    322, 323, 325
Kirsten, Peter 96, 104, 105,
    130
  Test matches 110, 140, 158
Kitchen, Merv 214, 248–9,
    263, 270
Klusener, Lance 202, 235,
    237, 334
  1999 World Cup 300, 302,
    303, 308–10, 312
Knight, Nick 82, 170, 215
Kuiper, Adrian 78, 93, 103

Lahore 219, 220
Lamb, Allan 51–2, 58–9, 80
Lampitt, Stuart 76
Lancashire League 197

Lara, Brian
  attitude 283–4
  dispute with West Indies
    Board 280, 282
  relationship with Dermot
    Reeve 166
  Test matches 284–5
  Warwickshire 165–6, 182,
    284
  West Indies captain 282–4
Lawry, Bill 223
le Roux, Garth 38
Leeds 148–9, 155, 234,
    250–60, 303–5
Lehmann, Darren 310
Lewis, Chris 107
Lewis, Rawl 282–3
Liebenberg, Gerry 227,
    254
lifetime achievement award
    2–3
Lindsay, Dennis 287
Lloyd, Andy 46, 82, 169
  leaves Warwickshire
    115–16
  Warwickshire captain 54–5,
    60–2, 65, 73, 76, 85–6
Lloyd, Clive 270
Lord's 227
  NatWest Trophy finals
    65–6, 118–20, 215–16
  Test matches 152–5,
    230–4
Lynagh, Michael 315

McDermott, Craig 101, 137,
    138–9
McGill, Stuart 206
McGrath, Glenn 139, 212,
    307, 309

McMillan, Brian 103, 107, 134, 141–2, 250, 252, 255

Malcolm, Devon 59–60, 156, 157–60, 191–2, 273, 274, 275

Man-of-the-Series
v England 1998 260
v India 1992 128

Mandela, Nelson
becomes President 153
constitutional reform 106
leadership 3, 6
personal qualities 4–5
presentation of lifetime achievement award 1–2
release from prison 69, 78
Rugby World Cup 173
support for cricket 131
support for sport 2, 5–6
West Indies 1998 tour 282

Marsh, Geoff 102
Marsh, Steve 62
Marshall, Malcolm 48, 109, 273
Martyn, Damien 138
Matthews, Craig 150, 194–5
May, Tim 138
Mbeki, Thabo 153, 155
MCC 153
Melbourne 220–1
Merrick, Tony 44–5, 48, 49, 53, 56, 60
Mitchley, Cyril 126, 130
Moin Khan 210–11, 218
Moles, Andy 32, 40–2, 62, 215
Moody, Tom 72–4, 76, 87
Moratuwa 133, 134
Morris, Willie 30

Moxon, Martyn 173
Mpitsang, Victor 289–90
Mullally, Alan 331
Mumbai 333, 334
Munton, Tim 63–4, 86, 170, 178, 215, 216
Muralitharan, Muttiah 134, 300
Mushtaq Ahmed 217, 218

Nationalist Party 18
NatWest Trophy 277
1989 64–6
1992 113–14
1993 118–20
1994 165
1995 170
1997 1, 215–16
New Delhi 94
New Zealand
1992 World Cup 103, 104
1996 World Cup 194
1999 World Cup 303
see also TEST SERIES
Newlands ground, Cape Town 70, 115, 124, 234, 324–7
Nissan Shield 50, 99
Noakes, Professor Tim 186, 198, 265
Nottingham, Stuart 272, 273
Ntini, Makhaya 235, 251, 258, 278, 289

Old Andreians Cricket Club 14
Old Trafford 235–40
Orchard, Dave 268
Ostler, Dominic 173

Oval, 1994 Test 148, 149,
    155–60

Page, Hugh 24–5
Pakistan
    one-day game
        Verwoerdburg 129
    one-day tournament 1996
        205
    touring in 219–20
    1992 World Cup 104–5,
        109
    1996 World Cup 194
    1999 World Cup 302–3
    see also TEST SERIES
Palmer, Roy 307
Patel, Dipak 98, 103
Patel, Min 172
Patterson, Patrick 110
Penney, Trevor 63
Pienaar, François 173, 315
Pienaar, Roy 31, 32
Piper, Keith 62, 215, 216
Player, Brad 30, 132
Pollock, Graeme 29–30, 36–7
Pollock, Peter 145, 276
Pollock, Shaun 9, 10, 197,
    203, 235, 240
    Test matches 222, 223,
        224, 242, 243, 253, 255,
        256–7, 287–8
    1999 World Cup 303,
        306–7, 308
Port Elizabeth 21, 35–7,
    37–8, 127, 128, 129–30,
    145, 190, 212, 224,
    286–7, 291, 320–1
Prabhakar, Manoj 129–30
President's XI v Australian
    rebels 24, 32–4

Prichard, Paul 47, 48
Princess of Wales Memorial
    Match 94–5
Pringle, Meyrick 104, 132,
    188
Procter, Mike 98, 145, 153,
    154, 160–1
Prue, Terry 140

Rackemann, Carl 32–3
Radford, Neal 76
Raju, S.L.V. 94
Ramprakash, Mark 65, 192,
    232, 237, 238, 242, 252,
    259, 263, 331
Randall, Derek 48
Randell, Steve 223
Rashid Latif 164
Rawalpindi 217
rebel tours
    Australian 21–5, 32–8
    English 69–71
Reeve, Dermot 55–6, 61–2,
    64, 65–6, 82, 86–7
    approach to cricket 116–18
    fitness 199
    support for AD over Lara
        169
    Warwickshire captain
        116–18, 165–6, 170–1,
        178, 181
Reiffel, Paul 309
Rhodes, Jonty 10, 141, 231–2
    fielding 63, 101–2, 104–5
    fitness 199, 201
    injury at Oval Test 156
    Test matches 126, 134,
        137, 230–1, 243, 255,
        287, 324–5
    1999 World Cup 301, 307

Rhodes, Steve 158
Rice, Clive 35, 36, 37–8
  coaching by 57–8
  dropped from South
    African team 96
  South Africa captain 90–2
  South Africa selector 236
Richards, Viv 115
Richards, Barry 229, 231
Richardson, Dave 102, 107,
  151, 191, 214, 223–4
Richardson, Richie 115
Riddle, Dean 278
Rishton 197
rugby, Bloemfontein 12–13
Rugby World Cup, 1995 5,
  172–4
Russell, Jack 188, 192, 193

St George's Park, Port
  Elizabeth 35–7, 37–8,
  287
Salim Malik 164
Salisbury, Ian 241, 253, 256
Saqlain Mushtaq 217
Scarborough 150
schooldays 10–14, 16–17
Schultz, Brett 133–4, 187–8,
  202
Searjeant, Neil 114
Sheikhpura 217, 219–20
Shepherd, David 269
Shipperd, Greg 36
Shoaib Akhtar 303
Sidhu, N.S. 94
Silverwood, Chris 323, 331
Slater, Michael 137–8, 141
Small, Gladstone 43, 60, 65,
  86, 178, 182, 216
Smith, Craig 187–8, 314

Smith, M.J.K. 75, 183, 332–3
Smith, Neil 66, 170, 172,
  216–17
Smith, Paul 57, 118, 119
Smith, Robin 80, 188
Smith, Steve 23
South Africa
  attitude to sport 15–16, 69,
    202–3, 302
  Cricket Development
    Programme 71, 78, 124,
    289
  integration of black players
    into mainstream cricket
    78
  one-day triangular series,
    2000 331–2
  pressure for non-white
    representation in Test
    sides 280–1, 289–96,
    324
  rebel tours to 21–5, 32–8,
    69–71
  referendum 106–7
  return to international
    cricket 80–1, 89–90
  South African Cricket Annual,
    Promising Young Player
    of the Year 31
South African Defence XI
  31–2
South African Schools 22, 25
Speed, Malcolm 332
Sports Science Institute, Cape
  Town 197
Sri Lanka
  one-day tournament 1996
    205
  1992 World Cup 103
  1999 World Cup 300

Sri Lanka – *contd.*
  see also TEST SERIES
Srikkanth, K. 94
Stephenson, Franklyn 98,
    132, 253
Stewart, Alec
  England captain 230, 233,
    239, 241–2, 256–7
  Test matches 229, 233–4,
    236, 237–8, 247, 267,
    318, 326
Stockhill, Nigel 271–2
stretching exercises 198, 201
Strydom, Joubert 27
Sunday League 87, 216,
    277
Sydney Cricket Ground 234
  Test matches 137–9,
    221–2
  World Cup 101, 107–8
Symcox, Pat 139, 193–4,
    196, 237, 251–2
  Test matches 134, 218–19,
    223, 286

Talat Ali 299–300
Tayfield, Hugh 128
Taylor, Mark 138, 144, 213,
    221
Technical High School,
    Bloemfontein 13
Telemachus, Roger 278, 289
television cameras, use in
    decision-making 125–7,
    264–6
television large screen replays
    266–7
Tendulkar, Sachin 94–5, 126,
    127, 129, 207–8, 209,
    283, 334

Terbrugge, David 324
TEST SERIES v.
  Australia
    1993/94 136–45
    1997 211–14
    1997/98 220–4
  England
    1994 147–60
    1995/96 186–93
    1998 226–60
    1999/2000 317–27,
      329–31
  India
    1991 89–90, 92–4
    1992 123–7, 128,
      129–30
    1996 205–10
    2000 333–4
  Pakistan
    1995 164
    1997 217
    1998 224
  Sri Lanka
    1993 133–6
    1998 224–5
  West Indies
    1992 109–10
    1998 280–8
  Zimbabwe 317
Thorpe, Graham 228, 232,
    238, 268
training 197–202
Trent Bridge 240–8,
    303
Triffin, Russell 269
Tshwete, Steve 2, 291
  support for cricket 131
Tudor, Alex 277
Tutu, Archbishop Desmond
    152, 155

Twose, Roger 120–1, 170, 173

umpires/umpiring 268–70
Adelaide Test 1993 140–1
Headingley Test 1998 251–2, 254, 256–7, 259, 261–2, 263
pressures 262, 264–7
third umpire/television replays 126–7, 264–6, 270
Trent Bridge Test 1998 244, 249, 263
United Arab Emirates 193–4
United Cricket Board of South Africa 78, 105, 183, 294, 328–9
Upton, Paddy 168–9, 197, 199, 201

van der Merwe, Peter 37, 096
van Zyl, Corrie 23, 24, 26, 29, 38, 51, 253, 290
Vaughan, Michael 330–1
Verwoerdburg 129, 145
Virginia 32–4
Voldstedt, Johann 11–12, 14, 50, 67
Vorster, Louis 52

Walsh, Courtney 110, 195, 273, 281–2, 285–6, 287
Wanderers ground, Johannesburg 27, 124, 163, 286, 288
Waqar Younis 176, 177, 217, 218
Warne, Shane 139, 142–4, 220–1, 307–8

Warwickshire 38–9
1987 (AD's 1st season) 40–9
1988 season 53–6
1989 season 57–66
1990 season 71–7
1991 season 81–8
1992 season 113–16
1993 season 113–14, 118–20
1994 season 165
1995 season 169–78, 181–2
1997 season 215–16
1999 (benefit) season 297, 314–15
2000 season 327–8, 333, 335
championship win (1995) 169–72
NatWest Trophy 1, 64–6, 113–14, 118–20, 165, 170, 215–16
preference for Lara over AD 182, 1671–9
Sunday League win 216
Wasim Akram 109, 175, 176–7, 217, 224, 273, 303
Waugh, Mark 138, 212, 222–3, 312
Waugh, Steve 84, 140, 143, 180, 211, 213–14, 222, 224
1999 World Cup 304, 305, 306, 310
Welch, Graeme 216
Wellington, New Zealand 103
Wessels, Kepler 11, 12, 50

Australian rebel tour 35, 36, 38
  dispute with AD 147–51
  South Africa captain 98, 115, 133, 138, 147–51, 152, 157, 160, 181
  Test matches 110, 152, 158–9
  World Cup 1992 102, 103–4, 105
West Indies
  dispute with Cricket Board 280, 281–2
  1992 World Cup 104
  1996 World Cup 185, 194–5
  see also TEST SERIES
White, Craig 177
Whitehouse, John 183
Whitfield, Brian 36
Willey, Peter 251, 256, 257, 259
Williams, Henry 331
Williams, Ray 29

Willis, Bob 275, 276
Wisden Cricketer of the Year 1991 88
Woolmer, Bob
  coaching of AD 174–5
  political pressure 294
  qualities as coach 81–5
  South Africa coach 161, 186, 187, 195, 214, 217, 228–9, 250–1, 298, 299–300, 305–6, 312–13
  use of technology 186, 228, 299–300
  Warwickshire 81–7, 165, 167–8, 328, 333, 335
Worcestershire 74–5
World Cup
  1992 97–8, 100–9
  1996 185, 193–6
  1999 298–314

Zimbabwe 105, 186, 208, 302, 317, 331